The Mandala

The Mandala

Sacred Circle in Tibetan Buddhism

Martin Brauen

Translated by Martin Willson

with photographs by
Peter Nebel and Doro Röthlisberger

Shambhala
Boston
1998

Dedicated to Sonam Dolma, Yangzom and Tashi

Shambhala Publications, Inc.
Horticultural Hall
300 Massachusetts Avenue
Boston, Massachusetts 02115
http://www.shambhala.com

First published as *Das Mandala: Der Heilige Kreis im tantrischen Buddhismus* (Köln: DuMont, 1992), on the occasion of the exhibition of that name at the Völkerkundemuseum der Universität Zürich (Ethnographic Museum of the University of Zurich), 1992.

Published by arrangement with Serindia Publications, London

9 8 7 6 5 4 3 2 1

Printed in Hong Kong

Distributed in the United States by Random House, Inc.,
and in Canada by Random House of Canada Ltd

Library of Congress catalogues the hardback edition of this book as follows:

Brauen, Martin
[Mandala. English]
The Mandala : sacred circle in Tibetan Buddhism /
Martin Brauen : translated by Martin Willson
p. Cm.
ISBN 1-57062-296-5
ISBN 1-57062-380-5 (paperback)
1. Mandala (Buddhism) I. Title
BQ5125.M3B7313 1997
294.3'437 – – dc20

96-35056
CIP

Frontispiece: Monk during the construction of a mandala of coloured butter on the occasion of the Butter Festival on the fifteenth day of the first Tibetan month. This popular festival commemorates the miracles of Gautama Buddha in Śrāvastī where the Buddha stayed during the rainy season for twenty-four years.

Contents

Sanskrit and Tibetan terms

Sanskrit terms and names have generally been transliterated in the standard manner, so as to give all the information needed for correct pronunciation and recognition. A few terms that have passed into the English language are spelt in the customary anglicized manner, e.g. 'mandala' (*maṇḍala*) and 'chakra' (*cakra*); the spelling 'Kālacakra' has, however, been retained.

The standard conventions have been followed in the transliteration of Tibetan terms. In some instances personal names are spelt phonetically, following the individual's preference in the case of modern personal names. Where technical terms are given in both Sanskrit and Tibetan, the Sanskrit precedes the Tibetan.

Foreword

by H.H. the XIV Dalai Lama

Mandalas are an aspect of Tantric Buddhism that, due to their colourful complexity, have attracted a great deal of interest. Taking a variety of forms, from simple diagrams and more elaborate paintings on cloth to complicated patterns of coloured sand and large three-dimensional carved structures, mandalas have a profoundly symbolic value. We Tibetans regard them as sacred.

Although some mandalas – for instance the symbolic representation of the Universe made of heaped grains – can be openly explained, most are related to Tantric doctrines which are normally supposed to be kept secret. Consequently, many speculative and mistaken interpretations have been published by people who viewed them simply as works of art or had no access to reliable explanations. Because the severe misunderstandings that can then arise are more harmful than a partial lifting of secrecy, I have often encouraged the writing of more accurate accounts.

In this work about mandalas, Martin Brauen has taken pains to consult authentic sources and organize his material clearly so that it can be easily understood. He explains the basic aspects of the Buddhist path, which provide the context for the use of mandalas. These include a strong wish to put an end to suffering, a strong wish to attain Enlightenment for the sake of others, and a correct view of Reality. He describes different kinds of mandalas, those which represent the outer universe, those which refer to a meditative view of the human body, and those visualized in the practice of deity yoga. This is preliminary to an explanation of the Kālacakra Mandala. The Kālacakra system was one of the last and most complex Tantric systems to be brought to Tibet from India. In recent years many Westerners have become acquainted with the Kālacakra tradition, as various lamas have given the Kālacakra initiation to large groups of people. I myself have given it several times in Western countries as well as in India. Moreover, there are already a number of reliable books concerning aspects of the Kālacakra system available in Western languages, to which this is a welcome addition.

I congratulate Martin Brauen for his sincere efforts to make a difficult subject clearer to others and offer my prayers that his good intentions will be fulfilled.

27 November 1991

Acknowledgments

This book could only have come about thanks to the energetic help of numerous institutions, the people working in them and many others, who made investigations, translated, discussed problems and specific questions with me, took photographs, produced models and drawings, gave me ideas, procured funding, went over my manuscript, and so forth. Quite a considerable part of this additional work was undertaken by Martin Willson, the translator, and Maria Phylactou, the editor of Serindia Publications, Peter Nebel, photographer at the Völkerkundemuseum der Universität Zürich, Susanne Grieder and Andreas Brodbeck. I wish to thank them from the heart, as well as Anthony Aris of Serindia, with whom it was a great pleasure to work, and all the institutions and people listed below, for their assistance, which often went far beyond what is customary.

My special thanks go to H.H. the XIV Dalai Lama, who showed his interest in the present publication by providing a Foreword.

Institutions:
Cassinelli-Vogel-Stiftung, Zürich: Council of the Foundation and its President, Mrs S. Staub; Zürcher Hochschul-Verein: the Committee and its President, Mr Thomas Freysz; The Office of Tibet, Zürich and the Private Secretariat of H.H. the XIV Dalai Lama, Dharamsala; The Ashmolean Museum, Oxford (Andrew Topsfield); British Museum, London (Wladimir Zwalf); Folkens Museum, Stockholm (Håkan Wahlquist); Liverpool Museum, Liverpool (Christina Baird); Musée Guimet, Paris (Gilles Béguin); Museum für Völkerkunde, Berlin (Claudius C. Müller); Sammlung für Völkerkunde, St. Gallen (Roland Steffan); Victoria and Albert Museum, London (John Clarke, Anne Buddle); Völkerkundemuseum der Universität Zürich (Karl H. Henking, Peter R. Gerber).

Individuals:
Jensine Andresen, Harvard; Alexander Berzin, Dharamsala; Robert Beer, London; Robin Brentano, New York; Andreas Brodbeck, Forch; Anne Chayet, Paris; Zara Fleming, Ruthin; Erich Frei, Zürich; Johannes Frischknecht, Zürich; Tenzin Geyche Tethong, Dharamsala; Rolf Glauser, Berne; Susanne Grieder, Zürich; Niels Gutschow, Absteinach; Amy Heller, Nyon; Michael Henss, Zürich; Reinhard Herdick, Munich; Julia Hintermüller, Zürich; Peter Iseli, Berne; Petra Jebens, Fosado; Martin Kalff, Zollikon; Britta Lanzerath, Cologne; Elisabeth Lauber, Zürich; Todd T. Lewis, Worchester; Helen Müller, Zürich; Peter Nebel, Werdenberg; Anna Nippa, Berlin & Zürich; Pema, Namgyal Monastery, Dharamsala; Maria Phylactou, London; Doro Röthlisberger, Zürich; Robert Rottermann, Bern; Frank Rainer Scheck, Cologne; Heidi and Ulrich von Schroeder, Wollerau; Ngawang Gyaltsen Sherpa, Kathmandu; Pema Namdol Thaye, Kalimpong; Khenpo Thubten, Williamsburg; Pia and Louis Van der Wee, Antwerp; Mark Webster, Zürich; Eugen Wehrli, Zürich; Martin Willson, Weymouth; Urs Wohlgemuth, Zürich.

Special thanks are also due to my family, especially my wife Sonam Dolma, and to Kunsang Wangmo, who have actively assisted me in many ways during the time this book was being written.

The Author
December 1996

Introduction
Approaching the Mystery

The mandala is fundamentally something secret. If you are interested in it in order to acquire reputation, and feel pride in showing what you have worked out to others, you do not have the right attitude. If however your work springs from efforts to offer help to other people, that is the right attitude of mind, which will contribute to the liberation of yourself and others.

The monk Khenpo Thubten to the author

The 'picture-friendliness' of Tantric Buddhism

To impart the most profound religious truths, Tantric Buddhism employs pictorial representations with an intensity found in no other form of Buddhism and scarcely in any other religion. This is not to overlook the fact that these figures and paintings only hint at what they are meant to represent; they are only aspects of the absolute and not the absolute itself in all its splendour and bliss. Rather, the absolute manifests itself in everyone and everything, and it is the goal of every visualization to discover and to realize clear, radiant divinity. For this, the practitioner uses special practices in which he purifies his consciousness through a sublimation called 'deity yoga' that brings him closer to the divine source; he 'becomes divine'.

Pictorial representations serve as an aid to the meditator. These are images that the meditator erects or hangs in front of him or herself. The cult figures of deities, as a rule of metal, wood or clay, do indeed show their three-dimensional character, but they do not convey the subtle materiality and radiance of the painted images, even though these are only two-dimensional.

This book seeks to interpret some fundamental Tantric symbols for the Western observer, reworking them in such a way that they satisfy Western visual conventions (though always with reference to the Tibetan Buddhist sources). Such adapted drawings or reconstructions should enable the reader to see the connections spontaneously, even though the traditional illustrations and the texts on which they are based may be hard to understand.

Thus – in the spirit of the 'picture-friendliness' of Tantric Buddhism – this book works extensively with pictorial representations.

The Kālacakra mandala as an example

Different traditions exist within Tantric Buddhism, each with its own, partly divergent, teachings and rites. The repertoire of symbols, deities and mandalas, is similarly extensive. It is not the goal of the present publication to portray as many of the different mandalas of Tibetan Buddhism as possible – for one thing because a wide range of mandalas has already been published in a Japanese and an Indian publication;[1] for another, because such an encyclopedic compilation imparts a great deal of detailed information but is of little help towards a better *understanding* of the mandala ritual.

Despite many differences, the two best known publications on the subject, *Theory and Practice of the Mandala* by Giuseppe Tucci, and *Mandala* by José and Miriam Argüelles, have one feature in common: by consulting the most varied source material they aim to present a study on mandalas that is of *universal validity*. Tucci drew his material from both Buddhist and Hindu sources, while the Argüelles' material was derived from the non-Indian as well as the non-Asian sphere. The analysis of mandalas and other mandala-like depictions by means of a comparative method of this kind, often without any convincing indication of the peculiarities of individual mandala traditions, is typical of many of the essays and a few of the main publications on the subject.[2]

In this book we have deliberately chosen another procedure. We concentrate mainly on a single mandala ritual, though not without going into a few other traditions here and there.

This is the mandala ritual of Kālacakra (*dus kyi 'khor lo*), which belongs to the highest class of Tantra, the Anuttarayoga Tantras. It was selected because the author has himself experienced this ritual and has received permission to document much of it in detail, from the preparatory rituals, through the production of the mandala in coloured powder, up to the initiation, and dismantling of the mandala; and because important publications on the Kālacakra ritual by several Tibetan lamas have appeared in recent years.

Statements which refer primarily to the Kālacakra mandala do not always apply to other mandalas. Divergences do exist, not only in the basic structure of the mandala, but also in important basic teachings. However, to prevent possible misunderstandings, it should be mentioned here that the *yogin* of the Kālacakra tradition works only with the moment of death and rebirth, not with the intermediate state (*bar do*); the *Kālacakra Tantra* is not therefore concerned with the sublime body of a deceased person in the intermediate state.

The symbolism and basic structure of the Kālacakra mandala also differ from those of other mandalas. The rings encircling the palace in the Kālacakra mandala are components of the cosmos: five great discs bearing the universe, namely: space, air, water, fire and earth. In many other mandalas such reference to the universe is not immediately evident. Moreover the colouring inside the mandala: black in the east, red in the south, yellow in the west, white in the north, and green and blue assigned to the centre, differs from that in other traditions.[3] In the Kālacakra tradition the eight charnel grounds – a component of many mandalas – are only hinted at as wheels in the air and fire circles, and are not described in detail below. It would be far beyond the scope of this publication to go into all the differences in detail. Where necessary, however, they are referred to in footnotes.

It is hoped that despite the focus on a single tradition, or perhaps because of it, the mystery of the mandala and with it a fundamental aspect of Tantric Buddhism, may be usefully revealed to the reader.

Tantric Buddhism: a short but demanding path

In the Tantric view, religion and ritual do not form an antithesis to the suffering-filled cycle of living. On the contrary, there are numerous correlations between religious practice on the one hand, and the structures and processes in the universe and in individual persons on the other, which it is necessary to understand and actively use. Knowledge of Tantric Buddhist cosmology and anthropology is therefore indispensable for an understanding of the *Kālacakra Tantra* and its mandala ritual.

Can a ritual as complex as the mandala ritual be explained in a book at all, without serious errors and misinterpretation? If we accept the Buddhist view of the relativity of knowledge, and with it the insight that there can be different levels of understanding and relative truths according to our state of knowledge and 'maturity', then it is surely permissible to present such a book knowing full well that the particular viewpoint of the author reveals some things, while leaving others in darkness, or perhaps even distorting them. Explaining the ultimate truth that Tantric Buddhism is about, namely 'emptiness' (see Ch. 2), as well as the complex path (deity yoga) that leads to it (see Ch. 5), is like walking a tightrope. It is a matter of approximating something that cannot be grasped in words, which the seeker him or herself will have to discern through arduous effort and under the guidance of an experienced spiritual teacher (*guru*).

How should an author deal with the religious rule not to make secret Tantric objects, images and teachings available to just anyone? How should he behave so as not to commit a root infraction and transmit Tantric secrets to those not yet 'ripe' for them? I have tried to resolve this problem by drawing exclusively on material already published. Principal sources were explanations by Tibetan lamas including H.H. the XIV Dalai Lama, Serkong Rinpoche, Geshe Ngawang Dhargyey and Geshe Lhundup Sopa. I have also used interpretations by Western scholars, mainly those of Alexander Berzin and Jeffrey Hopkins, who have already worked intensively and for a long time on Tibetan Buddhism and in particular on the *Kālacakra Tantra*, and have themselves been taught by distinguished Tibetan lamas. In addition, I submitted a synopsis of the text to H.H. The XIV Dalai Lama, Tenzin Gyatso, and received from him permission to publish the pictorial material produced on the occasion of the Kālacakra initiation. If despite the greatest efforts for truthfulness the book contains errors, this is evidently not to be blamed on the persons mentioned but is due to an incorrect interpretation for which the author accepts full responsibility. All the same, it remains to note that the sources mentioned do not agree in every point; divergences appear, some of which I refer to in footnotes.

As is often stressed in oral teachings, Tantra should not be offered to students as something complete, 'on a plate'. Rather, starting from certain basic data and insights, students are expected to work on the subject intensively themselves. The present book accordingly demonstrates some possible ways of approaching Tantra, not with the idea of transmitting incontrovertible truths, but as a stimulus for the reader to find his own way to analyse the Tantric understanding of the world and the person. To think that in Tantric Buddhism the ultimate goal can be easily attained, that is to say at once and without great efforts, is a well-known fallacy that some Tibetan authors themselves also share.[4] Tantric Buddhism does indeed place at one's disposal a short-cut path to release from the cycle of existence, but as ever the short-cut is just as laborious as the 'normal' path, if not more so. The material reappraised in this volume verifies how complex, many-layered and averse to conventional thinking the Tantric path is. With some justice it is claimed that the Tantric path is only for those endowed with considerable spiritual capacity.[5]

Since the ritual of the Kālacakra mandala belongs to the Anuttarayoga Tantra class, in principle two major phases may be found within it: the 'generation' and 'completion' stages. The first phase is one of ripening, in which the completion is prepared for and rehearsed. This is done through a slow recognition and experience of the various analogies to the dying process, and an anticipation or imitation of its individual phases, but also of the process of becoming, and the complex yoga practices of the completion stage closely related to them. As stated, the whole meditation process contains analogies to dying and being reborn, and is therefore like a spiritual rebirth. The death process is understood and 'cultivated' in detail. From this follows the overcoming of the fear of death. At the same time it becomes possible to consciously experience the 'clear light' that shines at the moment of death. However, the analogy between human life and the path of meditation goes beyond the parallels referred to: just as an embryo germinates in the womb and develops into a foetus and, after birth, into infant, child and adult, so the Tantric practitioner progresses through an analogous development with the difference that he goes through it all *deliberately* and *consciously*, and thereby creates for himself the prerequisites for perfect enlightenment.

Introduction to the mandala

Looking up the word mandala in popular or even specialist dictionaries, it becomes obvious how hard it is to do justice to the term in a short definition. There is talk of the mandala as a 'magic circle', a round 'ritual-geometric' or 'symbolic' diagram, or 'typically a circle which surrounds a square with a central symbol, which may be a numeral'. Alternatively mandalas are described as 'symbols of the cosmic elements, used as an aid to meditation', as 'models for certain visualizations', as 'an aid to self-discovery or to meditation on the transcendental'. All these definitions contain their own validity, but are not nearly precise enough, as will become apparent in our step-by-step approach to the Kālacakra mandala.

As a rule a mandala (*dkyil 'khor*) is a strongly symmetrical diagram, concentrated about a centre and generally divided into four quadrants of equal size; it is built up of concentric circles (*'khor*) and squares possessing the same centre (*dkyil*). Indeed, a great many mandalas are also aids to meditation, visualization and initiation.[6]

However the term 'mandala' also indicates other structures: among these we know of simple circles or discs which contain a sacred centre, or form the base of one, for example the discs of the five elements that constitute the lower part of the Kālacakra universe, or the discs of moon, sun and the two planets Rāhu and Kālāgni that serve as a throne for a deity. The palace that is home to the deities is also called a mandala, as are the deities themselves who reside in it, assembled in a clearly ordered pattern. The term 'mandala' can, moreover, be applied to the whole cosmos, namely when the entire purified universe is mentally offered in a special ritual (see Ch. 3, p. 24ff).

Numerous scroll paintings depict mandalas that are not recognizable as such at first sight. The characteristic type becomes clear when the composition of such paintings is analysed, and they are thereby revealed as three-dimensional, symmetrical structures, concentrated about a centre (see Ch. 5, p. 65ff). Even the *individual* deity can appear as a mandala: thus Kālacakra dominates the mandala of the same name. Like his partner Viśvamātṛ he has four faces, each facing one of the four cardinal directions. His arms, together with those of his partner, describe a circle around an (imagined) centre at the level of the heart (Plate 47, Fig. 37). Eventually, in the context of the image of the person in the *Kālacakra Tantra*, we shall discover that the human being is also seen as a mandala. For instance each of the wind channels, which according to Tantric conception flow inside the body, is linked to a particular direction, element, aggregate (*skandha*), and colour, thereby forming a mandala. In the so-called 'inner mandala', the human body is seen as a 'cosmos mandala' which is offered to one's own spiritual teacher (*guru*), and to the Three Jewels (Buddha, Buddhist teaching and community of monks).[7]

An important Tibetan source[8] mentions four types of mandalas. Two are outer mandalas: those made from powdered colours and those painted on textiles. Then there are the mandalas formed in meditatio. Finally, there is the body as a mandala. This enumeration omits three-dimensional mandalas, which is hard to understand, since spatiality is the most striking feature of the basic structure of mandalas. Another source, the *Dharmamaṇḍala Sūtra*, mentions mandalas of gold, silver, shell, stone, horn, wood and clay, besides those painted on cloth or made of coloured powder.[9] In fact, evidence of three-dimensional mandalas can be found at several places where Tibetan Buddhism spread, including the Potala in Lhasa (where there is a Kālacakra mandala); the Xuguang Ge (Yuanting Si) of Pule Si in Chengde (Jehol, China);[10] and Zangdog Palri Monastery in Kalimpong (West Bengal), to mention only a few examples

1 *The most famous yantra – a Śrī-yantra, Nepal. Four corner lions support a plinth, on which rises a building, simply suggested by four T-shaped gates represented in two dimensions. The actual yantra rests on two lotus flowers with 16 and 8 petals respectively; it consists of the central dot (bindu), 4 triangles pointing to one side, and 5 to the opposite side. A seated figure, Tripurasundarī, Lady of the Śrī-yantra, actually covers the yantra (Fig. 2). Her manifestations dwell in the 27 vertices and on the 16 outer lotus petals.*

2 *The Śrī-yantra (Fig. 1) with its Lady, Tripurasundarī.*

(Figs 46, 48, 50). In order to elucidate the intrinsic three-dimensionality of all mandalas, in this book we shall briefly depict the structure of a three-dimensional mandala (Plates 15–21), as well as some of its typical details (see Ch. 5). It should be noted that this is not a Kālacakra mandala, but a Zhi khro mandala with the one hundred (or one hundred and ten) peaceful and wrathful deities of the intermediate state (*bar do*), the deities that appear to the deceased immediately upon his entry into death. As the main point is to show the reader the *basic structure* of mandalas, it seems permissible in that context to switch to another mandala tradition.

Two-dimensional mandalas are either painted on a cloth ground or sprinkled on a flat surface with coloured powder. Whereas the latter are dismantled at the end of the relevant mandala ritual (Plates 41–3), painted mandalas can be stored away for a long time. The oldest drawn mandalas known to us come from the caves at Dunhuang in northwest China (ninth–tenth century AD), and already show the typical basic structure (Fig. 4).[11] Mandalas created later are considerably more complex representations. As a rule they display several concentric circles surrounding a square area (Plates 2, 10, 45, 46).

Let us now consider the square area at the centre of the mandala. Lines connecting the opposite corners of the square create four triangles of equal size, whose points meet in the centre of the mandala. Each triangle corresponds to one of the cardinal directions, and displays its characteristic colour. In Tibetan paintings, the east – which is black in the Kālacakra mandala – always occupies the bottom part. Each of the four outer sides of the square is interrupted in the middle

3 *Newar divination plate (Nepal), combining elements of yantra and mandala. From the outside inwards six circles that form a so-called Buddha mandala: lotus flowers as a border to the plate; charnel-grounds (Saṃsāra mandala); flames (Agni mandala); vajras (Vajra mandala); lotus/water (Padma/Jala mandala); and eight mantras (Wind or Vāyu mandala). In the centre further circles are added, comprising: consonants, which symbolize the various parts of the human body; vowels, which stand for the sounds of human speech; six triangles, probably representing the six possible realms of rebirth; a circle called Matsya mandala; and a yoni, symbol of the feminine, resting on a three-petalled lotus flower. The priest throws grains on the mandala plate and, from the pattern in which they fall, extracts information about the fate of the deceased, for whom the divination is being carried out in the so-called durgatipariśodhana ceremony (third to seventh day after death). Description according to Todd T. Lewis.*

by a T-shape. These are 'entrance gates', since the square in the mandala is none other than a building or the ground plan of a palace.[12]

Among the plethora of mandala representations there are a number in which the deities are only hinted at, for instance by their symbols (*samayamaṇḍala*), by dots or small circles, or by their seed-syllables (*bīja-* or *dharmamaṇḍala*) (Plates 2, 10, 45). Some mandalas may be completely empty, and these naturally demand greater powers of imagination.[13]

Even though *yantras* are hardly discussed in Tantric Buddhism, they should be mentioned here briefly, as they are frequently confused with mandalas. Their structure resembles that of a mandala (lotus flower circle, square area with four gates, orientation towards a centre, etc.). Functionally too they are not easily distinguished (Figs 1–3). Whereas *yantras* are linear and generally intended for repeated use, the more complex mandalas are coloured and in the past tended to be used only once.[14] Additionally most, if not all, *yantras* contain seed-syllables or short commands and, if drawn or printed on paper, after the relevant ritual they are often worn as an amulet, eaten as medicine, or buried as a magical protective diagram.[15]

Before going into the complicated structure of the Kālacakra mandala, its rich symbolism, and the individual steps and significance of the ritual, we should acquaint ourselves with some important Buddhist insights for, though there may be little expression of this in Western publications on Tantric Buddhism, the mandala ritual is, without doubt, based on Buddhist philosophy.

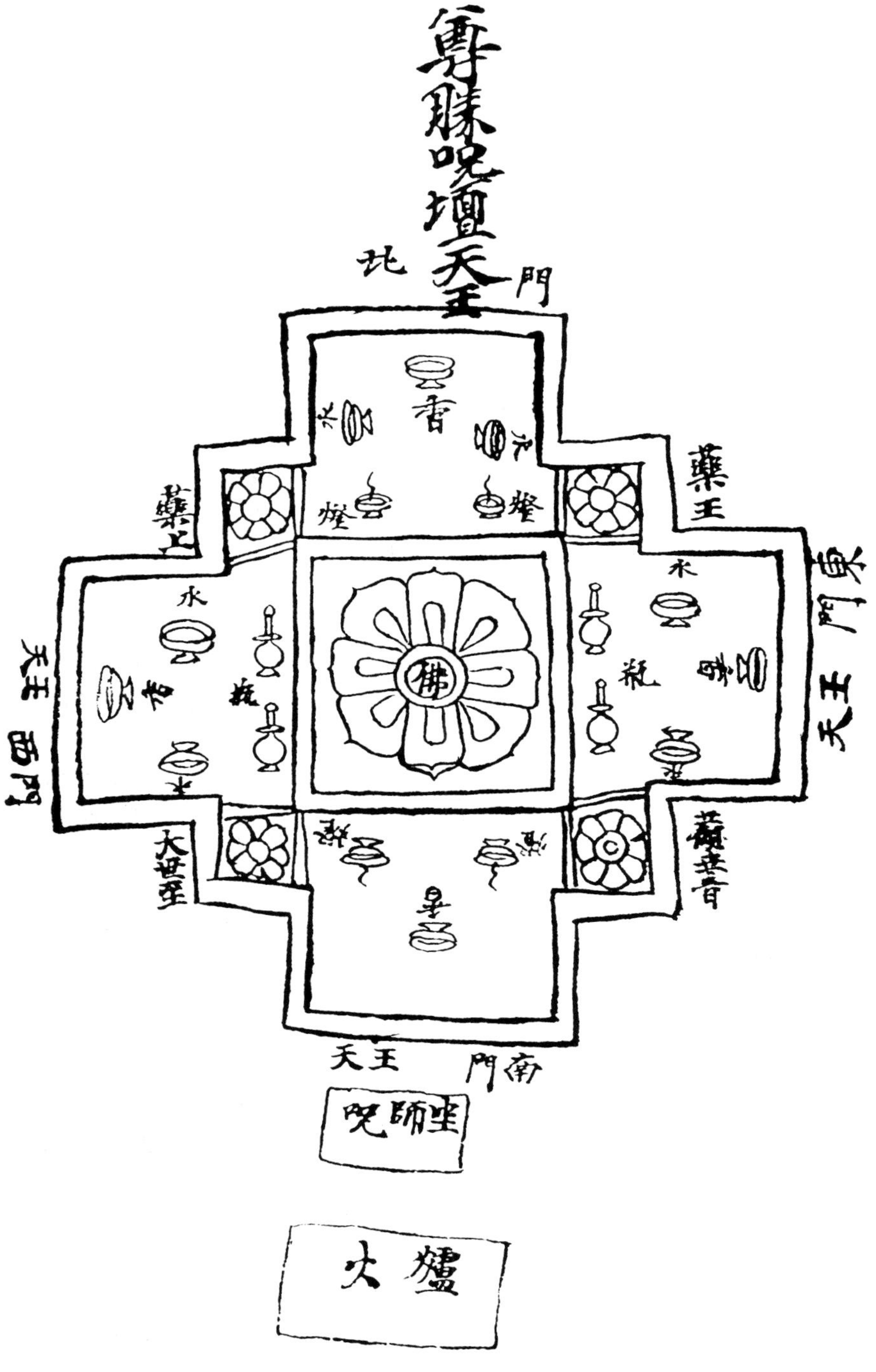

4 *One of the oldest ink drawings of a mandala known to us (9th–10th century), recovered from a cave at Dunhuang in northwest China, representing an altar prepared for the recitation of the Uṣṇīṣavijayā dhāraṇī. At the heart of the central lotus is written 'Buddha'. The surrounding small dishes, lamps and vases with their offerings are accompanied by the characters for 'water', 'incense', 'lamp'. In each direction are the names of the Four Lokapalas.*

The Centre of the Buddhist Wheel of the Teaching: Basic Ideas

Abandonment of self

Despite their partly divergent views and rituals, the different Buddhist schools and traditions of teaching share certain basic assumptions, in particular the theory of selflessness. What we in the West consider to be an individual, in the Buddhist view comprises five so-called aggregates or heaps (*skandha*). These are the *skandhas* of forms (corporeality, materiality, matter),[1] of feelings, of perceptions, of mental factors (volition, mental formations), and of consciousness (events of consciousness), which combine with each other in mutual interrelation. The five *skandhas* are transitory and subject to constant change, thereby also implying the transitoriness of human beings. That which is transitory can, moreover, possess no eternal soul – as Buddhists also say – no permanent self. In the West the individual is thought to possess a content, a core, which – for Buddhists – is a wrong view, the root of all our misery. The concept of 'I' and of 'self' leads to craving which continually gives rise to new dissatisfaction, anguish and sorrow. As a consequence of this realization the delusion of self has to be abandoned. If a person escapes from the shackles of the self, he or she escapes also from craving and with it from sorrow, and comes closer to the state known as *nirvāṇa*, which for Buddhists means freedom: freedom from bonds, freedom from attachments, freedom from craving. This state of freedom and independence permits an active life and a feeling of closeness to others to arise (see p. 16); giving up the self only makes sense if it goes along with a turning towards other living beings.

All Buddhist schools agree on the ideal of selflessness. Differences exist in the method, the way (*yāna*) in which the experience of non-essence can be attained. To simplify greatly, one can distinguish between the two ways of Sūtra or Pāramitāyāna (Way of Perfections), and that of Tantra or Mantrayāna (Way of Sacred Formulas); between the system of the *sūtras*, texts which emphasize instruction and time-consuming intellectual analysis of oneself and one's surroundings, and the system of the *tantras*, texts which explain how with demanding, partly secret, ritual practices, above all with deity yoga (p. 63ff), one can rapidly, though with greater risk, realize the ultimate goal of essencelessness or emptiness.

The Buddhas are said to have shown various ways to liberation according to the character, inclination and needs of suffering people; Buddhists account in this way for the different orientations of the separate schools. Tantrayāna, the vehicle of Tantra, from which stem the rituals of the Kālacakra mandala, is usually divided into four classes: Kriyā, Caryā, Yoga and, as the highest class, Anuttarayoga Tantra.[2] Anuttarayoga Tantra is further divided into two: 'male' or 'father' Anuttarayoga Tantra, in which particular stress is put on' method' or the path, and 'female' or 'mother' Anuttarayoga Tantra, which pays more attention to 'wisdom'. The *Kālacakra Tantra* belongs to female Anuttarayoga Tantra.

Emptiness: all phenomena are 'of the same taste'

Tibetan Buddhists regard what is generally called reality as being without essence, without a stable core or – to use a Buddhist expression – as 'empty'. Out of the wrong interpretation of perceptions and human longings arise contradictions, which the Buddhist wants to recognize with the aid of meditation. The meditator grasps that his or her 'reality' is not real, that another reality exists instead: 'emptiness' or the 'void' (*śunyatā*).[3]

But how can emptiness be reality? Emptiness is a central, exceedingly complex concept of Mahāyāna philosophy. From among the various concepts of emptiness, below we draw on the widely held concept of the Prāsaṅgika-Mādhyamika school. This school regards phenomena and beings as empty, in so far as they have no inherent or objective existence on their own, that is no existence inherent in the object. Thus it is not a matter of the complete non-existence of a phenomenon, but of the lack of a 'self'.[4] The Prāsaṅgika concept does not put in question the world of things and people around us, but rather the way we see the world.

Two examples may be used to illustrate the theory of emptiness. Tibetan texts often cite the example of a speckled, coiled rope, that is not clearly recognizable, and that may bring to mind the thought of a snake – though in reality the snake is only imputed by thought. With this example the Prāsaṅgika school wishes to prove that phenomena, appearances as separate entitites with their own inherent existence, exist only as a result of our thought or consciousness, which carries out classifications and descriptions.

Another example is provided by the well-known puzzle pictures in which blotches, lines and dots yield next to no meaning, and cannot be interpreted. After looking and searching for a long time, you suddenly recognize some content, for example a face or a shape. But the blotches, lines and dots of the first phase – of non-recognition – are exactly the same as those of the second phase – that of recognition of content. Nothing has altered; evidently it is the viewer who has changed. With his consciousness he has analysed, distinguished and organized the dots, lines and blotches. He has made discriminations and bestowed content and meaning onto that which is empty.

This demonstrates not only how with our discriminating, analysing consciousness, we create independent entities from that which is empty, but also how hard it is to return these entities to the undifferentiated state. Who does not know the difficulty of dissolving a puzzle-picture back into mere dots, lines and blotches once one has made out its hidden content? 'Order' can no more be led back into 'disorder', or only with effort. But this is precisely what someone meditating on emptiness must succeed in doing, because reversing the process of ordering, differentiating and constituting (seeming) entities, means recognizing the emptiness of all appearances.

Bodhicitta: liberating other beings in appropriate ways

Contrary to the view, widely held in the West, of the Tantric practitioner as disregarding all conventions without restraint, the person who has opted for the Tantric way must, like other Buddhists, observe numerous ethical rules. These include the basic Buddhist rules not to kill, lie, steal, commit adultery, or take intoxicating drink; in addition to keep the ten principal virtues (*pāramitā*) of giving, morality, patience, energy, etc; to avoid the so-called eighteen basic offences against the Bodhisattva vow (for instance praising oneself and disparaging others, not passing on the Buddha's teaching, not forgiving someone who has apologized, dissuading anyone from the intention of realizing highest enlightenment, giving up the teaching, and so forth). Furthermore it is necessary to avoid the fourteen basic offences against the *mantra* vow, even at the cost of one's own life:

> *Scorning and deriding the lama (bla ma), ... abandoning love,*
> *Giving up the aspirational and practical altruistic intentions,*
> *Deriding the doctrines of Sūtra and Mantra,*
> *Proclaiming the secret to the unripened, ...*
> *Not observing the pledges and deriding women.*[5]

The practitioner encounters one particular ethical precept again and again: the demand to cultivate the so-called 'mind of enlightenment' (*bodhicitta; byang chub kyi sems*), the altruistic mind of realization of emptiness that is guided by the wish to attain complete and perfect enlightenment for the benefit of others.[6] 'Self-less' means 'without self' or 'without any self' on the one hand, and on the other, being unselfish, willing to make sacrifices, altruistic and devoted to others, and thereby implies a demand for social action.[7] The utimate goal is not one's own liberation from the cycle of suffering, but the liberation – and so happiness – of all living beings. Regarding this, the *Kālacakra Tantra* says:

> *From this time until enlightenment I will generate the altruistic intention to become enlightened (bodhicitta). I will generate the very pure thought, and abandon the conception of an [inherently existent] I and mine. ... I will achieve the perfections of giving, ethics, patience ... I will cultivate [love wishing] that sentient beings have happiness, [compassion wishing] that they be free from suffering, joy in their abiding forever in bliss, and the equanimity of equality ...* [8]

The importance of the guru

The relationship between the disciple and his or her spiritual teacher (*guru; bla ma*) is of the greatest importance. This teacher can protect the adept from danger, from coming into contact with ideas and practices for which he or she is not yet ripe. The *guru* should thus lead his disciples individually. Moreover various teachings, particularly secret ones, are not fixed in writing but are simply transmitted orally from teacher to teacher; because of that the disciple is dependent on his or her teacher. Having at his disposal inner and outer qualities, the teacher is in a position to initiate, to draw mandalas and to meditate on them; he is practised in techniques of concentration, knows how the symbolic hand gestures (*mudrā*) and ritual dances should be performed, is experienced in the three lower classes of *tantras,* in making burnt offerings, and many other ritual practices.

The importance of the *guru* is illustrated by the following analogy which is said to go back to the great Sakya Pandita. However strongly the sun shines, the wood you wish to set alight will never ignite on its own. To kindle fire you need a lens to focus the rays. In the same way, you can only attain the blessing of the mighty Buddha through the mediation of a *guru*.[9] Sakya Pandita also held that worship of one's *guru* for the duration of just a fingersnap outshines the merit that has accrued during a thousand eons of practising the six perfections.[10]

A legend shows how the *guru* surpasses even one's personal protective deity. The teacher Nāropa once appeared to the translator Marpa as the *yidam* Hevajra. He gave his disciple the choice of prostrating to the deity or the teacher. Marpa decided in favour of the protective deity – a mistake since all emanated deities ultimately count as emanations of the *guru*.[11] So the meditator on deity yoga (see p. 63ff) sees in each visualized deity his own spiritual teacher, "undifferentiable from the Supramundane Victor, the great Kālacakra",[12] as it says in the *Guru Yoga* of the *Kālacakra Tantra*. The disciple places his trust in the great protector completely, as only he can show the path to supreme enlightenment, reveal the sacred words, and endow him with precious *bodhicitta*.[13]

The root of all causes producing
Happiness here and hereafter, is the practice
Of relying in thought and action
Upon the sacred friend who reveals the path.
Seeing this, follow him at any cost
And please him with the offering of practice.
I, a yogi, did that myself;
You, O liberation seeker, should do likewise![14]

This is the advice of Tsongkhapa, the famous reformer of Tibetan Buddhism.

Outer Mandala: The Cosmos

The cylindrical cosmos of the Abhidarmakośa

According to the *Abhidharmakośa*, a text written by Vasubandhu (fourth/fifth century), the universe comprises a virtually infinite number of world systems. Each of these systems consists of a gigantic cylindrical plinth and, on the plinth's surface, structured of water and mountains, there rests a heavenly realm. A thousand million such world systems or world units stand on a vast cylindrical base of air, whose height according to the *Abhidharmakośa* is 80,000 *yojanas*, but whose diameter is so great it cannot be expressed in numbers (Fig. 10).[1]

Before primeval times the power of the collective actions or collective *karma* of earlier living beings brought it about that from all the four directions there arose an incredibly strong wind. It filled the empty space and helped form clouds, from which water poured forth torrentially. From the water, the raging hurricanes shaped the lowest 'building block' of a world system: the gigantic cylindrical base. The winds moved more, and on the stirred water created foam, which grew ever thicker, heavier, and more yellow. In this way another component of the world cylinder was formed: the golden earth, in the centre of which rose a four-cornered mountain-column, made from the most precious elements of the whisked masses of water, namely gold, silver, lapis and crystal, Mount Meru, whose four sides each have four terraces. Around it, further whisking formed out of the elements of medium quality seven golden mountain walls. Moving away from Meru, each mountain is half the height of the previous one. Between the mountains the rain caused great seas of fresh water to develop, which collectively bear the name of the 'inner ocean'. On the other side of the outermost and lowest golden wall stretches an enormous salt-water sea, the 'great outer sea', in which float twelve continents – land masses formed in the third whisking. The rim of the golden earth-disc is encompassed by an eighth mountain wall, made of iron (Fig. 5). The world of human beings lies in the middle southern continent, Jambudvīpa, which lies on the southern side of Mount Meru whose lapis colour is the same as that of the sky.[2] This explains why people are unable to recognize the shape of the world mountain Meru from their continent.

At half the height of Meru, barely above the mountain wall nearest the world mountain, the sun and moon travel their orbits borne by the wind.

In the middle of the square summit-region of Meru lies the city of Sudarśana 'Beautiful to See', also laid out in a square (Fig. 7). In the centre of this stands Vaijayanta, the palace of the leader of the thirty-three chief gods who live in this realm of the world. The strongly symmetrical layout is evident: the mountain surface is subdivided into four regions which correspond to the four directions, and are oriented towards the centre – a plan typical of any mandala.

The idea of a city at the centre of the world is found also in other cultures. Thus for instance in the worldview of medieval Europe Jerusalem was accepted as the 'navel of the world', and Islam regards Mecca as the centre of the earth.[3]

The Buddhist world system clearly values upper regions more highly than those situated lower down. Thus above the heaven of the thirty-three gods (on Mount Meru) float further heavens or castles (*vimāna*), stacked concentrically one above the other, so that the purer they are the higher they are. Their arrangement and dimensions vary in the statements of the texts, but pictorial representations and writings alike lead us to assume that the heavenly strata become wider and thicker with increasing altitude (Figs 5, 8). Presumably the interval between successive heavenly strata also increases toward the top, though the pictures from Tibet and the Himalayas known to us are not clear on this point. This may be because a picture area in normal format (a scroll painting or a temple wall; Plates 4–7) does not permit cosmic distances to be represented to scale without also shrinking the part of the cosmos important to human beings – Mount Meru and the continents – to invisible dots.

According to Buddhist ideas, the worlds of the gods have their counterpart in the underworld, in the form of eight hot and eight cold hells beneath the southern continent of Jambudvīpa inhabited by human beings (Fig. 8).[4]

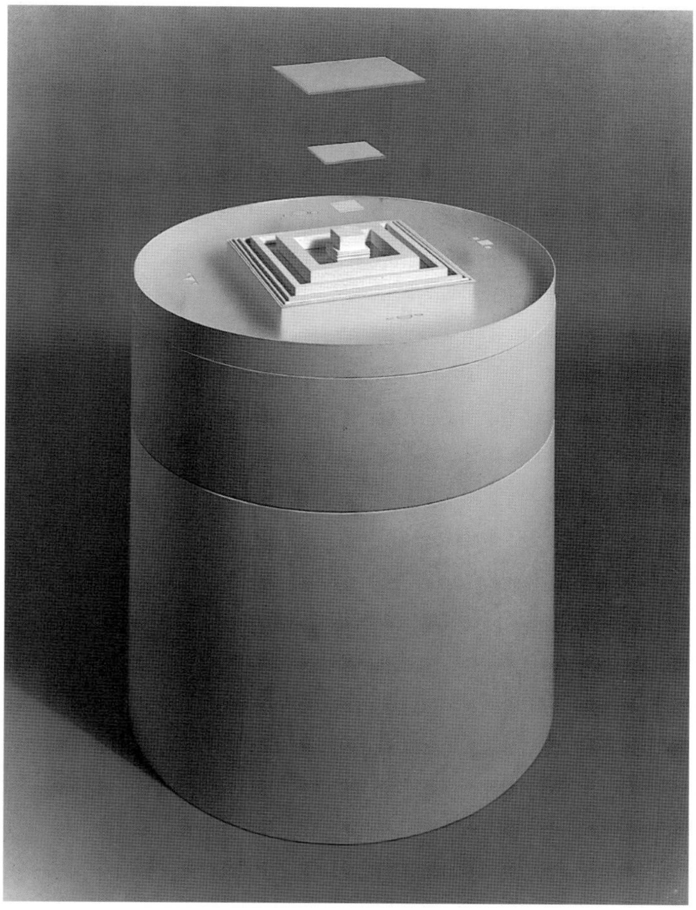

5 *Scale model of a cosmos according to sources going back to the Abhidharmakośa. The uppermost part of the cylinder (salt and fresh water seas) has a height of 80,000 yojanas (c. 600,000 km or 360,000 miles; in the Abhidharmakośa 1 yojana is equal to 7.5 km or 4.5 miles), the part below it consisting of gold is 320,000 yojanas high (c. 2.4 million km, 1.5 million miles), and the lowest region, full of water, measures 800,000 yojanas (c. 6 million km, 3.6 million miles); the radius of the cylinder amounts to 600,000 yojanas (c. 4.5 million km, 2.7 million miles). The continents in the ocean that washes round the mountain depart from scale, being magnified twenty times in the representation. An eighth mountain wall at the rim of the gold disc – the iron mountain – encloses the round ocean and ends only just above sea level. The rectangular pieces above Meru stand for the three lowest of the 25 heavens above the world mountain. According to one tradition, the distance separating them doubles from layer to layer.*[5]

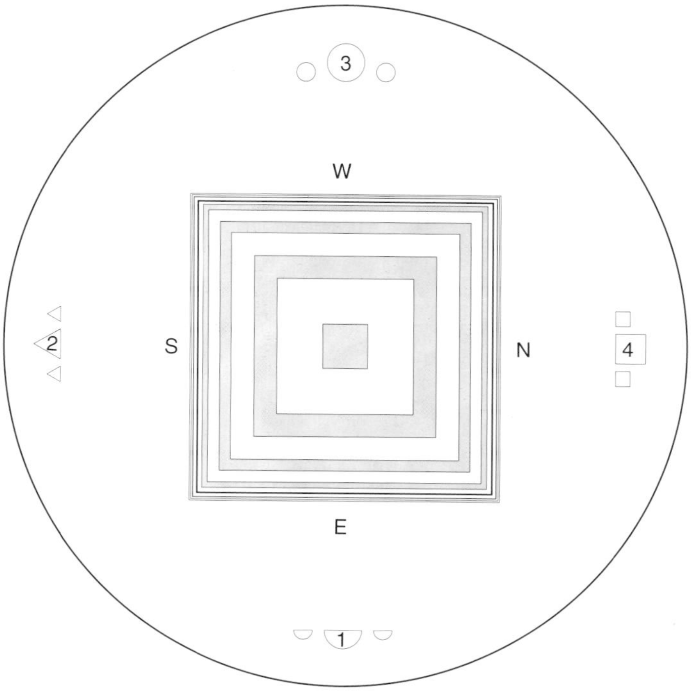

6 *Plan view of the cosmos according to Abhidharmakośa. The twelve continents are shown enlarged 25 times: (1) eastern continents; (2) southern continents; (3) western continents; (4) northern continents.*

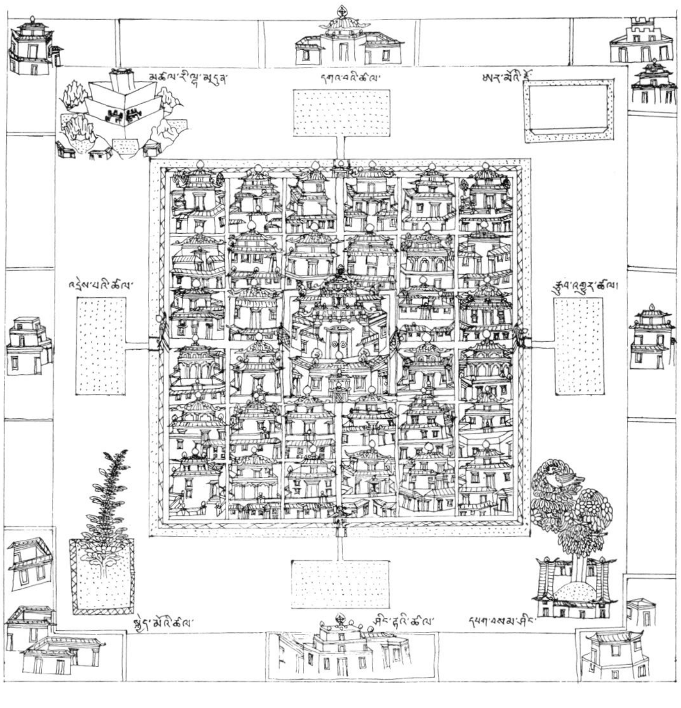

7 *Organization of the summit of Mount Meru according to the Tibetan Bonpo tradition.*[6] *In the centre, 32 smaller palaces – the residences of the 32 leading gods of this heaven – surround the larger palace of the chief deity. Parks, a mountain (in the top left-hand corner), and more buildings in the outer border, which shield the summit from the outside, hem the palace complex.*

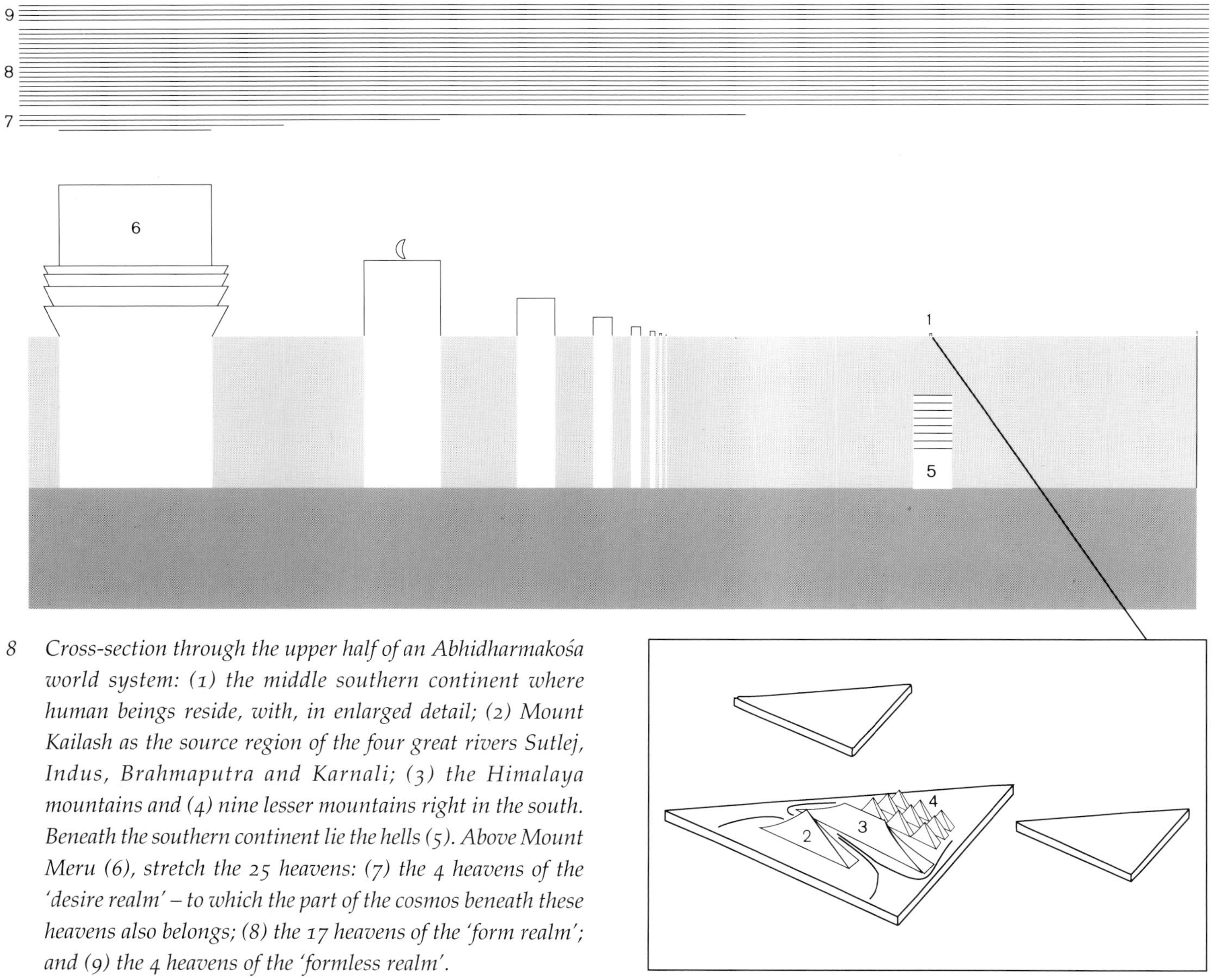

8 Cross-section through the upper half of an Abhidharmakośa world system: (1) the middle southern continent where human beings reside, with, in enlarged detail; (2) Mount Kailash as the source region of the four great rivers Sutlej, Indus, Brahmaputra and Karnali; (3) the Himalaya mountains and (4) nine lesser mountains right in the south. Beneath the southern continent lie the hells (5). Above Mount Meru (6), stretch the 25 heavens: (7) the 4 heavens of the 'desire realm' – to which the part of the cosmos beneath these heavens also belongs; (8) the 17 heavens of the 'form realm'; and (9) the 4 heavens of the 'formless realm'.

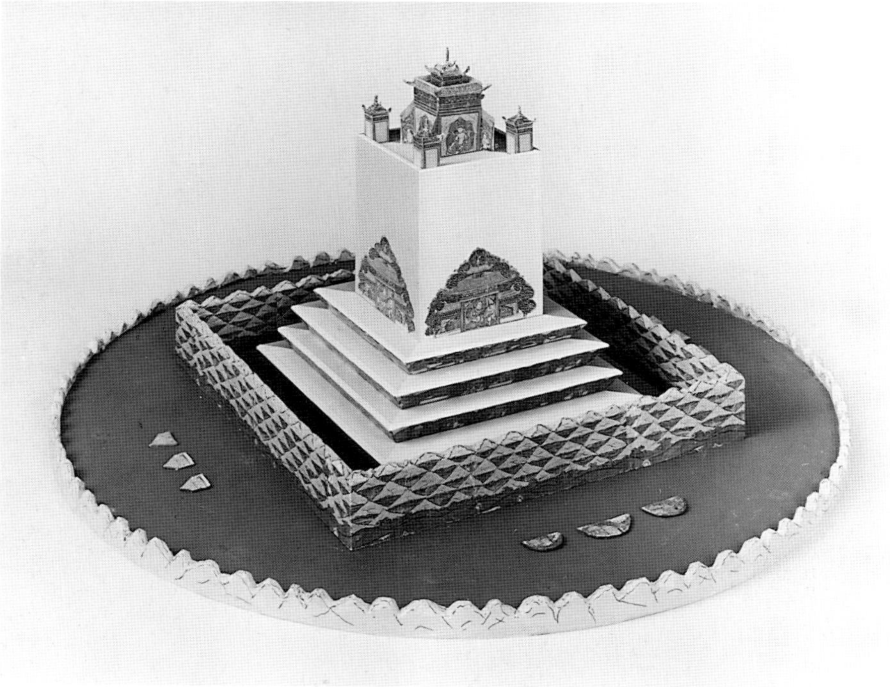

9 Model of the cosmos according to the Abhidharmakośa, showing the spatial arrangement of the world mountain and the twelve continents. For this a reproduction of Plate 7 was cut up into separate components and built up three-dimensionally; elements of the picture not belonging to the cosmos have been omitted (flowers, emblems either side of Meru); the seven mountain chains surrounding Meru also appear as a single wall.

Paintings of the cosmos – quite often found on the outside walls of Tibetan Buddhist places of worship, and more seldom in scroll paintings – do render the essential elements of this upper-world topography, but are often hard to interpret. In some, as stated, there is a lack of accurate scale; in others, Tibetan Buddhist art follows specific conventions when representing space. Thus for instance in the same work some parts may be depicted in 'plan' (i.e. from above), and others in 'elevation' (i.e. from the front or side), spatiality being portrayed in a way unfamiliar to the Western viewer (Plate 7; Fig. 9).

The divine at the centre of each world system

Unlike the cosmology of the European Middle Ages, the Buddhist conception of the world does not place the earth and human beings at the centre. Rather, here it is the gods – corporeal, subtle, spiritual and formless beings – and their worlds, that form the 'theocentric' axis of the universe, while human and other living beings eke out an existence on the margins of the centre.

Tantric visualizations, and above all the complicated mandala ritual, are invariably about reaching (returning to) this divine centre. The mandala as mirror of the cosmos – not just the outer cosmos but also the microcosm, the person – is based on the assumption of close relations between world, mandala and person.

Besides the concentration on the divine, Buddhist cosmology is notable for the multiplication of small cosmoses into an amassing of countless 'cosmos clusters' (Fig. 10) – a remarkable correspondence with the modern Western understanding of the universe. A thousand such world systems with a Mount Meru, sun, moon, god realms and so forth, form a 'small chiliocosm', a thousand small cosmoses form a 'middle' one, and a 'thousand middle' ones a 'great' or 'triple chiliocosm', embracing a thousand million world systems.

Also gigantic are the periods of time over which individual world systems arise and pass away, or in which only 'waiting space' remains, which is eventually moved again by a gently rising wind – whereupon a world system is built anew. Thus just as the *skandhas* are transitory, so too the world and the entire universe are susceptible to continual change.

The individual periods or 'cosmic pulse-beats', known as *kalpa* in Sanskrit, for their part embrace such enormous spans of time that they are often described in allegories rather than reckoned in years:

> *Imagine a cubical container, each side measuring one yojana (about 15 kilometres),*[7] *completely filled with fine hair. Take out a single hair tip each hundred years. The time it takes to empty it is a single solar day of a least eon. The measure of thirty such solar days makes up a month. Twelve months make up a year. A hundred years is called 'an eon'. Likewise the medium eon is a multiple of that (least eon). A superior eon is a multiple of the medium eon.*

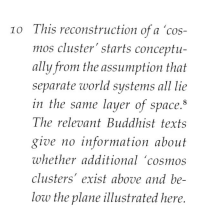

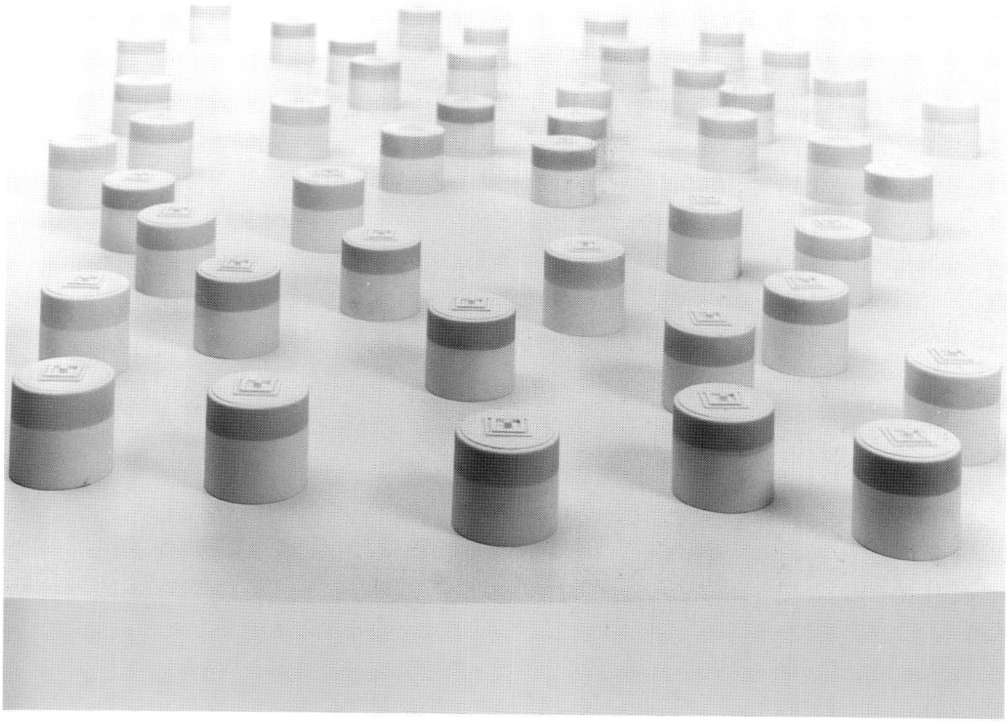

10 *This reconstruction of a 'cosmos cluster' starts conceptually from the assumption that separate world systems all lie in the same layer of space.*[8] *The relevant Buddhist texts give no information about whether additional 'cosmos clusters' exist above and below the plane illustrated here.*

The pyramidal cosmos according to the Kālacakra tradition

Different cosmologies are recognized by individual Buddhist traditions, but there is no contradiction in this, for as Kalu Rinpoche says:

> *Any one of these various cosmologies is completely valid for the beings whose karmic projections cause them to experience their universe in that way. There is a certain relativity in the way one experiences the world. This means that all the possible experiences of every being in the six realms of existence … are based upon karmic inclinations and degrees of individual development. Thus, on a relative level any cosmology is valid. On an ultimate level, no cosmology is absolutely true. It cannot be universally valid, given the different conventional situations of beings.*[9]

The second Tibetan Buddhist idea of the cosmos, that from the tradition of the *Kālacakra Tantra*, is only seldom described in Western publications as an independent one deviating from that of the *Abhidharmakośa*. Like the *Abhidharmakośa*, it too assumes that cosmoses arise, pass away and arise again in endless periods of time. However, according to the Kālacakra tradition, unlike the *Abhidharmakośa*, not all the atoms of the five elements disappear at the end of an epoch; they simply fall apart and become separated from each other by space atoms. As a result of the 'stockpile' of collective *karma* from earlier ages of the world the atoms again enter new combinations. The air atoms come together. This results in strong winds, which in turn make the fire atoms unite and because of this lightning, i.e. electriciy, arises. Next follows the formation of water atoms, which bring about rain. The rainbows which appear now are manifestations of the first earth atoms, which become thicker and thicker and eventually result in solid earth. The space atoms fill the space between the other atoms and float both below and above the world system.

Common to both notions of the cosmos is the concentric, mandala-type structure with a Mount Meru at the centre, though its form differs in the two systems. The base of the Kālacakra cosmos also differs (Plates 6, 8): it consists of four colossal round discs, of which the lowest (air) has the greatest diameter (400,000 *yojanas*, *c.* 6 million km, or 3.6 million miles; in the Kālacakra tradition 1 *yojana* is equal to 15 km or 9 miles), and the uppermost (earth) the least (100,000 *yojanas*, *c.* 1.5 million km or 910,000 miles).[10] Meru is not square as in the *Abhidharmakośa*, but round, and tapers towards the base. It is immediately surrounded by six concentric land masses, six mountain walls and six oceans. If one includes the water disc (Figs 11, 12), there are altogether seven oceans.

In the Kālacakra world model, one's attention is immediately drawn to the twelve circles arranged around Mount Meru. These are the wind-tracks on which the planets glide.[11] Pictorial representations of these twelve wind-tracks are found mainly on the walls of monasteries in Bhutan (Plate 4, left). The tracks are drawn in a bird's-eye view from a point directly above the cosmic centre.[12] Such illustrations admittedly do not demonstrate clearly the spatial arrangement of the tracks. Only a side view of a cosmos model reveals that the planets form a kind of cap or dome around Meru (Fig. 12). This model was constructed according to drawings made with a 3D computer program, based on traditional Tibetan sources.

It is further worth remarking, as regards the Kālacakra world picture, that the universe above Meru takes the form of a head, invisible to humans, with neck, chin, nose and forehead, as well as an upward extension in the form of a topknot (Plate 6).[13] The invisible shaping of the topmost part of the world into a head – in this region are found the twenty-five heavens of the Kālacakra universe – indicates that there is a special relationship between the Kālacakra universe and the form of a human being or of a deity (Plate 9; Fig. 31). In this the essential wisdom of the Kālacakra tradition is already apparent: the endless recapitulation of ordered structures from the breadth of the macrocosm down to the minuteness of the microcosm.

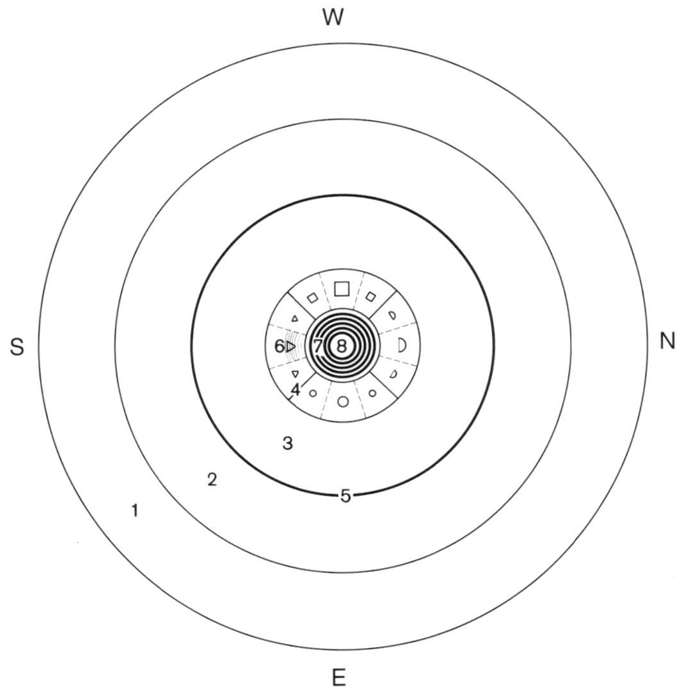

11 *Plan view of the cosmos according to the Kālacakra Tantra: (1) air disc; (2) fire disc; (3) water disc ('seventh ocean'); (4) earth disc; (5) fire or vajra mountain; (6) southern continent Jambudvīpa with seven mountain chains; (7) six rings each comprising a land mass, mountain wall and ocean (liquor, water, milk, curd, ghee, molasses); (8) base of Mount Meru.*

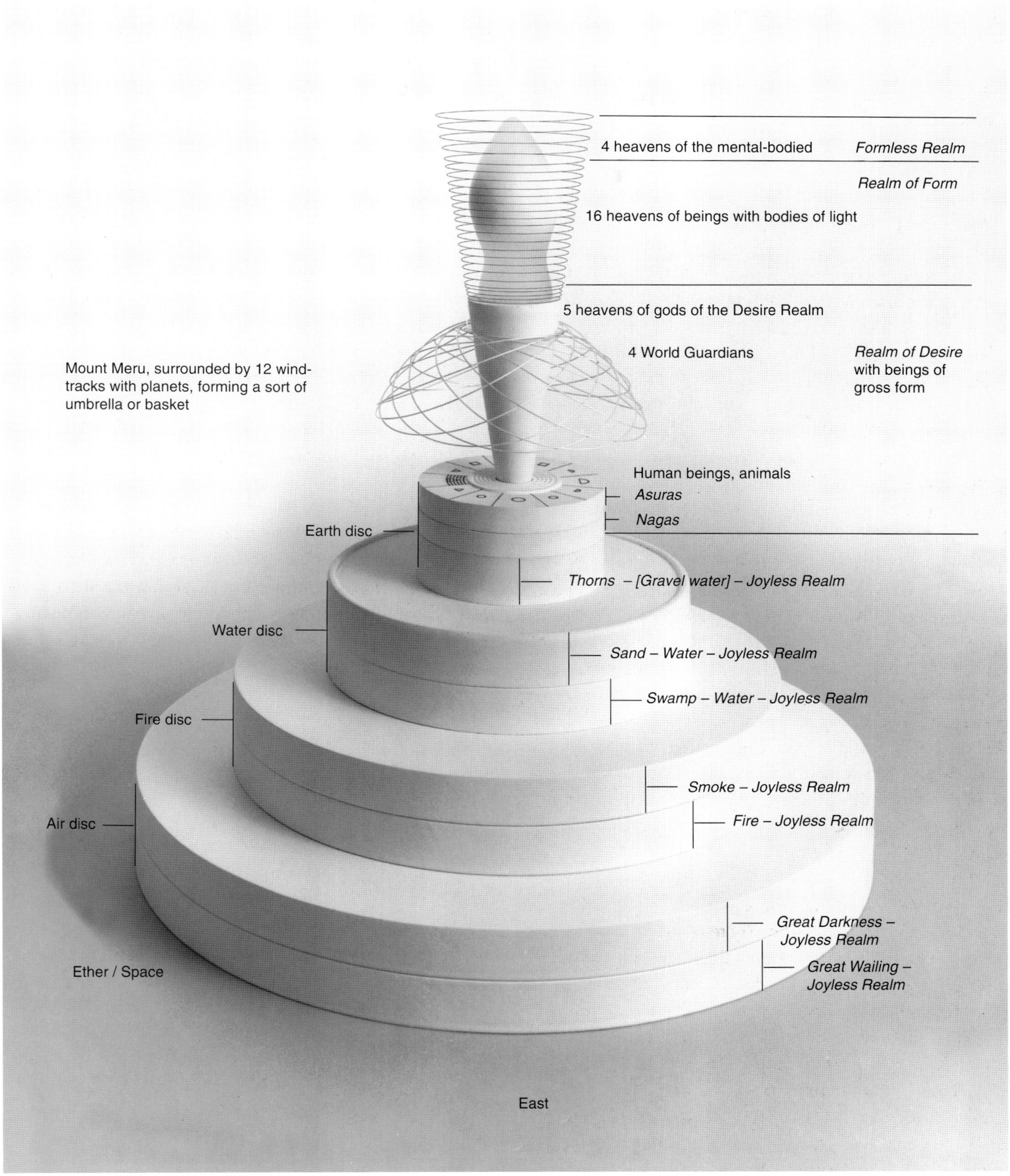

12 *Model of the Kālacakra cosmos: in the Kālacakra world system too there are twelve continents – three in each of the four cardinal directions, amid a great ocean around Mount Meru. The continents are depicted as square, circular, etc.*[14] *The middle, southern land mass, called Jambudvīpa, is the dwelling place of human beings and animals, and is divided into six regions.*

Offering of the universe: the grain mandala

The mandala-structure of the universe – whether according to the *Abhidharmakośa* or the Kālacakra tradition – is evident: circles or discs form the base for an inner realm that is aligned with the five directions (east, south, west, north and centre) and organized vertically (the highest point symbolizing the purest and most sacred realm). This basic structure of the universe is copied in a frequently performed offering in the form of a grain mandala. A silver plate fitted with a circular band serves as a base; it symbolizes the golden earth cylinder of the *Abhidharmakośa* cosmos (Fig. 13). The act of worship, during which the cosmos is presented as an offering, begins with careful cleaning of the surface of the plate – this purifies all the inner defilements of the worshipper. After taking refuge in the spiritual teacher and the Three Jewels (Buddha, Buddhist teaching, community of monks), and expressing the wish to attain Buddhahood for the benefit of all beings, the worshipper marks out with grains the surrounding circular 'iron mountain' that guards the universe outwardly, and in the centre, Meru, 'king amongst mountains' (Fig. 13/1). Then with a small pile of grain for each, the four main continents are built (Fig. 13/2–5), then the eight sub-continents (Fig. 13/6–13), the 'treasures of the four great continents' (Fig. 13/14–17), the 'seven precious things' (Fig. 13/18–24), and a treasure vase as an eighth (Fig. 13/25). Next the worshipper spreads the eight 'mothers' or offering goddesses (Fig. 13/26–33), and finally with a little pile for each, marks the sun and moon, an umbrella and a banner of victory (Fig. 13/34–37) and, again in the middle, marks the world of the gods above Meru (Fig. 13/38).[15]

The offering of the universe – which is eventually transformed into an absolutely pure Buddha-land – is regarded as one of the best methods of accumulating merits and of ripening the fruits of spiritual efforts.

On a higher level, this offering means still more: the analogies between universe and person, macrocosm and microcosm, mean that with the outer mandala of grains a worshipper offers not just the universe but his or her entire being. This becomes apparent when the so-called 'inner mandala' is offered. In this the parts of the body are correlated with different regions of the cosmos: the skin – imagined as golden – corresponds to the golden base of the universe; the trunk symbolizes the world mountain Meru; the legs and arms the four main continents; one's own head is regarded as the seat of the gods dwelling on Mount Meru; and one's eyes as the sun and moon.[16] Thus the whole body forms the cosmos as well as an (inner) mandala, which – transformed into a pure Buddha-land – is offered to both one's personal *guru* and the Three Jewels; a self-offering that represents an essential prerequisite for successful performance of Tantric rituals.[17]

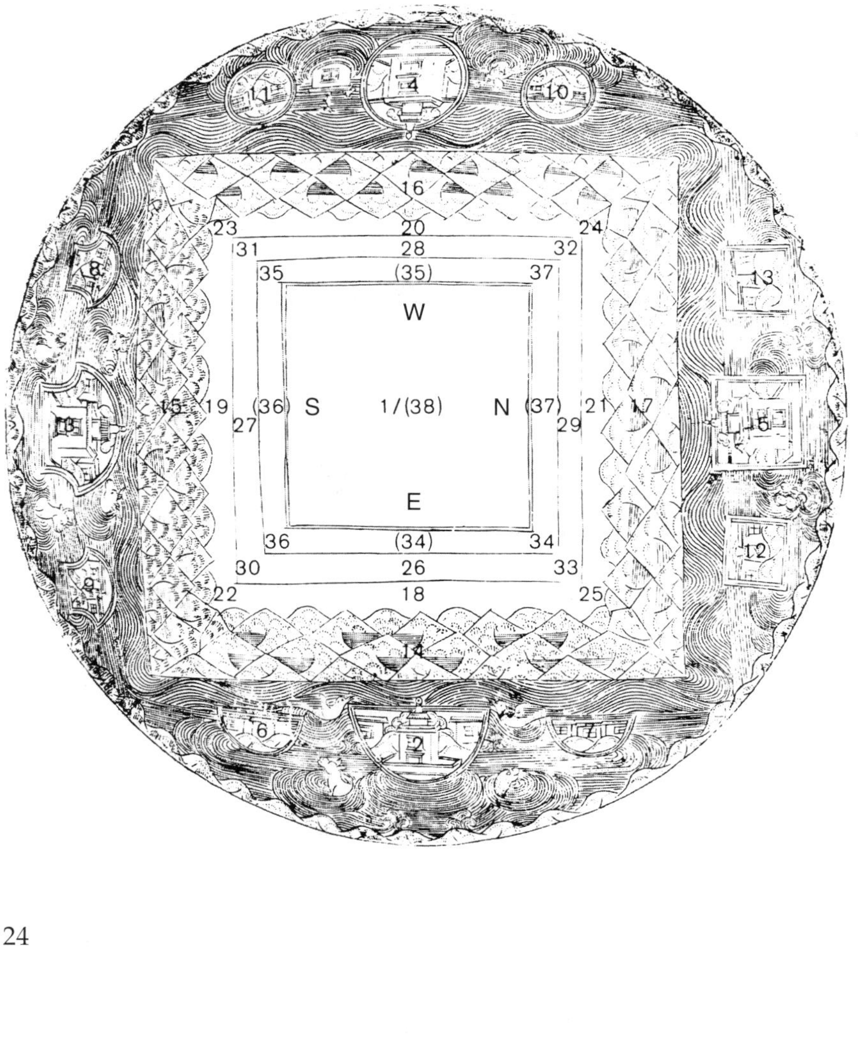

13 *Ground plan of the cosmos according to the Abhidharmakośa, engraved on the surface of a plate used as a base for the grain mandala. The components are: (1) Mount Meru; (2–5) main continents; (6–13) sub-continents; (14–17) treasures of the four great continents: [(14) mountain of jewels, (15) wish-granting tree, (16) wish-granting cow, (17) harvests from uncultivated land]; (18–24) the seven precious things:*[18] *[(18) wheel, (19) jewel, (20) queen, (21) minister, (22) elephant, (23) horse, (24) commander]; (25) treasure vase, as an eighth precious thing;*[18] *(26–33) eight mothers or offering goddesses:*[19] *[(26) goddess of gaity and laughter, (27) garland-bearing, (28) singing, (29) dancing, (30) flower-bearing, (31) incense-bearing, (32) lamp-bearing, (33) perfume-bearing]; (34) sun; (35) moon; (36) umbrella; (37) banner of victory;*[20] *(38) world of the gods above Meru. The numbers in brackets (in the drawing) give alternative arrangements.*

15 *An unusual form of representation of the universe: in the centre the square Mount Meru is recognizable, and on each of its terraced sides are portrayed the three continents of one cardinal direction (in fact these should have been on the level surface at the foot of the mountain).*

14 *The plate whose surface engraving is shown in Fig. 13 belongs to a set of silver hoops, which arranged one above the other make a three-dimensional representation of the 'outer mandala'. The symbols and figures (2–37 in Fig. 13) are engraved on the sides of the rings. Facing the viewer is the east side of the cosmos mandala; on the second ring from the bottom, for example, the 'mountain of jewels' is visible, above it the 'wheel', and above that the 'goddess of gaity and laughter'.*

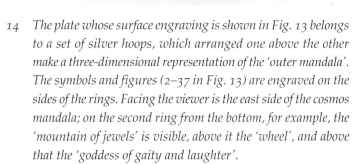

16 *This top view of the universe model in Fig. 15 makes clear the arrangement of the level surface. The outer ring shows, between mountains and water, the 'treasures of the four great continents' (Fig. 13/14–17) and the inner ring, the 'seven precious things' (Fig. 13/18–24, though in a different order).*

17 *The universe created out of grains of rice or other materials is first offered to the personal guru – here H.H. the XIV Dalai Lama during the Great Prayer Festival in Dharamsala in 1972 – and to the Three Jewels, combined with the request: "Accept this out of compassion for all beings, that it may be for the welfare of all beings!".*

Architectural reproduction of the universe: the stūpa

If we look at the scale model of the world according to *Kālacakra Tantra* from the side and prolong downwards the bell-shaped cap formed by the mutually interwoven astronomical wind-tracks, a structure resembling a *stūpa* is produced (Fig. 18). The cubical region above the dome, called the *harmikā*, is no attachment or superstructure but the uppermost part of Mount Meru, which is largely concealed under the 'cap'.[21] The vault itself corresponds to the dome of the sky, so that one can perfectly well speak, with Mus,[22] of a 'hemispherical' form of the *stūpa*.

The *stūpa*, a religious structure already known in early Buddhism, symbolizes the Buddha's teaching, but also the Buddha himself.[23] As a reliquary it can hold the mortal remains of a saint or pieces of his clothing, and in addition sacred texts, articles of worship and – in the regions of Tibetan Buddhism – *tsha tsha*, figures of clay mixed with the ashes of the deceased. In the course of time and depending on geographical situation, *stūpas* have developed quite different forms, but above all, always constitute an object of lay worship.

Several authors have already demonstrated the close relationship, in fact extensive correspondence, between the universe and the *stūpa*.[24] Some Western interpretations connect the levels of the *stūpa* with the five elements: the cubical plinth or the four-tier substructure with the element earth, the vaulted, virtually dome-shaped middle section with water, the thirteen superimposed discs of the *stūpa* spire with fire, the umbrella (sometimes also the sun and moon) with air, and the flame (sometimes with the sun and moon) with ether or space.[25] This attempt at interpretation refers to a late *stūpa* form (Fig. 21) quite common in Tibet, though no Tibetan text is known to the author that supports such an interpretation. It must therefore be viewed with some caution, even though it is traced back to the eminent Tibetologist Giuseppe Tucci.[26] Tucci based his attempt at interpretation on a Japanese source and made it clear that it was a matter of assumed correlations. The texts he cited make quite different alignments, bringing the various parts of the *stūpa* into relation with particular Buddhist concepts – notably the four perfect renunciations (*prahāna*), the five faculties (*pañcendriya*), the eightfold path (*astāṅgamārga*).[27]

This perhaps suggests that the original significance of the *stūpa* is to be sought rather in its equation with an entire world system or cosmos, and not simply with the five elements.[28]

The correspondence between *stūpa*-axis and world mountain appears clearly in older *stūpas* in Sri Lanka, which show stone central axes that local scholars call *Indrakīla* – the term for the stake that the Hindu god Indra used to join heaven and earth, identical with the Hindu world mountain.[29] In Tibetan too we find the expressions 'pillar of heaven' (*gnam kyi ka ba*) and 'earth-dagger' (*sa yi phur bu*)[30] used for sacred mountains, which, if we consider the downward-tapering Meru in the Kālacakra cosmos, are quite illuminating names.[31]

In ancient India, the pillar erected in the centre of a *stūpa* was called *yūpa*, a term that can mean a sacrificial stake, but also, and in this connection far more likely, the axis in the form of a cosmic tree that connects heaven and earth.[32] Ancient *stūpa*-depictions in Amarāvatī, in which branches of a tree grow out above the very middle of the dome,[33] indicate that this central axis, normally hidden deep inside the dome,[34] can actually be equated with a tree. Furthermore the expression 'life-wood' or 'life-tree' (*srog shing*) for the central axis of the Tibetan *stūpa* (Fig. 21) likewise suggests a correlation between the *stūpa*-axis and 'tree of life' that in the view of many societies marks the centre of the world.[35] In Buddhism, of course, this tree also signifies the most important of all trees, the one under which the historical Buddha attained enlightenment (*bodhi*); after all many Buddhists regard the place where the *bodhi* tree stands as the centre of the earth.[36]

In many pictorial representations a tree grows on Mount Meru – according to the *Abhidharmakośa* a magnolia – which is undoubtedly identical with this tree; in Buddhist legends, the gods and *asuras* are constantly quarrelling over its fruits and its roots reach down deep into Mount Meru.[37] In Tibetan Buddhism depictions are also known of the so-called 'field of accumulation' (*tshogs zhing*). This is a tree on which an entire pantheon is assembled. Such a 'gathering tree', which as a rule grows out of water, can be identified without hesitation as a world tree and world axis, all the more so as Mount Meru is also often depicted beside its roots.

Is the *stūpa*-centre then a cosmic tree or a cosmic mountain? Surely it is both, which need in no way imply a contradiction. For the world tree and world mountain stand in close relation to one another, often in symbols that are collapsed into one.[38] This means that Mount Meru and the *stūpa*-pillar, which remains largely hidden beneath the bell-shaped dome, could as has been demonstrated, be identical.[39]

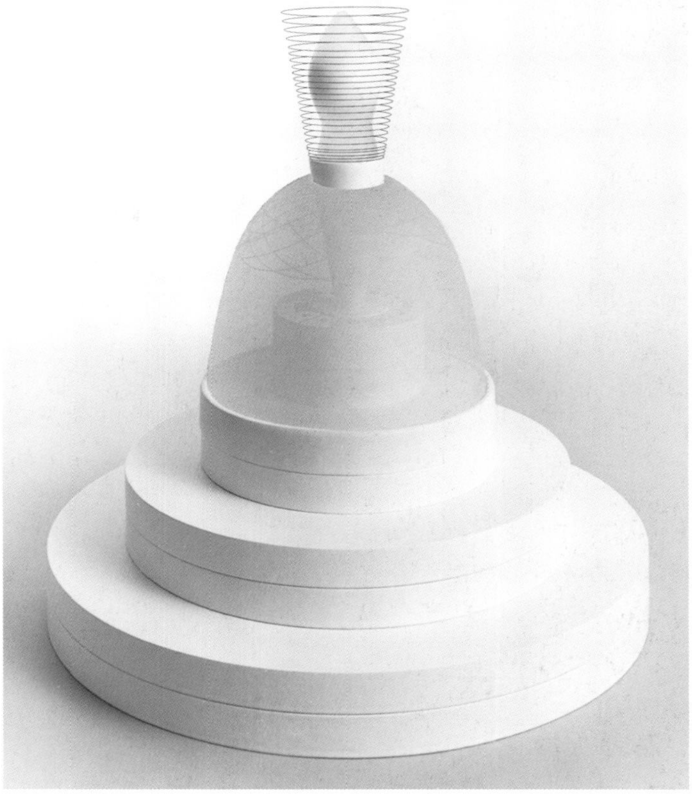

18 *Model of the cosmos adapted into a stūpa, according to the tradition of the Kālacakra Tantra.*

19 *Depiction of stūpa from Amarāvatī, Andhra Pradesh, India, from the so-called middle phase (second half of second century* CE*).*

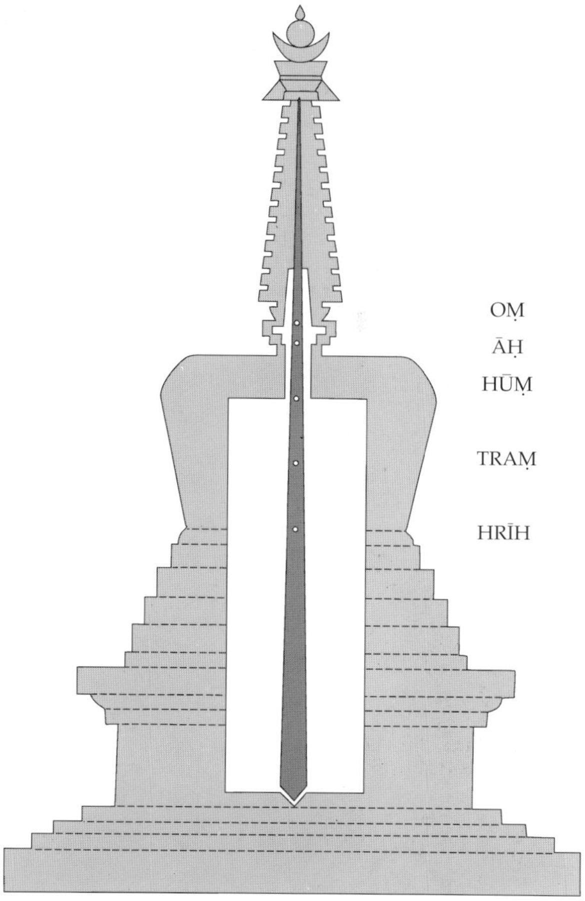

20 *Chendebji Stūpa, Central Bhutan. Like the Amarāvatī Stūpa, this stūpa too has much in common with the outer appearance of the Kālacakra universe.*[40]

21 *Cross-section through a Tibetan stūpa. In the centre is the cavity, in which rises the 'life-wood' (srog shing, axis); this should be of the best sandalwood, or at least of the wood of an unpoisonous fruit tree. That part of the piece of wood which was originally nearer the crown of the tree must form the point of the life-wood.*[41] *The places marked by dots on the life-wood are inscribed with a seed-syllable, from top to bottom,* OṂ ĀḤ HŪṂ TRAṂ HRĪH. *This recalls the power-centres (chakra) along the central wind channel in humans* *(see p. 54f)* *and suggests a close relationship between the human being and the middle region of the Tibetan stūpa.*

22 *Right: The Borobudur Stūpa (plan view). Clearly visible are the three concentric circles with 32, 24 and 16 stūpas, which emphasize the mandala character of this edifice. The partition into three regions corresponds to the tripartite division of the heavens above the cosmos into the realms of 'desire' (kāmadhātu), 'form' (rūpadhātu), and 'formlessness' (arūpadhātu).*

But the *stūpa*-pillar could also be a tree, a channel of life – an idea that becomes particularly interesting when we equate Meru, and with it the *stūpa*-pillar, with the spine of the human body (Fig. 31). This equation really suggests itself, because the central axis of a Buddhist metal statue, likewise called *srog shing*, together with two blades of grass situated to its left and right, symbolize the three main channels (*nāḍī*) along the human spine (see Ch. 4).[42]

Following on from this, it is hardly surprising that in Tibetan the *stūpa* axis is also called 'Brahmā-line' (*tshangs thig*), a term that according to Tucci signifies the 'spinal column' (*Brahmādaṇḍa*).[43] Tucci further recognizes in the trinity of sun, moon and flame (which frequently crowns the Tibetan *stūpa*) a suggestion of the three main channels in the human body,[44] one more indication that there are correlations between the *stūpa* and the human body – or rather the body of the Buddha.[45] In a late Javanese Buddhist text, this leads to the following observation: "The body of the Buddha, seen from without, is a *stūpa*."[46] The correspondence between Buddha body and *stūpa* also becomes clear when one examines Tibetan scroll paintings, on the reverse of which there is sometimes a drawing of a *stūpa* which coincides with the main figure portrayed on the front.

The stūpa as stepped path to enlightenment

Buddhists are rarely conscious of the above-mentioned symbolism of the *stūpa*. The faithful regard *stūpas* as objects of worship, in the niches of which they lay sacred objects and which they circumambulate clockwise many times in order to gain merits which is how the original form (Ur form) of a mandala arose. Anagarika Govinda surmises that the first mandala may have been created when the devout transformed the *stūpas* that sheltered the relics of the Buddha by adding a path that was surrounded by a stone railing with four gates. Each of the gates marked one of the four important events in the life of the Buddha.[47]

Some *stūpas* are circumambulated not only on the level of one *stūpa* plinth but spirally on several storeys, up to the most important sanctuary, where a symbol of the absolute is kept (Figs 22–4). This traversal of a *stūpa* recalls the meditative 'walk' through a mandala palace, that stepped path to enlightenment on which the disciple progresses from the grossly material via the subtly material to the formless, mental realm, so as to experience eventually highest bliss and emptiness.

The best known traversable *stūpa* is undoubtedly that of Borobodur in Java, over 30 metres high, of the ninth/tenth century (Figs 22, 23). This clearly elucidates elements of the picture of the universe. It constitutes a three-dimensional mandala and also symbolizes the world mountain, or more precisely the uppermost 'storeys' of the universe, those of the gods.[48] For the Buddhist, however, Borobodur is primarily a processional way:

> *... which leads the pilgrim up from the misery of saṃsāra portrayed in the reliefs of the plinth ... to the future Buddhas Maitreya and Samantabhadra and finally, with the three round terraces of the summit, into the region with neither images nor forms of the arūpa heaven.*[49]

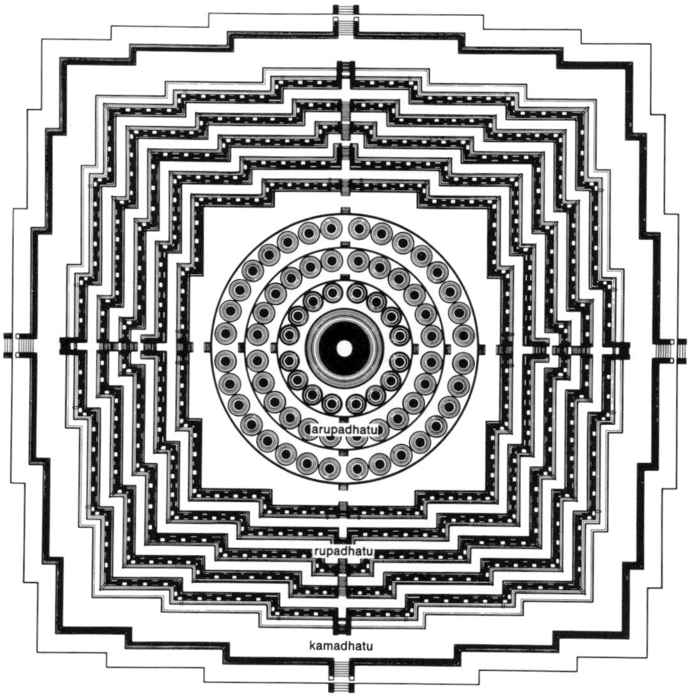

23 *Borobodur Stūpa in Java.*

24 *Cilañco shrine in the eastern part of Kirtipur, Kathmandu Valley, Nepal: a stūpa precinct far more modest than Borobodur but comparable with it and likewise traversable.*

Replicating the cosmos in structured space

The *stūpa* is a single cosmos edifice created in a relatively small space. However, the universe can also be reproduced by the architectural structuring of a larger area. Thus studies of old pictures and research on site reveal that Samye (*bSam yas*), the oldest monastery in Tibet, was originally designed in accordance with the Buddhist conception of the cosmos, though it later lost much of its initial character through extensions and demolitions. The surrounding wall at Samye corresponds to the iron mountain which, according to the *Abhidharmakośa,* rims the golden earth disc (Fig. 25/1). The four buildings, one in each cardinal direction, correspond to the four main continents (Fig. 25/2). The intermediate directions are marked by four *stūpas* (Fig. 25/3), which seem to indicate the world mountain Meru, while two smaller buildings on the north-south axis symbolize the sun and moon (Fig. 25/4). The central temple (Fig. 26), with its square ground plan, two courtyards laid out around the inner temple, and four gate-like extensions – one in the middle of each outer wall – clearly corresponds to the palace, as we have to imagine it both on the world mountain and in the mandala (see p. 69ff).

The mythical kingdom of Shambhala too (Figs 29, 30), follows cosmological principles in its structure. The historical Buddha is said to have been entrusted the *Kālacakra Tantra* to Sucandra, King of Shambhala, who took it with him to his kingdom. In Shambhala all people live in wealth and happiness without sickness and without being threatened by animals or having to go hungry; they spend their time wholly in the practice of religion. In this 'Shangri-la' there is never a sign of non-virtue or evil.[50]

The central temple of Lhasa, the Jokhang, which according to legend was erected on a round pond (*'O thang mtsho*) in 639 CE, likewise conceals within it a mandala structure, which is also a symbol of the cosmos: a wall encloses the round pond in a square (Fig. 28). The legend reports that a king wanted to erect a *stūpa* in the middle of this round lake. He asked his ministers to throw stones into the lake while reciting the mantra *oṃ maṇi padme hūṃ*, whereupon a square, stone *stūpa* was miraculously produced. Over it was placed a framework of tree-trunks, which serpent spirits had coated beforehand with clay so that they would neither rot in water nor burn. Boards were laid over the tree-trunks and the gaps filled with molten bronze. In this way the lake disappeared and the foundation for the central temple of Lhasa was created.

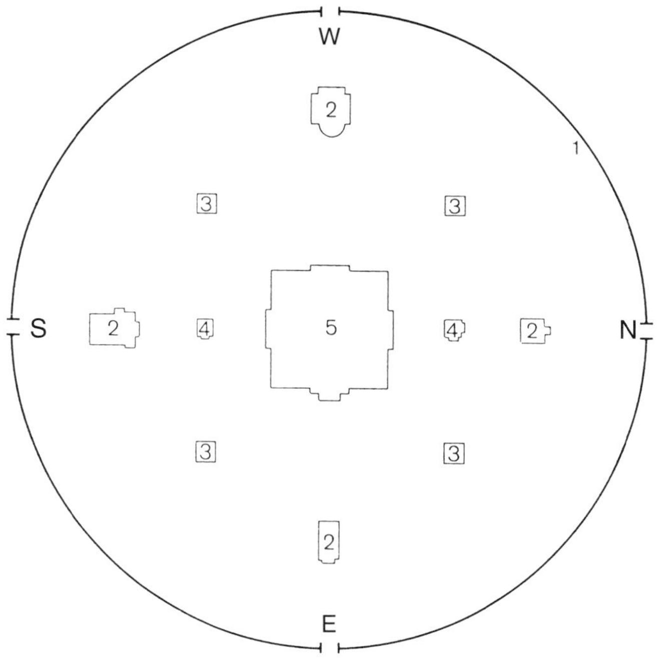

25 *Reconstruction of the original monastery precinct of Samye. In contrast to the form visible today, the front, east-facing side, is drawn just like the other three sides, as one must assume the temple complex initially had this strongly symmetrical form. Supposed arrangement of the oldest parts of the building: (1) surrounding wall = symbol of the 'iron mountain' that fences off a world system; (2) four temples = symbols of the four continents of a world system; (3) four stūpas in the four intermediate directions; (4) small buildings = symbols of the sun and moon; (5) main temple = symbol of the world mountain Meru or the palace on top of Mount Meru.*

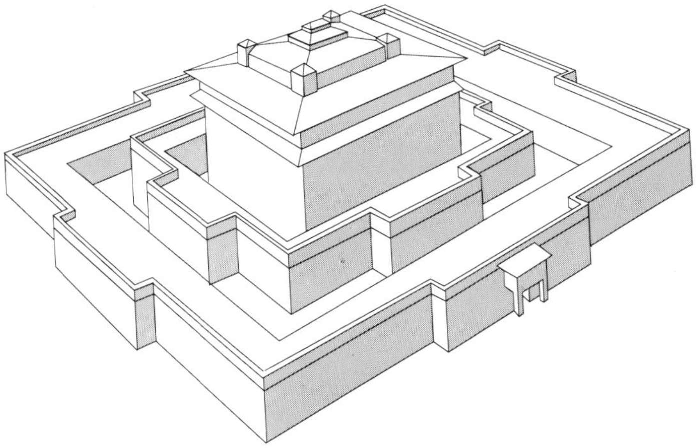

26 *Reconstruction of the main temple of Samye in its original form.*

Since the Jokhang has been extended many times, the present state of the building no longer reveals this basic conception.

Architectural precincts with a mandala-type or cosmological structure are widespread in Asia. Let us recall the temple-towns of South India (e.g. Tiruvanamalai), in whose centre stands the shrine of the chief deity; Bhaktapur in the Kathmandu Valley whose (ideal) town plan depicts a mandala with the shrine of Tripurasundarī in the middle;[51] the cosmological structuring that is just begininning to be discovered in the towns of Kirtipur in the Kathmandu Valley and Leh in Ladakh; the Mingtang, the Imperial Palace of pre-Buddhist China, as revealed by excavations in the capital of the western Han Dynasty; and also the Tang capital Chang'an (present day Xi'an), which was aligned on the four cardinal directions and had twelve gates, one for each month.[52] The ground plan and form of the ancient Khmer monuments also, especially the former capital Angkor Thom (built in the thirteenth century), and the shrines in its neighbourhood, clearly display a cosmological character.[53] Towns in Burma such as Pegu, Pagan and Mandalay were likewise designed as reflections of the cosmos, whose centre they symbolized.[54]

Let us mention that an emphasis on the centre is in no way restricted to the architecture of Asia:

> *The architecture of many towns mirrors an ever-recurring shape (gestalt) of the town, and this shape of the town … mirrors an ever reappearing pattern, the mandala.*[55]

A mandala-like structure and a plan representing the world are shown, for example, by the cities of Jerusalem, Rome, Gur, the capital of the Sassanids, Baghdad, the capital of the Abbasid Caliphate, and Ecbatana, the first capital of the Indo-European Medes, in the centre of which, on the testimony of Herodotus, stood the royal palace, behind seven circular walls, each of a different colour.[56]

Captions for Colour Plates 1–22

1 *Footprint of Buddha Śākyamuni on a maṇḍala-like lotus disc, Newar, Nepal. The two gold-coloured feet are both adorned with a 'wheel of the teaching' and four lucky symbols. The text in the lower margin of the picture says that Man Singh and his wife commissioned the picture when he returned from Lhasa. This was done as a substitute for a mourning ritual not carried out, possibly after a prolonged absence. The commissioners hope, says the text, that the entire world and all its living beings may find liberation from cyclic existence.*

2 *Vajrakīla mandala, Tibet. This mandala can be identified only with difficulty, since neither the principal deity (centre) nor the attendant deities, who should be standing or sitting on the ten blue triangles, are depicted. They have to be projected into the picture by the meditator in visualization. The mandala is surrounded (from the outside inwards) by circles of flames, vajras, the eight charnel grounds, and lotus flower. Clearly discernible are the crossed vajra on which the palace rests, and the colour scheme, typical of the majority of mandalas (the colours of the Kālacakra mandala differ): white in the east, yellow in the south, red in the west and green in the north.*

3 *Scroll painting depicting the five Tathāgata-Buddhas with Uṣṇīṣavijayā (lower left) and White Tārā (lower right), Tibet. Each of the five Tathāgatas is recognizable by his colour and hand gesture; four-faced, white Vairocana in the centre is moreover identifiable by his emblem – the 'wheel of the teaching' that he holds in his hands; in the case of the others the emblems are missing, nevertheless we give them here: east (lower left), blue Akṣobhya (vajra); south (top left), yellow Ratnasambhava (jewel); west, red Amitābha (lotus); north, green Amoghasiddhi (crossed vajra or sword). At bottom centre can be seen the offerings of the five sense organs: fabric, incense, mirror, music and fruit, as in Plate 7, and right at the bottom wealth symbols such as ornaments, rhinoceros horn, elephant tusks, jewels, etc. (cf. Plate 7).*

4, 5 *Wall paintings in Punakha Dzong, Bhutan. For a detailed description of the representations, see pp. 18–23.*

6 *Cosmos according to Kālacakra Tantra, modern painting of 1991 by Kumar Lama, Yolmo, Nepal. In the lower half of the picture can be made out, in plan view, the discs of the elements (two for each, as in Fig. 12), and the living beings that dwell in them.*

From the outside inwards, the discs can be identified as follows: green/black – air; red/blue and red – fire (the latter is smoke); pale blue/dark blue – water; yellow-green – earth, with human dwellings on its surface and some of the hells below. In the centre, ringed by mountain walls and seas (one set shown in the picture, standing for the six), rises Mount Meru, widening upwards, with the serpent-tailed planetary deity Rāhula in the innermost small circle guarding its base; above it lie the heavenly strata, with a transparent head visible in the middle of them (see pp. 22ff).

7 *Abhidharmakośa cosmos, Tibet (side view of a single world system). In the centre is the world mountain Meru, with its white, eastern face turned towards the viewer. In the 'great outer ocean' (outside the seven mountain walls) in each of the four cardinal directions, lie three continents (the western ones are not visible, as they are concealed by Mount Meru). The middle southern continent (left of the mountain) is Jambudvīpa, where human beings live.*

On the four terraces on the sides of Mount Meru live the demigods and lesser gods. On top of the mountain one can make out the city 'Beautiful to See', or the palace Vaijayanta that stands at its centre (see p. 18), with the 33 gods who rule this region of the world (in the centre, Indra or Śakra, around him 32 [28 + 4] other gods). In the lower part of the picture, five goddesses make offering of the five sense organs (from left to right: incense for the sense of smell, music for the sense of hearing, a mirror for the sense of sight, fruit for the sense of taste, and fabric for the sense of touch). Beneath are the 'seven precious things', the 'eight lucky symbols', and in the plate right at the bottom, symbols of wealth.

8 *Detail from a rare scroll showing the four discs of the Kālacakra cosmos (respectively, black/grey – air; red flames – fire; blue waves – water; yellow – earth) from the side, and from above. On the earth disc stands Mount Meru, surrounded by twelve continents (square, round, halfmoon, and triangular in form), mountain rings and oceans. The twenty-four heavens above Mount Meru can be clearly seen; the twenty-fifth heaven is on the surface of Meru. The invisible 'cosmos head' within the heavens and the wind-tracks are not shown.*

9 *An extremely rare representation (from the same scroll as Plate 8) which shows the correlations between the size/measurements of the human body and of the Kālacakra cosmos. The distance between the feet and the crown corresponds exactly to the distance between the fingertips of the extended arms, and, in the cosmos, to the height and width of the cosmos. Vertically as well as horizontally the body and the cosmos can be divided into eight sub-measures (here deliniated by fine red lines). The distance between the middle of the neck and the shoulder (or in the cosmos the distance between the centre and the brim of the earth disc) comprises one sub-measure. The knees (two sub-measures) correspond to the top of the (red) fire disc, the hips (four sub-measures) to the top of the (yellow) earth disc. Mount Meru correlates with the spine of the human being (see also Fig. 31).*

2 *Vajrakīla maṇḍala, individual deities are not portrayed*

3 *The five Tathāgata-Buddhas, forming a simple mandala (upper two-thirds of picture)*

4 *Wall paintings in Punakha Dzong, Bhutan: Kālacakra cosmos from above and from the side …*

5 … *left, Abhidharmakośa cosmos; right, Wheel of Life.*

7 *Cosmos according to Abhidharmakośa*

8 *Kālacakra cosmos*

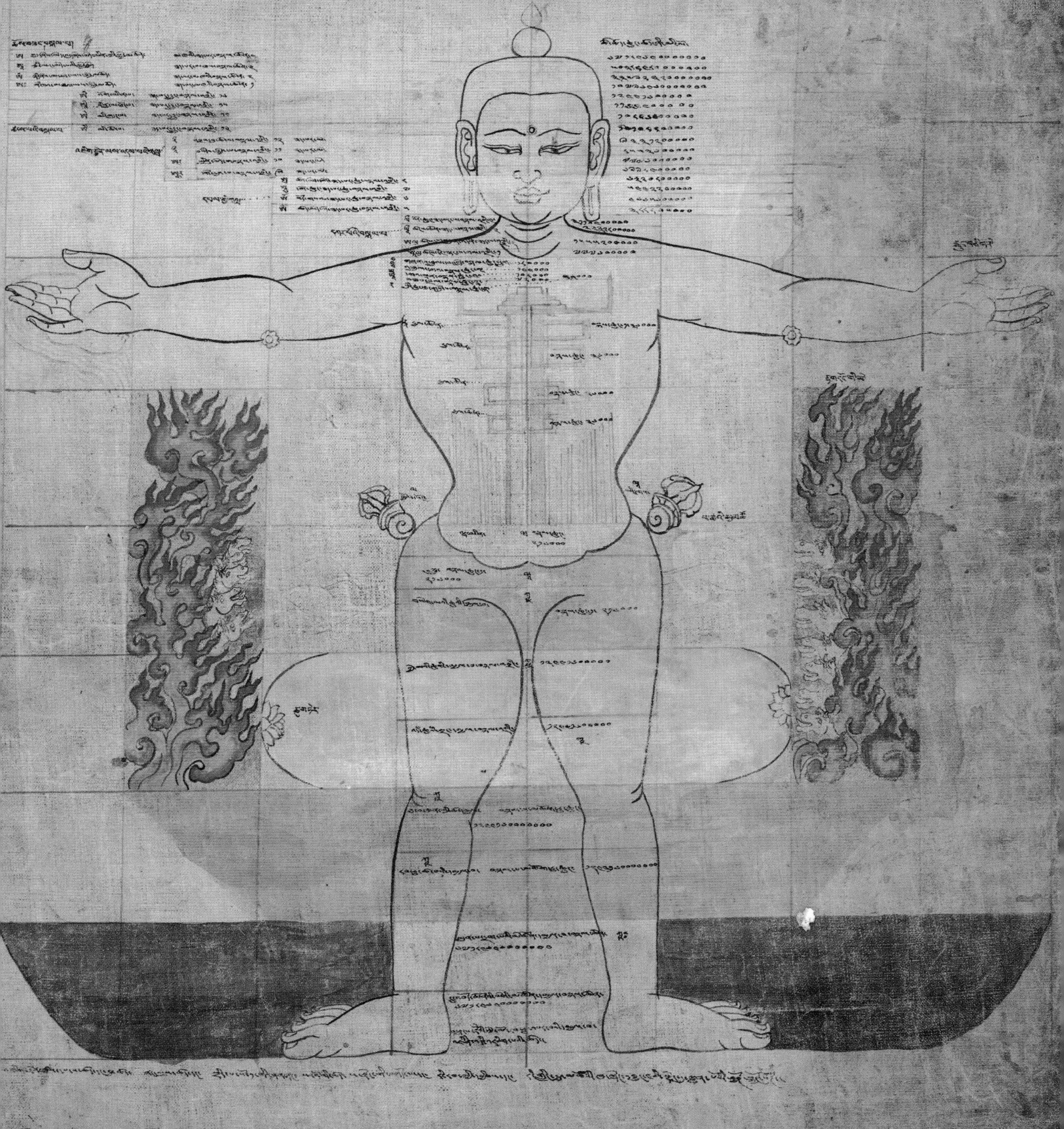

19 *(Uṣṇīṣa-)Sitātapatrā maṇḍala, in which the deities are represented only by symbols*

11 *Mandala of Simhanāda-Lokeśvara*

12, 13 *Offering of the universe, from above and from the side*

14 *Altar-stūpa, a shrine with deities reminiscent of a 'gathering tree'*

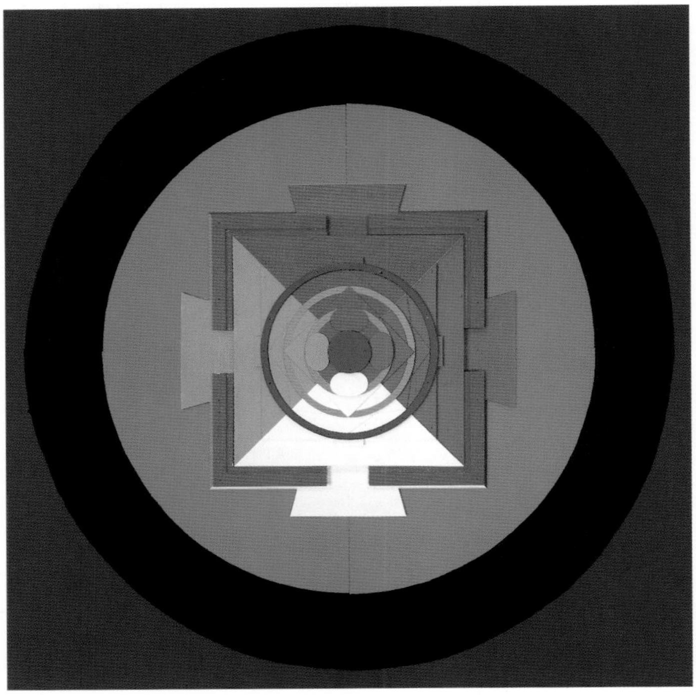

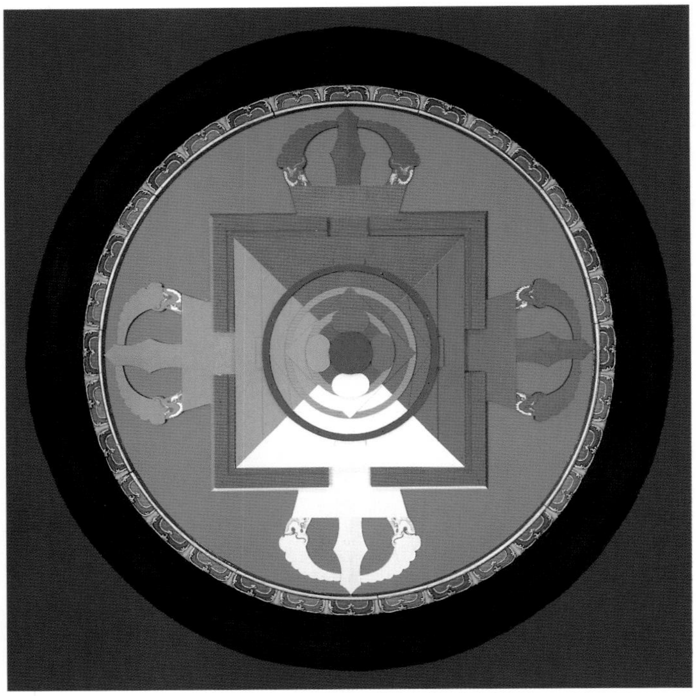

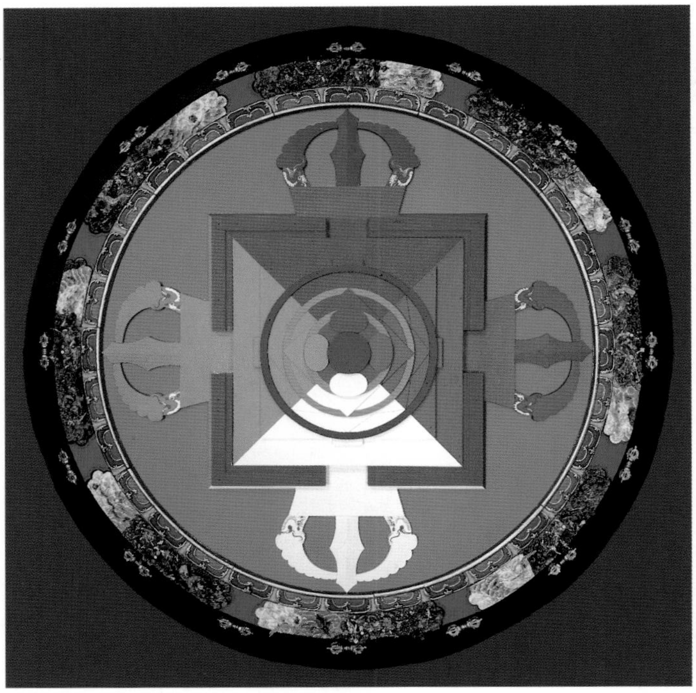

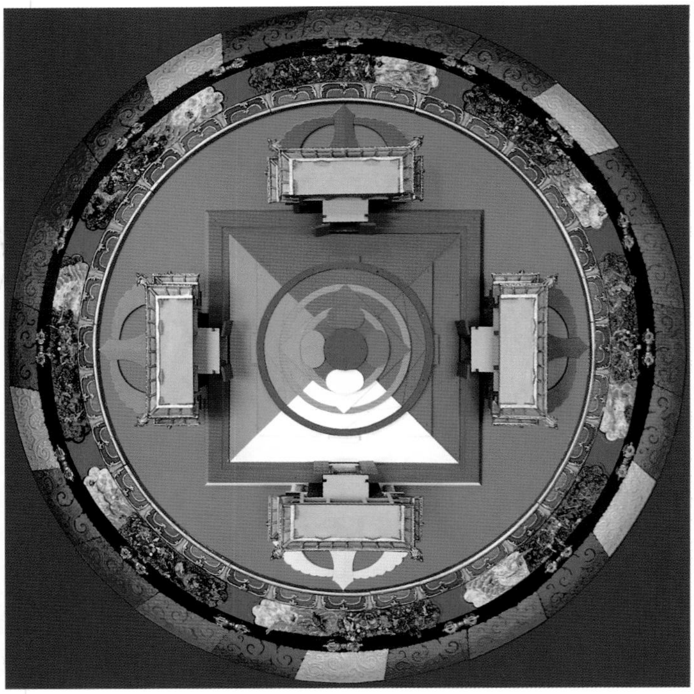

15 *Ground plan of a three-dimensional Zhi khro mandala (east at bottom): interior of the palace …*

16 *… which rests on two crossed vajras and is enclosed by a lotus-flower circle …*

17 *… followed by further circles: charnel-grounds, vajras …*

18 *… and, on the outside, flames. The four entrances to the palace are clearly visible …*

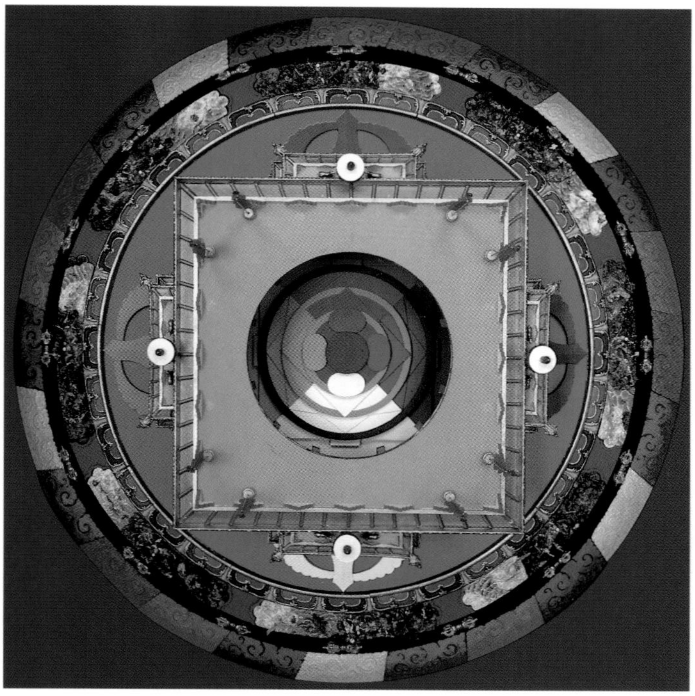

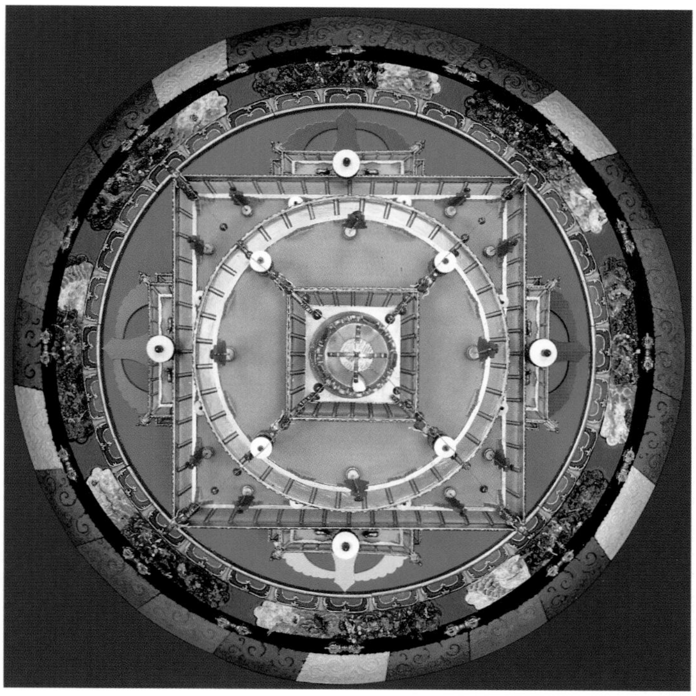

19 *... which together with the transparent walls support the palace roof.*

20 *Complete Zhi khro mandala viewed from above ...*

21 *... and from the south side.*

10 (Uṣṇīṣa-)Sitātapatrā mandala, Tibet. In this mandala, symbols take the place of the deities. Thus an umbrella symbolizes the principal goddess; vajras, crossed vajras, jewels and so forth stand for other deities of the mandala. One can clearly make out the elaborately constructed portals as well as the standards placed in vase-shaped stands on the roof of the palace.

11 Mandala of Siṃhanāda-Lokeśvara, Tibet. Avalokiteśvara is sitting on a lion surrounded by eight serpent (nāga) kings; a ninth nāga (or more likely a nāgī) can be seen at the Bodhisattva's feet. The structure of this mandala is atypical, with none of the usual circles (of flames, vajras, etc.) that surround the palace region. The palace appears to be built upon water, which is reasonable as nāgas live in water as fertility deities.

12, 13 Universe-offering of metal, Tibet. The individual parts of the universe (Figs 13, 15, see p. 24f) are here reproduced in three dimensions; however, the sun on the right of Mount Meru is missing. The base (six round mountain walls) and the form of the world mountain indicate that this is a representation of the Kālacakra cosmos. Such elaborate depictions of the universe were presented as offerings to the spiritual teacher (guru) and with him the Buddha (Fig. 17; see also p. 108).

14 Altar-stūpa, Tibet or Bhutan. This folding wooden stūpa – called 'tashi gomang' in Bhutan – recalls both a 'field of accumulation' (tshogs zhing; see p. 27) a 'gathering tree' on which a whole school is united, as well as a mandala palace, which likewise houses particular groups of deities and is similarly constructed. Altar-stūpas of this type are still used today in Bhutan by travelling tellers of religious stories.

15–21 This series of pictures shows the various levels of a three-dimensional Zhi khro mandala. The sequence of individual circles can be clearly seen (from the inside outwards): lotus flower, charnel grounds, vajra and flame circles. The circle of the charnel grounds is not found in all mandalas, but only in those of the higher tantric classes (according to some sources, in mandalas of wrathful or protective deities); the circles surrounding the Kālacakra mandala deviate somewhat from this tradition (see p. 10). The Zhi khro mandala shown here was made by Pema Namdol Thaye, Kalimpong (India), and Ngawang Namgyal Sherpa, Kathmandu (Nepal), in 1990 for the Völkerkundemuseum der Universität Zürich.

22 This sixteen-tiered mandala belongs to the tradition of the Kadampa school founded by Atiśa (982–1055). Atiśa (with red hat) is shown outside the mandala, at the side of Buddha Śākyamuni. It is quite easy, even for a person not trained in visualization, to grasp the three-dimensionality of the mandala: a pyramid viewed from above.

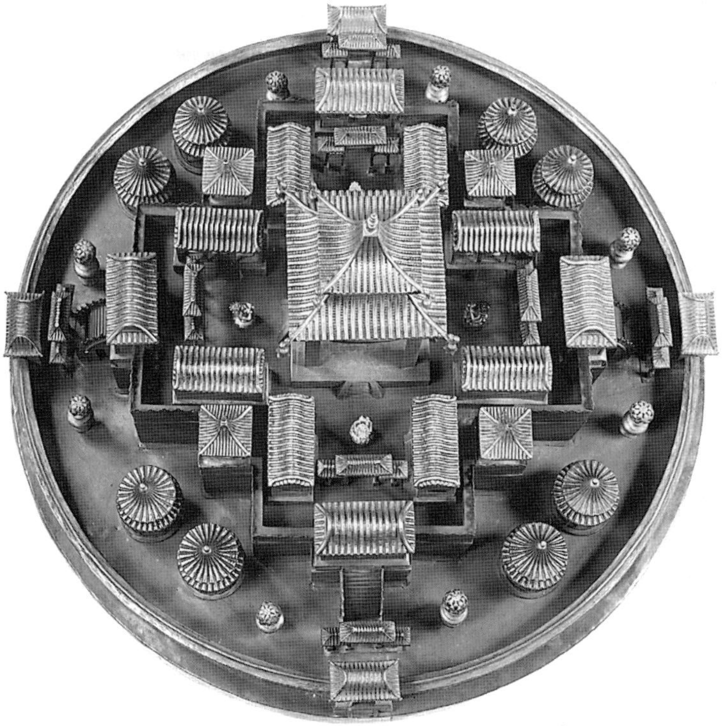

27 Model of a Mongolian monastery precinct which, like Samye, recalls the Buddhist cosmos in its structure.

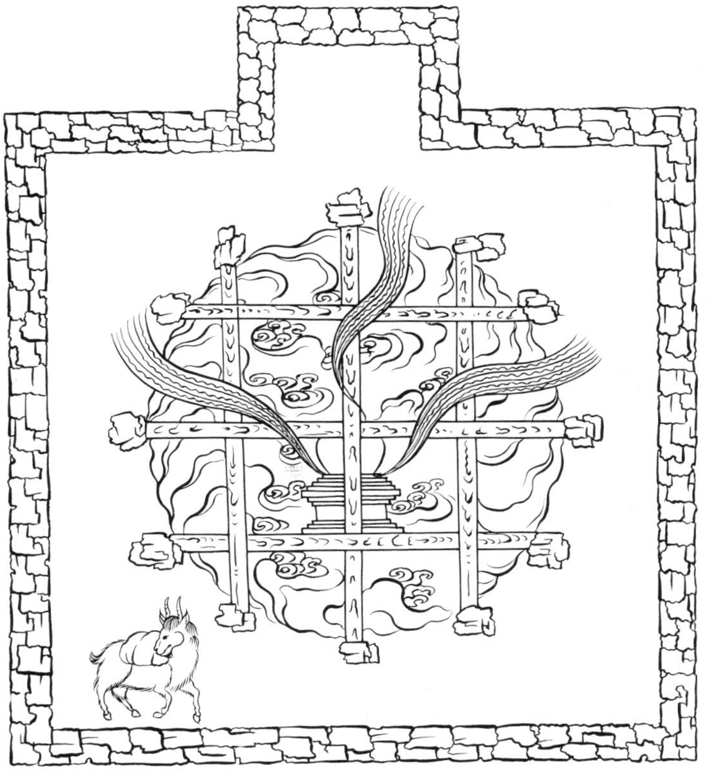

28 The beginning of construction at the Jokhang Temple in Lhasa. The mandala-like structure is clearly visible.

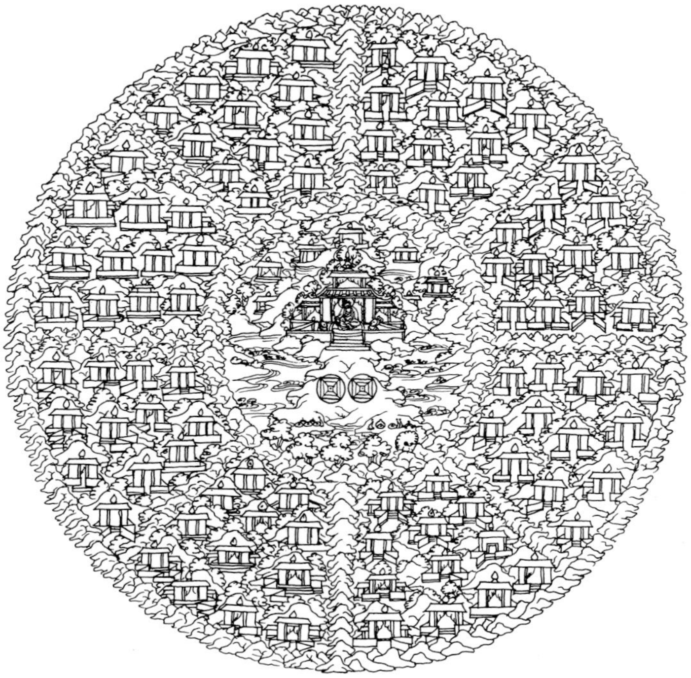

29 *Shambhala, a paradise surrounded by high mountain ranges and glaciers believed to be somewhere to the north or north-west of Tibet, which only those virtuous and experienced in the tantras are able to see and get to. It consists of an enormous lotus flower with eight petals; each petal, washed round by water, sustains 120 million townspeople (making 960 million in all),*[57] *each 10 million forming an administrative unit, represented in the drawing by a palace. In the brightly shining city of Kalapa*[58] *in the centre of Shambhala rises a nine-storey palace, which, like the main temple of Samye, recalls a mandala palace: square, with four gates, encompassed by three ring walls and adorned with pearls, diamonds, silver and turquoises. Inside it shelters a large, three-dimensional Kālacakra mandala.*[59]

30 *According to the Tibetan commentary on this picture from the Bonpo tradition, this realm constructed in mandala form is a paradisal land that is known by various names. The people of Oḍḍiyāna (Udyana) call it Sukhāvatī (the Paradise of Amitābha); it is also called Land of the Unchanging Swastika, Land of the Initiation Circles, … Land where Desires are Fulfilled; Indians call it Shambhala, the Chinese, Treasure Continent … ; the Kashmiris know it as Indestructible Vajra Continent, and in the Gesar tradition it is Land of the Turquoise-winged Cuckoos; in Nepal they speak of the Continent of Wish-granting Trees, and the Tibetans call it Ol mo lung ring … '*[60]

Inner Mandala: The Person

Analogy between person and cosmos

The theory of structural correlations and parallels among all things and in particular between universe, mandala and human body, is well-developed in the *Kālacakra Tantra*.

The *Kālacakra Tantra* – 'Tantra of the Wheel of Time' – speaks of three closely interwoven levels, the so-called 'outer', 'inner' and 'alternative' or 'other' wheels of time. The 'outer wheel of time' comprises the outward appearances of the whole human environment, namely the universe with its element discs, Mount Meru, the winds and its rhythm of time. The 'inner Kālacakra' is made up of what lives in this environment, human beings, whose structure, composition, and 'inner periodicity' correspond exactly with that of the outer wheel of time. The 'other Kālacakra', finally, is the teaching of these analogies and correlations, as well as the resulting yoga practice, a kind of 'mental judo' (Berzin): one uses the powers in the outer and inner wheels of time instead of opposing them.

The outer and inner Kālacakra agree in a great deal (Plate 9; Fig. 31). The conspicuous head-shape above the Kālacakra universe corresponds to the human head; the greatest horizontal extent of the universe corresponds to its maximum height, just as in the human being the distance between the two outstretched hands at either side of the body is equal to its overall height (four cubits); the four superimposed discs of the elements comprise half the height of the universe, which corresponds to the span between the feet and hip-bones in the human body; Mount Meru coicides with the human spine, a correspondence Tucci also pointed out;[1] and the tracks of the planetary winds correspond in the upper part of the body to the lungs, and therefore to the most important winds in the person, which in Tantric Buddhism – and thus in the mandala ritual too – must be purified and brought under control.[2]

Further correlations exist between the human body and the Kālacakra mandala. If a drawing of a person is projected onto a drawing of the palace that forms the centre of the Kālacakra mandala (see p. 69ff), the lowest part of the palace, the so-called 'body realm' of the mandala (body mandala) coincides with the legs; the 'middle realm' (speech mandala) coincides with the extent of the trunk, especially the chest and lungs; and the 'mind mandala' with the head. In addition it is clear in Figure 32 that the distance between the shoulders correlates with the extent of the 'mind realm'; the distance between the elbows with the extent of the 'speech realm'; and the distance between the fingertips of the right and left hands with the extent of the 'body realm'. It deserves particular mention that the point between the eyebrows, which plays an important role in meditational practices of the highest yoga class (see p. 117f), coincides exactly with the centre of the 'mind mandala'. This is the realm in the centre of which stand the two highest mandala deities, Kālacakra and Viśvamātṛ.

That there exists a relationship between architecture and the person – at least the divine person or 'cosmic man' – is an ancient Indian idea that also receives attention in the construction of an Indian temple.[3] The *vāstumaṇḍala* determines the plan of an Indian temple, and it represents the *vāstupuruṣa*, the celestial person. His body, face-down, forms the foundation of the temple; his limbs and the vital points on his body are occupied by forty-five deities. In the temple, therefore, the different deities congregate in a single, ordered being, the *vāstupuruṣa*.[4]

To return to the Kālacakra tradition, further analogies come to light when universe and mandala palace are superimposed on one another (Fig. 33). There is a correspondence between the discs of the four elements (the fifth element, space, does not appear here as it displays no vertical extension), and the realm of the body mandala; between Mount Meru with its orbiting winds and the planets riding on them, and the speech level; and finally between the 'cosmic head' and the heavens, and the realm of the mind in the mandala.[5] The height of the palace is the same as the width of the palace base (inside measurement, not counting the entrance gates; both are 32 arm-spans, about 60 m), just as the height of the cosmos is equal to its width. The same goes for the lowest disc of the cosmos (air) and the body mandala (inside measurement); for the fire disc and

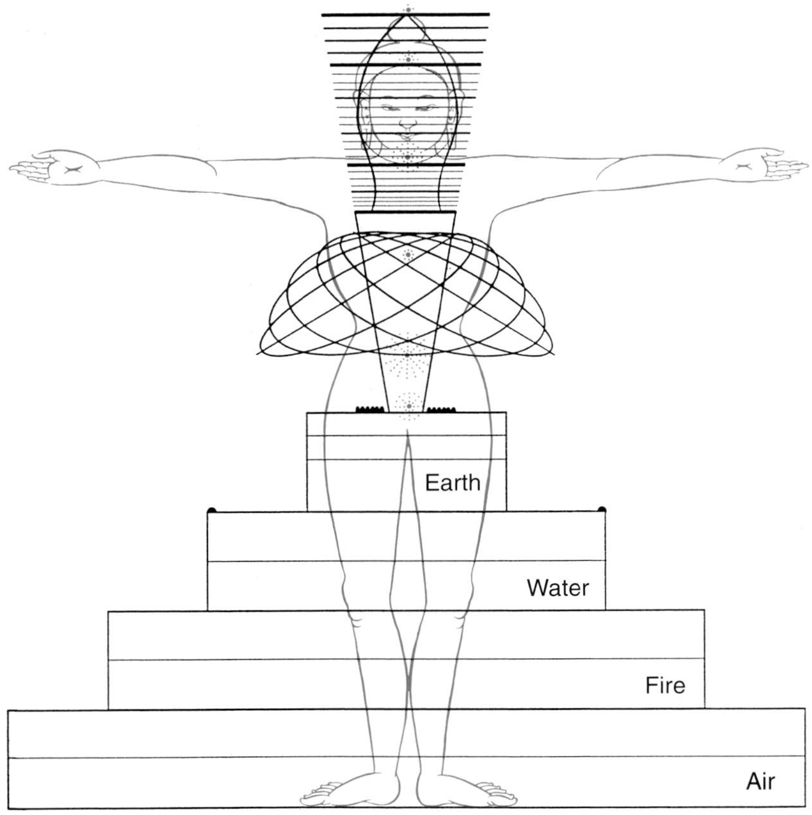

31 Structural correspondences between Kālacakra universe and human body.

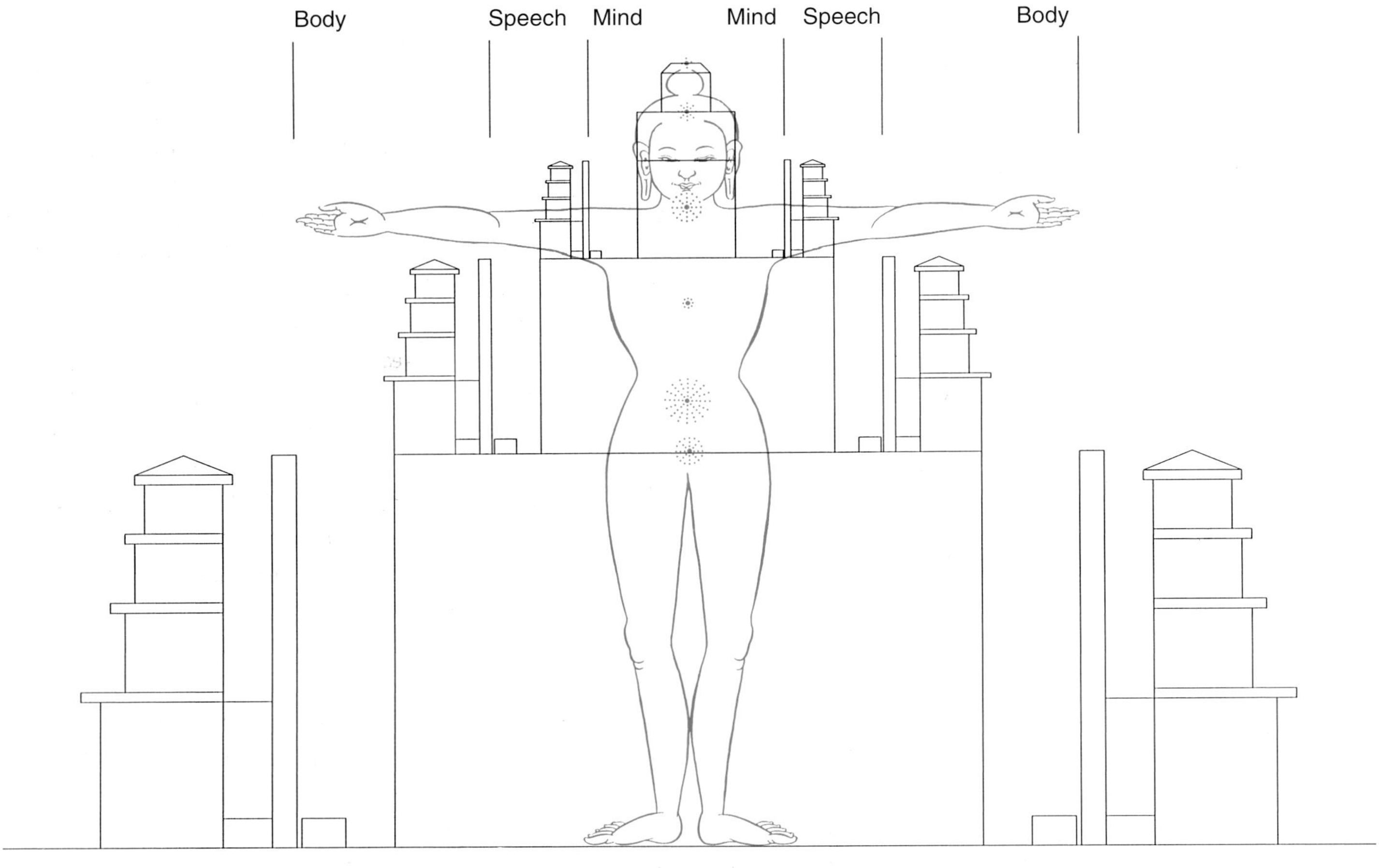

32 Structural correspondences between human body and Kālacakra mandala palace.

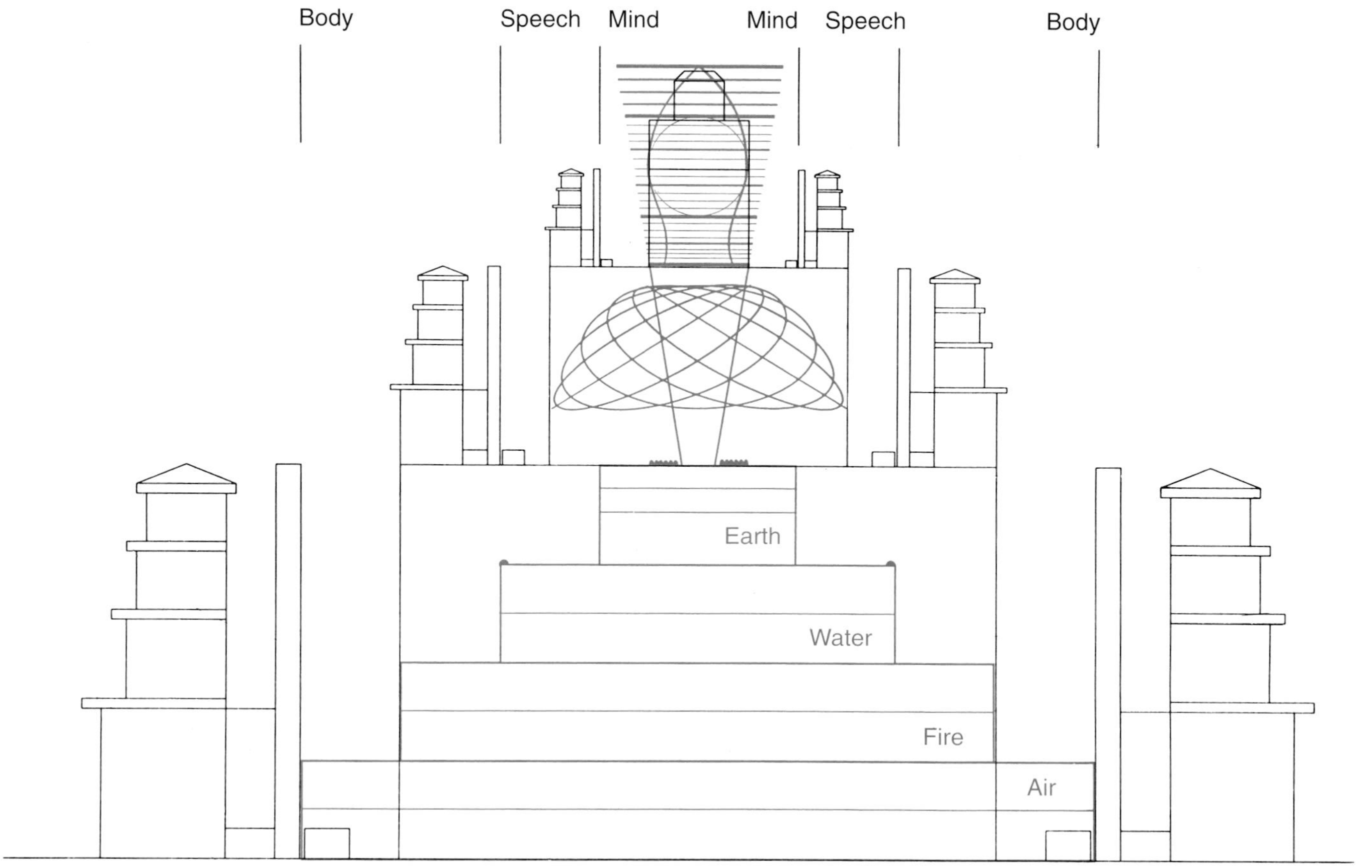

33 *Structural correspondences between Kālacakra universe and mandala palace.*

the plinth in the body mandala, and for the water disc and the speech mandala (inside measurement), while the earth disc correlates with the uppermost realm of the mandala – the mind mandala (inside measurement). Finally, there is a correspondence between the diameter of the summit region of Mount Meru and the cube within the mind mandala.

The person as mandala

The universe and the human body, according to the Kālacakra tradition, do not only agree outwardly, that is to say in their structure, but also display many more subtle correlations.

The mandala palace consists of several levels: those of body, speech and mind, the last of which is again divided in two (Fig. 45). This division, as we shall see below, applies also to the person.

Body

For the Buddhist, each individual consists of five transitory aggregates (*skandha*) combined with one another in mutual interrelation. These are: forms, feelings, perceptions, mental factors and consciousness. In the Kālacakra tradition as a rule, a sixth *skandha* is added, 'deep awareness' (wisdom). The five elements – space, air, fire, water and earth – are further components (or constituents) of the person. Deep awareness ('great bliss') may be included as a sixth.[6] Aggregates as well as elements belong to the level of the body. In the Kālacakra mandala and in the mandala initiation (see p. 114, *The seven basic initiations*) the aggregates and elements are assigned definite symbols and directions. Their positions in the mandala are set out in Table 1. This makes it clear that the human body can be understood as a mandala.

The aggregates and elements of the human body can also be arranged vertically, as each is linked to one of the six chakras that lie along the body's 'central axis' (see Tables 8 and 11).

In addition, the limbs and joints, which also belong to the body level, can be assigned to particular directions. Here let us simply note that the limbs and joints of the left half of the body are linked to the cardinal directions (with the male deities of the mandala), and those of the right half to the intermediate directions (with the female deities).[7]

Speech

According to the Tantric conception, 72,000 invisible channels (*nāḍī; rtsa*)[8] run through the body. Through these flow energy-laden winds (*prāṇa* or *vāyu; rlung*). Winds and wind or energy channels count as the most important components of the person on the level of speech. Two of the three main channels lie to the left and right of the spine

SW Ṝ fire element (1.3)	W Ḷ forms aggregate (2.5)	NW Ḹ earth element (1.5)
S Ṛ feelings aggregate (2.3)	C Ā space element (1.1) A consciousness aggregate (2.1)	N U perceptions aggregate (2.4)
SE Ī air element (1.2)	E I mental factors aggregate (2.2)	NE Ū water element (1.4)

Table 1 The five elements and five aggregates. The first number after each element or aggregate indicates the mandala initiation in which the component is purified, the second gives the position of the purification in the relevant initiation (thus fire (1.3) is purified as an element in the first initiation – in third place; perceptions (2.4) as an aggregate in the second initiation – in fourth place).

respectively; the third, the central one, slightly in front. The central channel (*dbu ma*)[9] runs from the genitals through the middle of the body to the crown of the head, where it bends forward a little and ends between the eyes. The left, white channel (*rkyang ma*)[10] extends from the left nostril to a finger-breadth below the bottom end of the central channel, while the right, red channel (*ro ma*)[11] correspondingly runs down the body from the right nostril. The left channel is related to the moon, the right to the sun. The central channel is associated, in the region above the navel, with the eclipse planet Rāhu (the 'Howler'), and in its lower part with the eclipse planet Kālāgni ('Fire of Time'). On the other hand Rāhu and Kālāgni are identified with the ascending and descending points of the moon's orbit – its intersections, 180° apart, with the ecliptic, the track of the sun – which in India from the early eleventh century were regarded as planets.[12]

The six chakras[13] or lotus flowers (*padma*) already mentioned are located at certain points along the central *nāḍī*. According to the Kālacakra tradition these power centres are found at the level of the sexual organs, the navel, the heart, the throat, the forehead, and the crown. Normally the power centres are portrayed as lotus flowers (Fig. 34). The number of petals each has depends on the energy channels joining the relevant chakra.

At the height of each chakra, the left wind channel coils round the central channel clockwise, the right anticlockwise. According to the Kālacakra tradition this hinders the free flow of wind in the central channel severely, though not completely.[14] If we follow the explanations of the First Dalai Lama, Gendun Drup,[15] the three main channels appear to form a mandala and are divided into an upper and a lower part; respectively navel to crown, and navel to genitals or anus. Taking into account the colours, elements and directions mentioned and assigned by the First Dalai Lama, the following picture emerges (Fig. 35).

The scheme of three, or six, main channels is instructive in two respects. It makes it clear once again that in Tantric Buddhism the human body is perceived as a mandala; at the same time it provides a key to better understanding of the Kālacakra mandala. In the mandala a red deity always forms a pair with a white one; a black with a yellow one; and a green with a blue one. The reason becomes clear in the diagram. Only 'equal' or complementary partners can form a sensible couple,[16] for instance the upper left and upper right channels. Thus there result the colour combinations red and white (upper right–upper left); black and yellow (lower left–lower right); and green and blue (upper central–lower central).[17]

The winds pulsating in the channels serve as a vehicle or carrier for the components of consciousness and in general enable all mental and bodily processes. Thus the downward-emptying wind controls the movement of white and red *bodhicitta* (male and female 'drops'),[18] urine and excrement;

34 *Human being with six energy or power centres (chakra) according to the Kālacakra tradition.*[19]

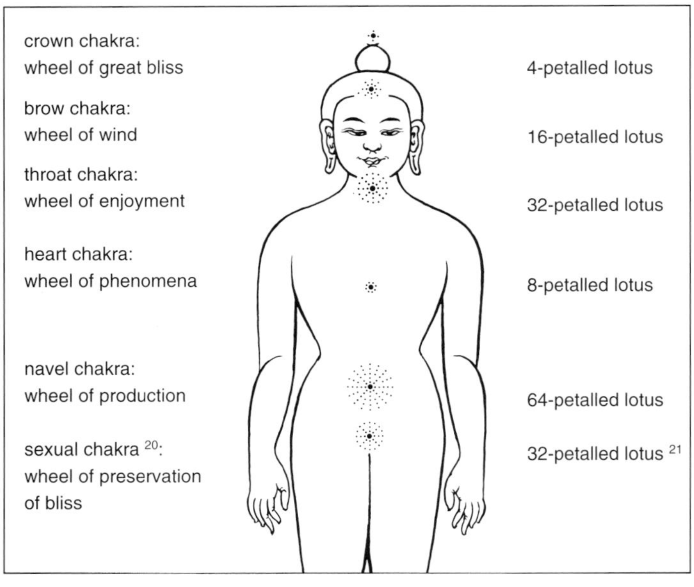

the fire-accompanying wind separates the nutrients from the unusable components and kindles the inner fire (*gtum mo*); the life-holding wind maintains the flow of inhalations and exhalations through the nose, etc.[22]

In Tantric Buddhism the winds are regarded as contributory causes of cyclic existence, but also contain the seeds of enlightenment. That is why the yoga of the mandala ritual sets great store on understanding the importance of the winds, purifying them and using them in a positive sense, to wit, to attain enlightenment. According to the Kālacakra system there exist in a human being ten principal winds,[23] which are related to the elements and the directions,[24] and thereby ideally form a mandala in the human body (Table 2).

35 *Attempt at a pictorial representation of the three principal channels above and below the navel chakra. Water, space and air are regarded as belonging to the male side; fire, earth and wisdom to the female side.*

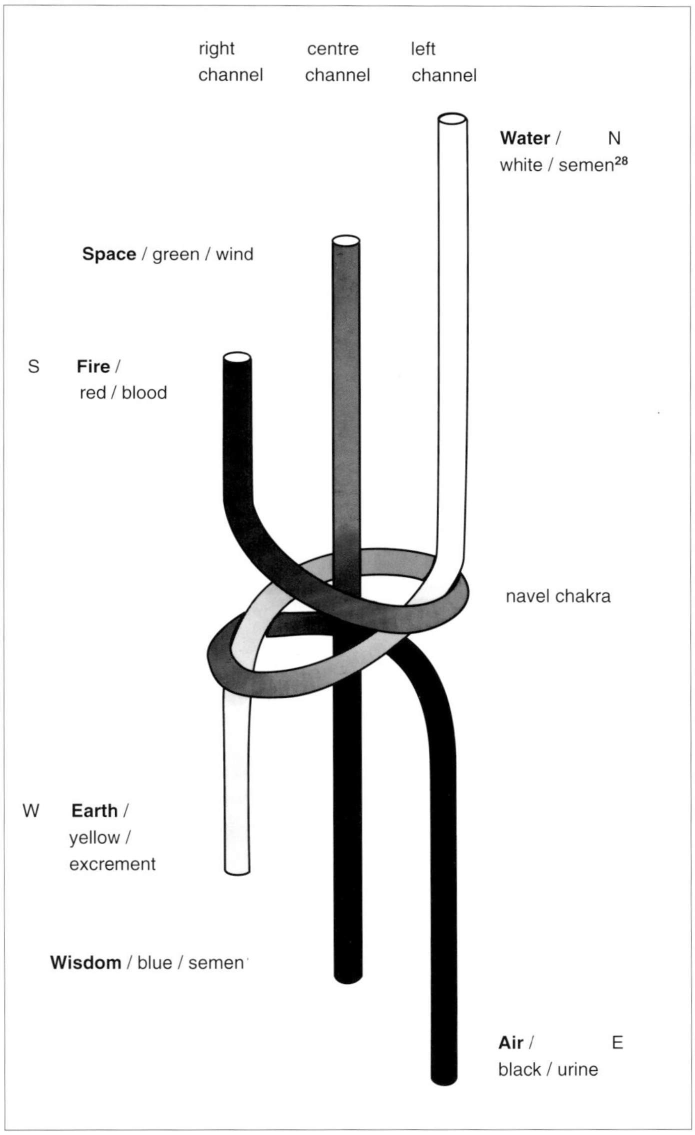

[SW] *kṛkala* wind[25] (3.4) HAḤ fire element	[W] *nāga* wind (3.7) Ā earth element	[NW] *dhanaṃjaya* wind (3.8) HĀ earth element
[S] upward-moving wind (3.3) AḤ fire element	[C] vitalizing/life-holding wind[26] (3.9) HOḤ space element --- downward-emptying wind[27] (3.10) PHREṂ deep awareness (great bliss) element	[N] pervading wind (3.5) AṂ water element
[SE] tortoise wind (3.2) HA air element	[E] fire-accompanying wind (3.1) A air element	[NE] *devadatta* wind (3.6) HAṂ water element

Table 2 The ten principal winds, their directional assigments in the human body (or the places in which they flow into the heart chakra), and the seed-syllable and element with which each wind is connected. The first number indicates the mandala initiation in which the wind is purified (here always the third), the second refers to the position of the relevant wind purification in the sequence of purifications (see also detail from Plate 46, p. 98f).

If the ten winds are arranged according to 'their' directions, a simple mandala results, which corresponds to the inner and highest part of the Kālacakra mandala (Table 2; Figs 45, 64), and is used in the third mandala initiation (Tables 6, 16). The first eight winds correspond to the eight goddesses (Śakti)[29] who surround the divine couple Kālacakra and Viśvamātṛ, while the last two are related to the centre and correspond to the goddess Viśvamātṛ.

However the correspondences between outer world (universe) and inner world (person) go still further. The twelve months and the twelve signs of the zodiac correspond – in the course of a human life – to the twelve 'shifts of the breath' (*pho ba*) in a span of twenty-four hours, a complete day-night unit (Table 3). Just as there are months in which the day 'waxes' and gets longer and some in which it decreases, so too, according to the Tantric Buddhist view, there is a comparable change of the breath within a day. In one half of the day the breath flows predominantly through the right nostril, in the other mainly through the left. In this way, at times the breath flows mainly through the right energy channel related to the sun, and at others it flows mainly through the left channel, which is assigned to the moon.

Outer Kālacakra (macrocosm)				
1 year	= 12 months	= 360 days	= 21,600 (360 x 60)	*nāḍī*
	1 month	= 30 days	= 1,800 (360 x 5)	*nāḍī*
		1 day	= 60 (5 x 12)	*nāḍī*
Inner Kālacakra (microcosm)				
1 day	= 12 shifts of breath	= 60 (5 x 12) *nāḍī*	= 21,600 (360 x 60)	breaths[32]
	1 shift of breath	= 5 *nāḍī*	= 1,800 (360 x 5)	breaths
		1 *nāḍī*	= 360 (60 x 6)	breaths

Table 3 Correspondence of Outer Kālachakra (cosmos) and Inner Kālachakra (person), as regards time units.

In one 'shift of the breath', a person makes 1,800 breaths, also described as karmic (inner) wind, so that in a day one breathes in and out 21,600 times (12 x 1,800). Each of the twelve groups of 1,800 winds must be purified one by one in the completion stage (see pp. 118).

Winds determine outer as well as inner processes. While the outer winds develop through collective *karma*, the inner ones are formed through individual, that is personal, *karma*. The ten principal winds that pulsate in the right or left channels correspond in the outer Kālacakra to the winds around Mount Meru, on which the ten planets[31] ride through the twenty-seven constellations or lunar mansions in the northern and southern zodiac (see p. 22ff).

Mind

According to the concepts of Tantric Buddhism, besides the realms of body and speech, the person possesses distinct mind components: 'six sense powers' (or faculties) and 'six sense objects', as well as 'six action faculties' and 'six actions' (or activites) which, on the basis of the symbols attributed to them in the fifth and sixth initiations, can be arranged in the form of a mandala.[32] Tables 4 and 5 seek to illustrate these relationships.

A fourth level, or rather a sub-level of the mind realm, is that of 'great bliss', with the aggregate of 'deep awareness' (symbolized by a *vajra*), and the element of 'deep awareness' (symbolized by a bell), which are related to the fourth initiation and the centre of the mandala (Fig. 45).

Four states of existence and four drops

In the *Kālacakra Tantra* four states of human existence are differentiated: waking, dreaming, deep sleep and ecstasy, states in which the human energy winds are concentrated in so-called drops (*thig le*) in certain places, namely the chakras.[33] In the waking state, which brings forth appearances of the objects of the five sense organs (Table 4), the energy winds of the upper part of the body are gathered in a drop in the brow chakra,[34] the so called 'body drop'.[35] In the dream state which gives rise to syllables, words, speech and so forth – which is why the drop belonging to it is called the 'speech' or 'dream drop' – the upper body winds are located in the throat chakra.[36] In the two remaining states the shift of the winds to lower chakras continues: in the state of deep sleep, with its 'mind' or 'deep sleep drop', in which the consciousness is developed, the upper winds concentrate in the heart chakra,[37] and finally, in the state of sexual ecstasy they slip into the second lowest centre, the navel chakra.[38] The corresponding drop is called the 'drop of deep awareness'.

Since the winds gathered in the chakras contain impurities, appearances at the body, speech, mind and bliss levels are sullied (impure appearances of objects, impure sounds, impure mind, impure orgasmic bliss). The meditator should gradually purify these soilings and create 'empty forms', 'empty sounds', 'non-conceptual clear mind' and 'immutable great bliss', with which ultimately – in the last phases of the so-called 'generation stage' – are attained the pure diamond Buddha body, the pure diamond Buddha speech, the pure diamond Buddha mind and the pure diamond Buddha bliss.[39] Thus despite their impurites and supposed imperfections, at all times the drops also contain the nucleus of enlightenment.

ĀR tastes (5.6)	AL sense of touch (5.9)	ĀL smells (5.10)
AR sense of vision (5.5)	Ā other phenomena (5.2)[40] A sense of hearing (5.1) ---------------------------- AḤ sounds (5.12) AṂ mental sense (5.11)	O sense of taste (5.7)
AI tangible objects (5.4)	E sense of smell (5.3)	AU forms (5.8)

Table 4 Mandala-style arrangement of the six sense powers (senses) and six sense objects. The first number indicates the mandala initiation in which they are purified (here always the fifth), the second refers to the position in the sequence of purifications.[41] Contrary to this schematic representation, in the actual mandala the Bodhisattvas who correspond to the senses or their objects in the centre are not depicted in the centre of the mandala but on the left of the four entrances of the mind mandala (for Tables 4 and 5 see also Plate 46; p. 100f).

RĀ going (6.6)	LA faculty of defecation (6.9)	LĀ speaking (6.10)
RA arm faculty (6.5)	HA f. of urination (6.1) HĀ ejaculating (6.2) ---------------------------- HĀṂ f. of ejaculation (6.11) HAḤ urinating (6.12)	VA leg faculty (6.7)
YĀ defecating (6.4)	YA mouth faculty (6.3)	VĀ taking (6.8)

Table 5 Mandala-style arrangement of the six action faculties and six activities. The first number indicates the mandala initiation in which the relevant faculty or activity is purified (here always the sixth), the second refers to the position in the sequence of purifications.[42] Contrary to this schematic representation, the wrathful deities who correspond to the action faculties and activities in the centre are not depicted or visualized in the centre of the mandala but above the mandala (6.1, 6.12), or in the body realm of the mandala (6.2, 6.11).

Birth of a person: development of a cosmos

According to the *Kālacakra Tantra*, a person orginates in a manner analogous to the deities of a mandala (see p. 109ff). The consciousness of a person who has died (symbolized by the syllable HŪṂ) and – serving as a vehicle – the wind (represented by the syllable HI),[43] on sight of a couple making love enter by the man's mouth or crown and reach his penis and from there the woman's womb. There they get between a red *bodhicitta*-drop from the mother and a white *bodhicitta*-drop from the father. Blood from the mother and sperm from the father, as well as the consciousness of the new being ready for rebirth and the wind which serves it as a vehicle, mix to form the indestructible drop of the heart centre, about the size of a mustard seed and symbolized by the syllable HAṂ, and with that the prerequisite for a new body.

Later, during the process of maturation, part of the white *bodhicitta* ascends from the heart centre into the central channel in the crown chakra, from where it can spread into the whole body, while part of the red *bodhicitta* descends in the central channel into the navel centre and from there is responsible for the increase of the red *bodhicitta*.[44] As long as the child is in the womb, it remains unacquainted with the four states of waking, dream, deep sleep and ecstatic bliss. Not until shortly before birth, when the body is fully formed – though the ten principal winds still rest motionless in the central channel – is the baby 'awoken' by the songs of the four goddesses or female Buddhas (Table 13):[45] at this moment the winds of these goddesses penetrate into the womb and activate the winds of the foetus.[46] The four goddesses cause certain winds to abandon the blissful state in the central channel and leave the body. In the final stage of meditation this process must be reversed and the winds brought under control (see p. 118).

These winds leave the body from the heart via the navel chakra, the two side channels and both nostrils. The newborn begins to breathe at this moment, and at the same time the sense organs take up their functions – namely the six kinds of consciousness that 'ride' on the above-mentioned winds (consciousness of the mind, hearing, smell, sight, taste, and touch), take possession of their objects and bring them back as sensory impressions into the navel chakra and into the central wind channel, a process that will be activated again in meditation. With the beginning of the sense functions the child attains the six action faculties (Tables 5, 6).[47]

Table 6 is a summary of what a person consists of according to the *Kālacakra Tantra*. Body, speech and mind realms are distinguished, as they are in the mandala palace (body, speech and mind mandalas).

Analogies exist between the development of a person and certain phases of the mandala meditation. Abiding in the womb corresponds to the phase of the 'supreme victorious mandala' (see p. 110ff). The next phase, the moment of birth, has its parallel in the so-called 'yoga of supreme victorious actions' (= second phase of the *sādhana*, see p. 113ff).[48] There follows the ripening and movement of the two drops – semen and blood – a process analogous to the 'yoga of the drops' (= third phase of the *sādhana*), and the 'subtle yoga' (= fourth phase of the *sādhana*): the white, male *bodhicitta* rises to the crown chakra and at the age of sixteen reaches full power. The number sixteen is related to the waxing moon: in fifteen days the moon waxes, on the sixteenth it is full, and correspondingly, according to ancient Indian tradition at sixteen a man reaches the age of adulthood and marriage. The red, female *bodhicitta* on the other hand, which after birth slowly flows down to the sexual chakra, ripens in twelve years, a phenomenon related to the sun, the twelve signs of the zodiac and the twelve months, as well as to the fact that a woman attains sexual maturity at the age of twelve years.

Death of an individual according to the Kālacakra Tantra

According to the Kālacakra tradition, the process of death begins with the consciousnesses of the various senses disappearing, leaving only the mental consciousness and its related life-holding wind, both of which find their way into the central energy channel. The process of disappearance of the various consciousnesses has as a consequence that the atoms of the individual elements no longer hold together.

Body	
Six elements	**Six aggregates**
air	mental factors
fire	feelings
water	perceptions
earth	forms
space	consciousness
Seventh Initiation	
deep awareness (great bliss)	deep awareness (wisdom)
6 female Buddhas	6 male Buddhas
First Initiation	Second Initiation

Speech		
Ten winds		**Six (or two) channels**[49]
fire-accompanying wind + tortoise wind	(1) (2)	lower left
upward-moving wind + lizard (*kṛkala*) wind	(3) (4)	upper right
pervading-wind + *devadatta* wind	(5) (6)	upper left
serpent (*nāga*) wind + *dhanaṃjaya* wind	(7) (8)	lower right
life-holding wind	(9)	upper central
downward-emptying wind	(10)	lower central
10 Śaktis		Kālacakra and Viśvamātṛ
Third Initiation		Fourth Initiation

At death, as at the dissolution of a universe, earth dissolves into water, water into fire, fire into air, this into space and finally space into wisdom.[50]

The mental consciousness and the life-holding wind become completely refined, and retire into the heart centre. The knots in the central energy channel unravel and thus enable the white *bodhicitta* from the crown to flow down into the heart, to enter there the 'drop that is indestructible during the lifetime'.[51] While the white *bodhicitta* is sinking from the crown to the heart, the dying person perceives a pale light, "like the moon just rising from beneath the horizon, casting a pale sheen upon the sky".[52] Next appears to the dying person a reddish vision, resulting from the rising of the red *bodhicitta* from the navel to the heart chakra, so that the white and red *bodhicitta* now completely enclose the indestructible drop in the heart. The dying person perceives this as total darkness, ultimately succeeded by a bright, radiant, clear light, the 'clear light of death'.[53] In this vision, like an exceedingly clear, light-coloured and bright sky, the subtle consciousness and subtle wind of the deceased reveal themselves, nestling in the drop in the heart chakra already mentioned. The state of the clear light of death is comparable to the 'effective' or 'actual clear light', but not identical with it. The 'effective clear light' can only be perceived by an experienced *yogin* or *yogini*, in fact during the completion stage. Herein lies the crucial difference between the death process and enlightenment.[54]

After the appearance of the clear light of death, the consciousness of the deceased and the subtle wind which serves as its vehicle leave the indestructible drop through one of the apertures of the body (e.g. the nostrils). In this phase the white and red *bodhicitta* situated in the heart chakra also separate: the white flows downwards and leaves the body by the sexual organ, while the red rises and comes out of the nostrils.

According to the Buddhist view, rebirth ensues under the influence of diverse 'impulses' or movements accumulated in previous lives, which can be described by the collective name *karma*. The 'impulses' use the winds as a vehicle, and it is these very winds that after entering death cause rebirth, a cycle that only settles after all the winds have been purified and dissolved in the yoga of the completion stage.

Mind		
Six senses	**Six action faculties**	**Emblem/ Direction**
sense of smell	mouth faculty	sword (E)
sense of vision	arm faculty	jewel (S)
sense of taste	leg faculty	lotus (N)
sense of touch	faculty of defecation	wheel (W)
sense of hearing	faculty of urination	vajra (above)
mental sense	faculty of ejaculation	bell (below)
6 Bodhisattvas	6 wrathful deities	
Fifth Initiation	Sixth Initiation	

Table 6 The most important components of a human being and their correlations with the mandala deities and inititations. As a rule 36 components are counted altogether, thus not six channels but only two (left and right channels); the element and aggregate of deep awareness are not purified in the first and second initiations but separately in the seventh. Through the details of the individual emblems and directions, assignment to one of the six Buddha 'families' results (Table 7, p. 78).

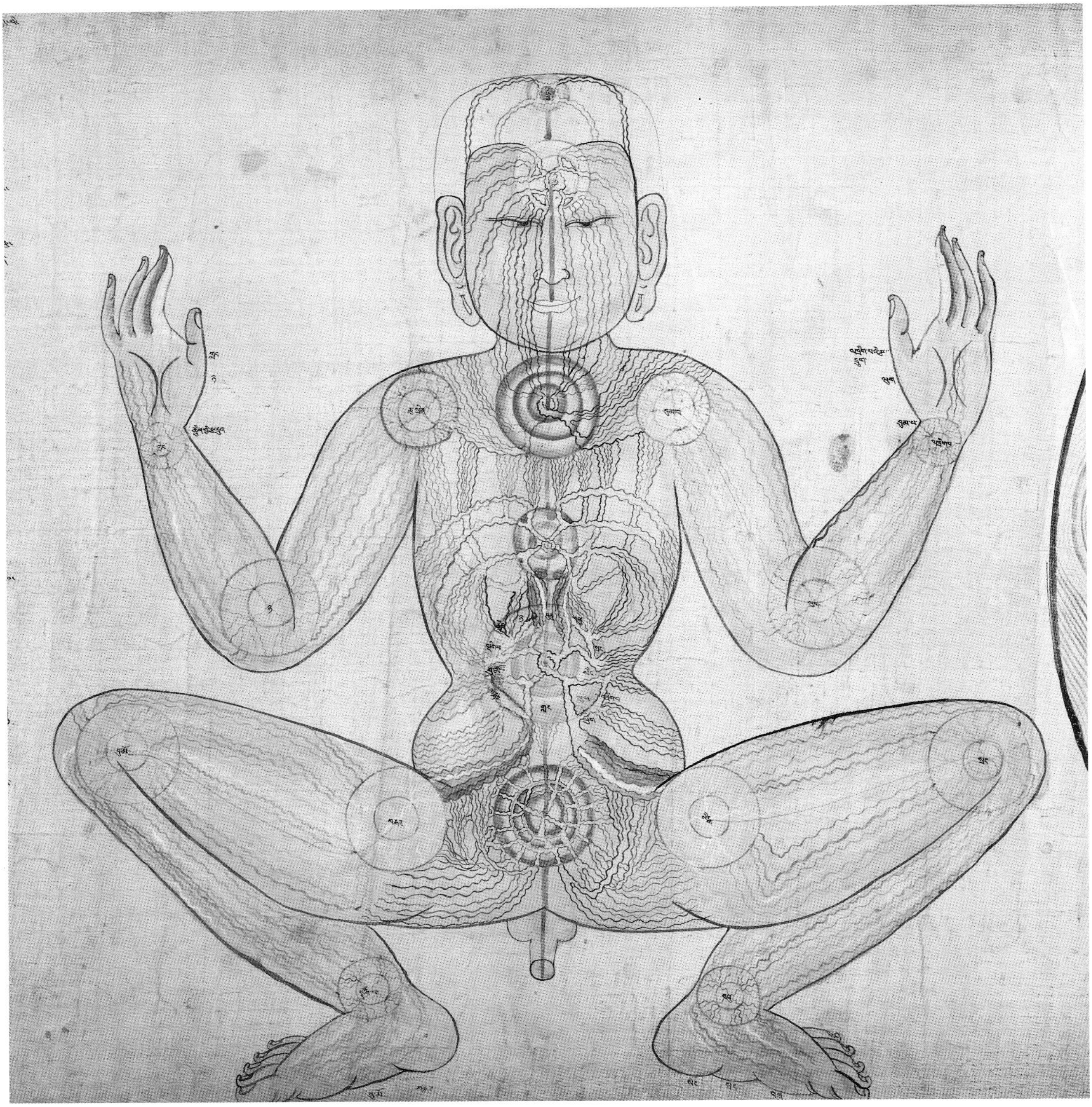

36 *Human figure with six chakras. Clearly visible are the six principal chakras: sexual, navel, heart, throat, forehead and crown, aligned on the central axis. Also shown are the major channels (nāḍi) through which flow the energy-laden winds (prāṇa).*

The Other Mandala: The Tantric Method

Intersection of universe and person in the mandala ritual

The essential goal of Tantric Buddhism is to cleanse the winds and the four principal drops of impurities. For this the meditator must realize emptiness while taking on an empty form. As an aid he or she creates for him or herself a mandala, which shows clearly and intelligibly the correlation between the adept's body and the universe. This lays the foundation for conscious control of the forces operating in this holistic system. The meditator must dissolve the winds of his or her own body in a progressive process of purification by cleansing the outer (cosmos) and inner (person) wheels of time; the winds related to the four states, the six connected with the elements as well as the six connected with the aggregates (which flow more or less uncontrolled in the left and right wind channels), must be brought to rest and directed into the central channel, where the practitioner purifies them and dissolves them in the six chakras along this channel.[1] In addition, the 21,600 breaths or karmic winds and the 21,600 red, female drops and the 21,600 white, male ones connected with them are also purified. In this way the practitioner makes the last impurities vanish and attains the body, speech and mind of a Buddha.

It is only possible to master and dissolve the winds, and to perform the 'completion stage' of the Kālacakra *sādhana* when one has attained the necessary maturity. The adept must have gone through the 'generation stage', thereby gaining a detailed awareness of the correspondence between outer and inner cosmos and purifying him or herself. The mandala meditation with the visualization of deities should foster this process; for whoever visualizes a deity and assumes its form – which is endowed with a high degree of purity – is close to the state in which the false view of things is abolished. In its stead the realization dawns that nothing exists of itself. By using the subtle energies and the visualization of deities, Tantric Buddhism differs from other Buddhist schools, although the final goal remains the same.

Thought and action by analogy

A widespread Buddhist method consists of meditating on the opposite of what is to be attained: to achieve freedom from all bonds, you meditate on your own bondage and lack of freedom; to develop compassion, the meditator must first think about his or her greed and selfish conduct and thus create the preconditions for a change for the better.

Another (Tantric) possibility lies in imitation, or 'thought and action by analogy', which stems from the recognition that the ultimate goal – the attainment of the mind, speech and body of a Buddha – is fundamentally most closely bound up with a body subject to death and rebirth. For at the moment of death, as also at the full attainment of Buddhahood through meditation, all the winds dissolve and the subtle consciousness manifests in its pure form, clear light. At the moment of death every individual finds him or herself for a short time in the state of clear light, but is propelled by his or her own *karma* to leave it and search for a new existence.

The goal of Tantric Buddhism is to become aware of the nature of that light and eliminate the accumulated effects of previous actions, ultimately attaining Buddhahood. The latter is already latently present and therefore not basically different from the state that must be overcome. The inner kinship of all beings forms the basis for the complicated Tantric system of analogies and correlations, and through 'thought and action by analogy' death and rebirth eventually lead to an awareness of blissful emptiness and the attainment of an (immaterial) divine body.[2]

The path to Buddhahood is complicated and proceeds on several levels. The practices on the lower levels only simulate the higher practices; it is thus a matter of anticipation by analogy, a systematic rehearsal, which leads towards the actual decisive performance of the completion stage. Thus at the generation stage (*utpattikrama; bskyed rim*) the *yogin* imagines his own existence in ever new variations as emptiness in the shape of deities, so that after this 'ripening'

37 *Kālacakra and Viśvamātṛ*

he may, with the aid of special yoga practices during the completion stage (*sampannakrama; rdzogs rim*) fully 'divinize' his body and mind, that is to say be actually and completely liberated. The generation stage is an understanding by analogy or simulation, an 'as if'; the completion stage is the actual event and experience.

For the better appreciation of the Kālacakra mandala ritual we shall explain below some important aspects of its chief deity Kālacakra (Plate 47; Fig. 37), in particular the relationship between him and the outer and inner world, so as to demonstrate the correlations and the Tantric theory of 'interconnectedness'. Kālacakra has tamed the winds (see p. 118), and has thereby succeeded in preventing the white, male *bodhicitta* and the red, female *bodhicitta* from leaving the body. He can thus retain the state of supreme bliss. This ability is symbolized by his posture; Kālacakra's outstretched right, red leg indicates the flowing down of the red *bodhicitta*, while the bent left, white leg symbolizes the hooking up of the white *bodhicitta*. Kālacakra stands with each foot on a deity; symbolizing that – as Buddhahood made form – he controls the karmic winds in the right and left channels and guides them into the central channel. This wind channel is symbolized by the body of the deity, whose blue colour signifies profound wisdom. His two legs also symbolize the two halves of a year, as well as the two halves of a day, during which the breath flows mainly either through the right or left nostril.

Kālacakra's three necks – black (centre), red (right), and white (left) – symbolize the three most important channels in the person, as well as the three groups of four time-periods, or the four shifts of the breath, depicted by the deity's four faces. The six collarbones correspond – in the outer wheel of time – to the six seasons of the year (spring, hot season, rainy season, autumn/harvest, early winter and late winter/thaw), as well as to the six watches of the day and night. The twelve shoulders (six each on the left and right) symbolize the twice-six shifts of the breath; the twenty-four arms symbolize the dark and light phases in a year (twelve waxing and twelve waning phases of the moon) and the twenty-four half-shifts of the breath. Kālacakra's twenty-four hands comprise 360 phalanges and finger-joints (three in each of the five fingers of the twenty-four hands). These are analogous to the 360 days of the year and, internally, to the 360 units of the day (each consisting of sixty breaths). Even the colours of the individual fingers have a deeper significance: the yellow outer part of the thumb corresponds to the element earth, the white of the index finger to water, the red of the middle finger to fire, the black of the ring finger to air, and the green of the little finger to space, while the colours of the insides of the individual finger-joints symbolize the trinity mind (black), speech (red), and body (white).

Tantric Buddhism misunderstood: unio mystica

Like other Tantric deities, Kālacakra holds a female partner in mutual embrace. In the West, these so-called father-mother representations (*yab yum*) have given rise to the widespread view that Tantric Buddhism is closely linked to eroticism and sexuality. Not least, numerous books have contributed to this notion in recent years, books with highly suggestive titles like *'Tantra for People of Today: Spiritual and physical development through eroticism and sexuality'*, *'Tantric Sexual Magic'*, *'Tantra, Round Dance of Perfect Desire'* and so forth, whose pictures and text are devoted to sexual contact between god and goddess. On the basis of these books, the practice of *maithuna*, sexual intercourse of a *yogin* with a female partner, could be regarded as a main element in Tantric Buddhism. However, this overlooks the fact that the sexual union of a male deity or *yogin* with his partner, or a female deity with her partner, is a symbol of *unio mystica*, the mystical union of 'wisdom', or 'insight into the emptiness of everything' (in the form of the female deity), and 'method' or 'compassion' (in the form of the male deity).

Sexuality is indeed openly depicted in Tantric Buddhism. This arises from the recognition that it has an important role in life; in fact it is a precondition for life and must therefore be taken into proper consideration in the system of analogies and correspondences. Body and sexuality are not denied, but taken as a starting point for the attainment of the experience of emptiness. Anyone who generates a visualization undertakes a 'journey' through a deity and in the process penetrates via the male deity's penis (*vajra*, 'diamond sceptre') into the female deity's vagina (*padma*, 'lotus'). This does not necessarily mean actual sexual intercourse with a partner. This path is only recommended to those driven by strong desire, while the most subtle meditation on the union of 'method' or 'bliss' (male principle) and 'wisdom' or 'emptiness' (female principle) is intended for those who have no more desire.[3] In the case of an actual partner, certain qualities are necessary. She must comply with vows and instructions, follow Tantric practices, and have received the relevant initiations.[4]

Visualizing Buddha-nature: deity yoga

"Everyone has Buddha-nature and thus is basically fit to become enlightened as a Buddha."[5] A Tantric practitioner strives for the source of his or her true being, wishing to experience the pure state that is often likened to a diamond (*vajra; rdo rje*) – solid, unbreakable, but also completely clear and transparent. Because it aspires to this diamond-like state of Buddha-nature, Tantric Buddhism is also called Vajrayāna.

Buddha-nature is manifested on different levels and in different forms: as *dharmapāla, yi dam*, Bodhisattva, Tārā, ... or as Kālacakra. According to his character, disposition and destiny, a meditator selects one aspect of Buddha-nature, one divine being out of the virtually innumerable throng of Buddha manifestations, each of which belongs to one of the five Buddha classes. These stand for the 'five wisdoms' (Table 12), which in turn portray aspects of the 'mind of clear light'. Once chosen, the deity becomes the personal protective and meditational deity.

The imitation of a deity is carried out in so-called 'deity yoga' (*deva yoga; lha'i rnal byor*), in the course of which one imagines oneself as an ideal, altruistic being, in the shape of a Buddha.[6]

The practitioner must prepare for the demanding meditation of becoming a deity by means of a simpler kind of visualization. To this end he invites a deity to take a seat on a lotus flower in a clean place in front of him.[7] The meditator visualizes it in all its details and presents it with offerings: water for bathing the feet and the body, clothing, ornaments, music, perfume, flowers, incense, food, lamps and so on. Further steps follow in the course of which the meditator confesses his or her faults, takes refuge in the deity in question, prays, and finally cultivates the four immeasurable virtues: loving-kindness, compassion, sympathetic-joy and equanimity.[8]

To be able to practise the actual self-generation of deity yoga one must have accumulated merits (for instance through innumerable prostrations and recitation of the *mantra*), know the basic teachings, have taken part in an initiation ceremony, feel the wish to develop in oneself *bodhicitta* – the 'thought of enlightenment', and have taken refuge in a *guru* and the Three Jewels. In addition, and this is particularly important, the practitioner must be under the guidance of an experienced *guru*. After a purifying bath the meditator sits in the Vairocana position,[9] with crossed legs, straight back, senses under control. Breathing steadily and cultivating the altruistic thought of enlightenment, he begins self-generation as the deity.

There are then six steps to perform.[10] First the practitioner meditates on the ultimate deity: the ultimate absolute, emptiness or the non-dualistic, undifferentiable suchness of the self, which is the nature of the meditator but also that of the deity he has generated in front of himself as "All phenomena are of the same taste in their final nature, emptiness."[11] In the second step, the mind of insight into emptiness uses as a basis for generation a clear white moon disc, level with the place where the meditator wishes to appear as the deity himself. The sounds of the *mantra* of the visualized deity vibrate above the moon disc; this is therefore called the generation of the 'sound deity'. The third step transforms the sounds into the corresponding letters, which are strung round the edge of the moon disc; the 'letter deity' is generated. Next, numerous light-rays are emitted from the moon disc and its letters, on the end of each of which emanates a form of the meditational deity; these deities emanate clouds of offerings and clouds with nectar, and bring every being what it needs. In the fourth step, the emanated deities and light-rays are withdrawn back into the moon and *mantra* letters, which turn into the form of the deity being meditated upon. The 'form deity' has been generated. After 'blessing' certain points of the deity body, such as the heart, the place between the eyes, the throat and the shoulders, with special gestures (the 'seal deity'), the meditator invites the so-called 'gnosis being' (*jñānasattva*), that is the actual deity that was already present *in front* of him, to merge with the deity he is visualizing himself as (the 'pledge being', *samayasattva*), and to be 'as water in water'. Now the meditator has attained a clear vision of himself as the deity and feels divine pride. This is called the 'sign deity'.

The meditator must endeavour to see the divine emanation ever more clearly, by choosing certain parts of the body as objects of meditation: the face or faces, the crown on the head, the hair, the emblems etc., details that all possess a deeper, hidden meaning.

When the meditator has become the deity, he brings his breath under control so as to calm his mind, which rides on the wind, and concentrate it on a single point. He observes either the form of the *mantra* letters in the heart of the deity in front of him or in his own heart, or simply the sounds of the *mantra*, so that he may then refine the meditation on emptiness in various stages, and eventually realize that even the deity's body and mind are without inherent existence.

The description of the principal deities of the Kālacakra mandala – Kālacakra and Viśvamātṛ – may serve as an example of a visualization:

... In the centre are the syllables HŪṂ *and* HI, *wind and mind.*
These mix together into the form of the syllable HAṂ.
Through its transformation I [appear as] Kālacakra
Bearing the brilliance of sapphire and blazing with
magnificence,
Having four faces and twenty-four hands, the first two
Holding vajra and bell symbolizing Great Bliss
Supreme and immutable, and the actuality of Emptiness
The nature devoid of [dualistic] elaborations.
Holding these I embrace the Mother.
The remaining hand-lotuses, right and left, are adorned
With hand-symbols, sword, shield and so forth.
My outstretched red right leg and bent white left leg
Sport in dance on top of Māra and Rudra.

With hundreds of such features I charm.
My body is adorned with many types of amazing ornaments,
Dwelling in the midst of the five stainless lights ablaze,
Like the expanse of space beautified by the constellations.
Facing the Supramundane Victor, Viśvamātṛ
Of saffron colour has four faces and eight hands,
Holding various hand-symbols, knife, skull and so forth.
In the posture with the left leg extended,
She embraces the Supramundane Victor.[12]

Appearance of light

The body of the deity is indeed visible but does not consist of tangile, perceptible material, rather it is a body of light or rainbows. Deities are visible because of the emitted or intrinsic light that radiates from them.[13] They can be described as luminescent, opalescent or scintillating, or regarded as a kind of light-fluid that lights up everything it comes in contact with. The equation of supreme state and luminosity led the Tibetologist Giuseppe Tucci to the conclusion that in all manifestations of the religious experience of Tibetan man, from Bon religion to Buddhism:

> *... a common fundamental trait is evident: photism, the great importance attached to light, whether as a generative principle, as a symbol of supreme reality, or as a visible, perceptible manifestation of that reality: light from which all comes forth and which is present within ourselves.*

Tucci mentions as an example, among others, the Tibetan idea of the time of death, according to which "the consciousness of the spiritually mature person becomes identified with the light which shines out at the time of death."[14]

The worship of light can be confirmed throughout the Indo-Iranian sphere, from Vedic to late Buddhist times.[15] In this connection it appears all the more remarkable that according to the creation story in the *Abhidharmakośa* human beings originally had a natural radiance, similar to that of the gods, which was lost when they began to take solid food. As their own bodily light disappeared, however, the sun, moon and stars began to shine.

Central arrangement of deity pictures and mandalas

The practice of deity yoga makes great demands on the practitioner's powers of imagination; particularly complicated is the visualization of multiple deities arranged in clear geometric patterns in space, and forming whole mandalas. That is why pictures of the relevant deities are readily used as an aid, as mental supports. The meditator hangs such pictures up in front of him or her, or – in the case of mandalas made of coloured powder[16] – sprinkles them on a flat surface.

Tibetan Buddhist visualizations and the images underlying them obey their own representational regularities. As a rule the individual figures, objects and surfaces are so represented in them that the painter, and thus also the viewer, seems to face head on each element of the picture – gods, human beings, mountains, trees, or as in a mandala, individual parts of a building – even if in reality the individual elements are side by side or on top of one another.

To elucidate this factor, and make it apparent even to an unpractised viewer, we shall compare the arrangement of a two-dimensional mandala with that of a three-dimensional one. We choose for this comparison a Zhi khro mandala.

In the middle of this mandala (but not of the Kālacakra mandala) is enthroned white Vairocana, and in each of the four cardinal directions another of the five Buddhas: red Amitābha in the west, green Amoghasiddhi in the north, blue Akṣobhya in the east and yellow Ratnasambhava in the south (upper two thirds of Plate 3). Deities can be identified not only by the colours of their bodies but also by their gestures, the emblems in their hands and their ornaments and clothing, as well as by the number of legs, arms and heads they each possess.

Referring again to the upper part of Plate 3, one should imagine a white Vairocana in the middle surrounded by the four other deities, all seated on the same plane. This plane coincides with the surface of the picture. What complicates matters is that in addition to their arrangement on this plane, the individual figures are also depicted in side view. Consequently one and the same figure in a painted picture is viewed simultaneously from two angles: from above ('plan' view) for its spatial position or location, and from the front or side ('elevation' view) for the depiction of outward appearance.

A further characteristic of Tibetan Buddhist paintings is their alignment on a vertical central axis, which roughly coincides with the 'axis' of the principal deity, its spine (though departures from this basic pattern are known). The other figures are disposed with strong symmetry about this central line. As a rule the principal deity sits or stands 'higher' than the surrounding figures (Figs 39, 40); this emphasizes his special place within the Buddhist hierarchy. Centring in the mandala can go so far that the secondary figures are turned towards the principal deity, like protectors, and surround him or her attentively, as a lotus mandala confirms (Figs 40, 41).

38 Detail of a Tibetan scroll painting depicting the five Tathāgata-Buddhas[17] and their attendants. In the central circle can be seen in addition the Ādibuddha Samantabhadra, above.

39 *Clay figures of the deities in Fig. 38 are here set out in the same arrangement on the surface of a Zhi khro mandala (Plates 15-21; the three deities shown either side of the central figure in Fig. 38, the four wrathful deities, and Samantabhadra, who actually floats above all the other figures, are omitted).*

41 *In plan view the mandala structure of Fig. 40 is clearly revealed.*

40 *The Tathāgata-Buddha Akṣobhya, surrounded by eight Bodhisattvas on lotus petals; the flower can be closed so that its petals completely enclose the Tathāgata. Divine figures protect the lotus flower. According to the inscription on the base, the sculpture was made on the instructions of the layman Dantanāga; Burma or Bihar.*

42 *Kālacakra mandala with 'elevation' components emphasized in the upper half of the picture and 'plan' components in the lower half. The platforms and the base are not emphasized in either segment.*

The example of a Kālacakra mandala will be used to show how in a painted or coloured powder mandala individual elements are portrayed from different viewpoints. In the upper half of Figure 42 the 'elevation' components – those depicted from the side – have been especially emphasized (for instance wall decorations such as pearl garlands, gems, etc., as well as gateways and gate superstructures) so as to differentiate them from the 'plan' components. In the lower half the reverse has been done; the walls are emphasized as 'plan' elements depicted from above.

To further understand the complexity of the Kālacakra mandala, a three-dimensional model was prepared (Fig. 43). This three-dimensional depiction of the (vertical) levels of the two-dimensional mandala makes it evident that the five circles correspond to the five (or four) element discs which, according to the Kālacakra tradition, form the foundation of the universe (see p. 22ff): space, air, fire, water and earth (in the two-dimensional depiction, from the outside in, Plate 45; in the three-dimensional one, from bottom to top, Fig. 43). The three square blocks arranged on top represent the different levels of the mandala palace that stands on Mount Meru. The mountain itself – not depicted – is situated between the earth element (the innermost and smallest element disc) and the palace. In this mandala representation

43 *Division of the Kālacakra mandala into the five levels of the elements, and the three regions (body, speech and mind) of the mandala palace. Effective vertical distances are ignored and Mount Meru, on which the palace is raised, is not depicted.*

the proportions of the universe which forms the base, and the mandala palace are not reproduced accurately. If one takes effective scale into account, the palace (measuring 32 armspans at the base) takes up only a fraction of the surface of Mount Meru, whose diameter amounts to 400 million spans.

The basic structure shown in the model is generated, i.e. visualized, on the basis of a text that runs as follows:

> *In the beginning, in the infinite element of space beyond all measure, there comes from* YAṂ *a symbolic black wind disc, bow-shaped,*[18] *400,000 yojanas wide [equivalent to about 6 million kilometres or 4 million miles], marked with a banner of victory. On this, from* RAṂ *arises a red fire disc, triangular,*[18] *300,000 yojanas across, marked with a lucky symbol (svastika).*
>
> *On this, from* VAṂ, *a white, round water disc, with a diameter of 200,000 yojanas, marked with a lotus. On this, from* LAṂ, *a yellow square*[18] *earth disc, 100,000 yojanas wide, marked with a vajra.*
>
> *Each of these four symbolic discs has, arising from* HUṂs, *two crossed vajras, one above and one below.*
>
> *On top of all this comes from* MAṂ, *the great central Mount Meru, of the nature of vajra, with a diameter of 16,000 yojanas at its base, and 50,000 at its highest point. In its centre arises from* KSAṂ *a multi-coloured lotus, half as wide as the upper surface of Mount Meru, its corolla making up a third of it. On this, from* HAṂ *comes a moon, from the aspiration sign (visarga) a sun, and from the nasalizing dot (anusvāra) together with its flame (nāda), the symbolic discs of the eclipse planets Rāhu and Kālāgni, the same size as the corolla of the lotus. All these unite and from them arises the series of syllables* HAṂ KSAḤ MA-LA-VA-RA-YA *(written in the form of a single, unpronounceable syllable* HKSMLVRYAḤṂ, *cf. Fig. 66).*[19]

The mandala palace

After this creation of the universe the *yogin* once again lets space, air, fire, water, earth and the central mountain arise from the individual letters, together with lotus, moon, sun, Rāhu and Kālāgni, and above, from a HŪṂ a *vajra* tent.

> *Inside this, from* OṂ *comes an exquisite palace, square with four gates and four portals, made of gold and sparkling with the light of gems.*[20]

This palace comprises three principal regions: body, speech and mind.[21] The 'palace of the splendour of flawless jewels' so essential in the mandala meditation is regarded as an emanation of the Buddha, and its various parts as different facets of the enlightened Buddha.[22]

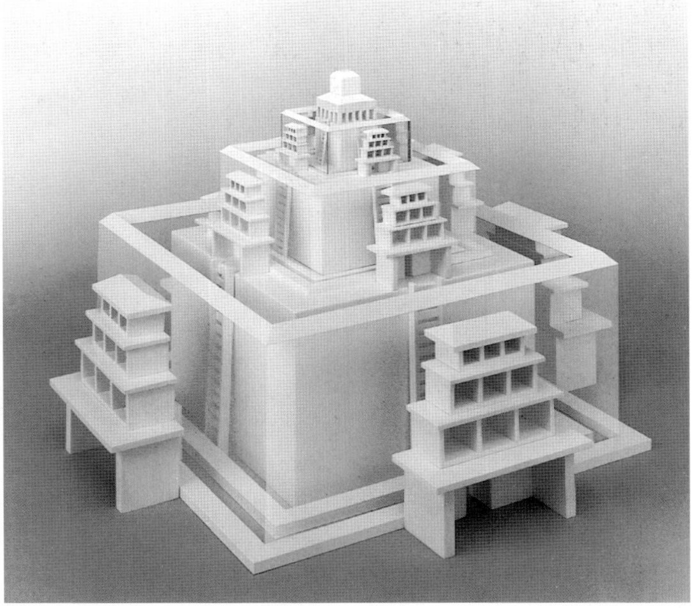

44 *Model of the Kālacakra mandala palace reduced to the essential elements.*

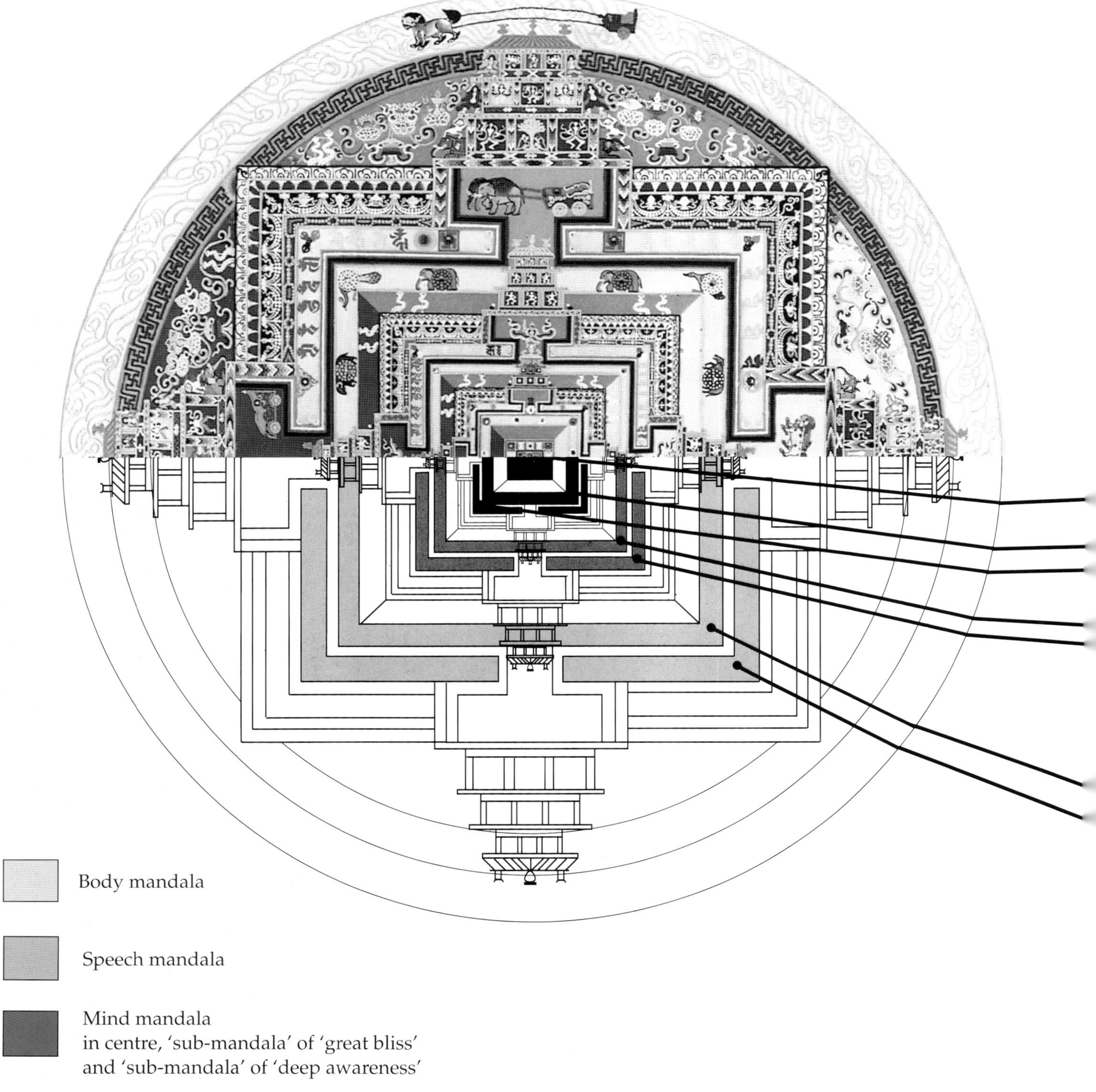

For the present publication the palace of the Kālacakra mandala was drawn to scale in three dimensions with the aid of a special computer program (AUTOCAD), and from this reconstructed as a model (Figs 44, 45).[23] The horizontal measurements (widths and lengths) were taken from the Kālacakra mandala sprinkled in coloured powder (Plate 45), while the vertical measurements – in particular the heights of the individual plinths and of the walls surrounding them – are derived from various sources.[24]

45 *View inside the Kālacakra mandala palace:*

(1) *Realm of the body mandala –* W1 *wall around the body mandala, shining in five rainbow colours –* P1 *outer and inner platforms for the deities of the body mandala;*

(2) *Realm of the speech mandala –* W2 *wall around the speech mandala, shining in five rainbow colours –* P2 *outer and inner platforms for the deities of the speech mandala;*

(3) *Realm of the 'sub-mandala' of 'deep awareness' in the realm of the mind mandala –* W3 *wall around the mind mandala, shining in three rainbow colours –* P3 *outer and inner platforms for deities of the mind mandala;*

(4) *Realm of the 'sub-mandala' of 'great bliss' in the realm of the mind mandala, comprising the 'floor' of the most important deities of the mind mandala: Kālacakra and Viśvamātṛ, the ten Śaktis, male and female Buddhas;*

(5) *Apex of the palace.*

In the mandala sprinkled from coloured powder (Plate 45), the deities enthroned on these platforms are not portrayed in their bodily appearance, but simply marked with dots. These are each divided into two, symbolizing the partnership of female and male deities (see also Plate 46).

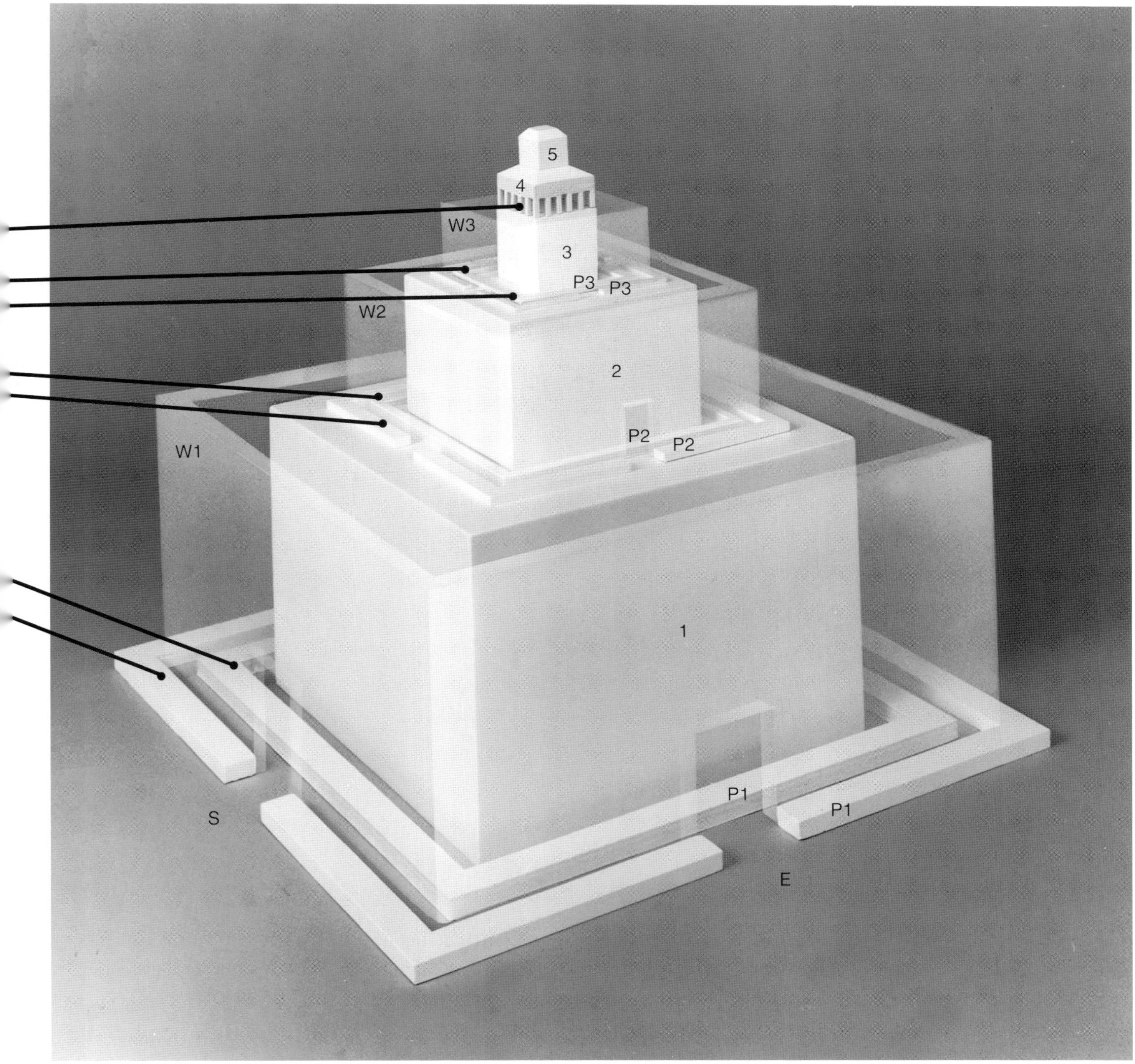

46 *That the reconstruction of the Kālacakra mandala palace (Fig. 45) corresponds to traditional ideas is confirmed by this Kālacakra mandala made of metal in the Potala, Tibet.*

47 *Detail of a mandala palace: corner. Thanks to the three-dimensional Zhi khro mandala, we can clearly recognize in the two-dimensional Kālacakra mandala: (1) outer platform; (2) wall, shining in five rainbow colours; (3) garlands of pearls; (4) beam; (5) ornaments under the roof; (6) end of roof; (7) flags and banners.*

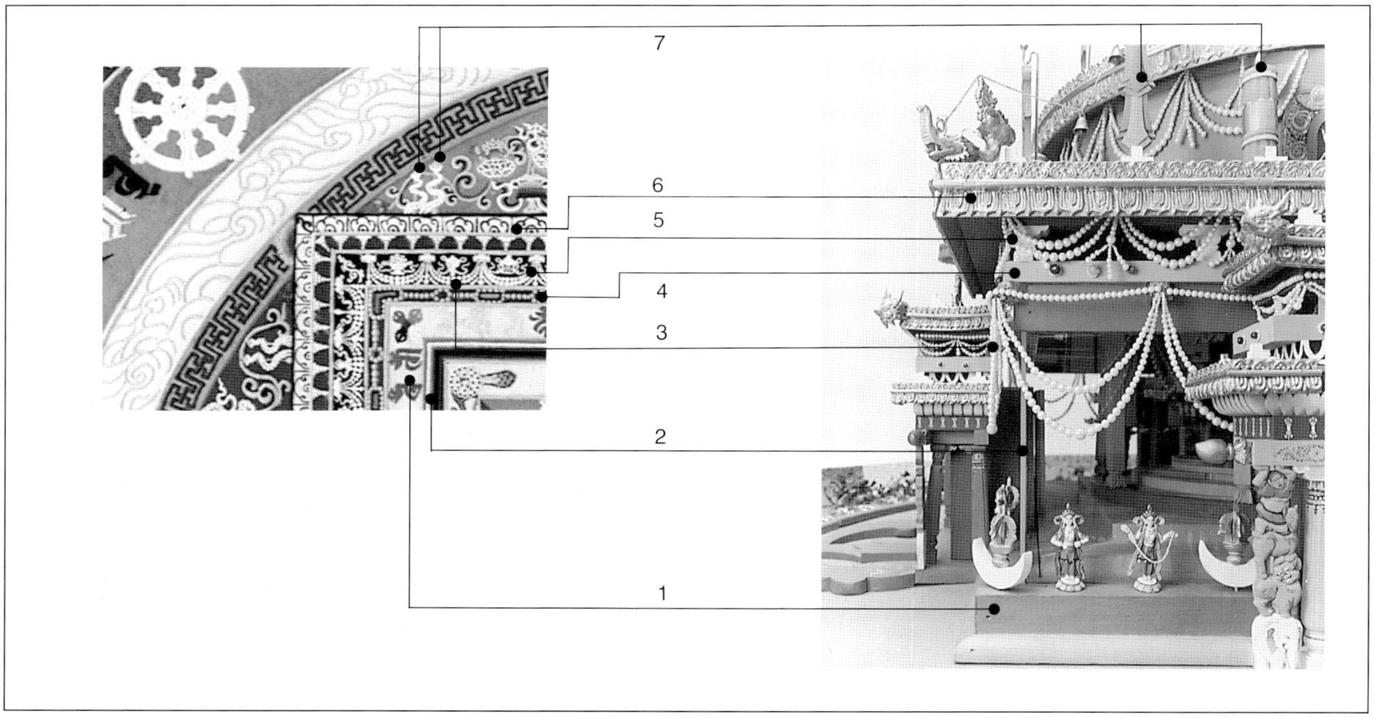

48 *Rare three-dimensional mandala from Nepal. The mountain peaks visible in the bottom third recall the structure of the cosmos (mountain walls around Mount Meru). In the middle region one can make out the circles of the charnel grounds (incised on the side wall of the lowest circle), flames, vajras and lotus flowers, upon which rests a crossed vajra. Above this rises the palace, clearly displaying characteristics of Nepalese style. In the centre of the mandala palace (see Fig. 49) stands Caṇḍarosaṇa, surrounded by eight deities (two of them now missing). The palace is sheltered by a roof in the form of a canopy, on the highest point of which Amitāyus sits enthroned.*

The details missing in the model can be gathered from Figures 46 and 47. The following quotation conveys a further impression of the radiant palace of the Kālacakra mandala:

> *On the upper edge of the wall is a jewel cornice, on which rests a fourfold row of columns, draped outside with a filigree lattice of strings of pearls. This wonderful palace is endowed with every classical feature, eaves embellished with hanging emblems, parapets and so forth. It is ... black in the east, red in the south, white in the north, yellow in the west and blue in the centre.*[25]

Inside the palace dwell most of the deities that are invoked in the mandala ritual.

Plates 15–21 demonstrate several steps in the manufacture of a three-dimensional Zhi khro mandala, which contains the hundred deities of the intermediate state (*bar do*) – the deities that appear to a deceased person after death and before a new rebirth. Apart from sixteen goddesses bearing offerings, they are all within the transparent palace or temple walls, on several levels graded upwards towards the centre. As they are not of any importance for the Kālacakra mandala and have already been described in detail in the various translations of *The Tibetan Book of the Dead*,[26] we shall not discuss them closely here. Rather, we shall use the three-dimensional Zhi khro mandala to elucidate certain elements which, in the two-dimensional mandala, are often only recognizable with difficulty. Thus Figure 47 compares a detail from a two-dimensional Kālacakra mandala with the corresponding region of a three-dimensional Zhi khro mandala.

In its structure, the mandala palace recalls the religious architecture of India. As for instance Stella Kramrisch and Mircea Eliade have shown convincingly, the Indian temple offers an image of the world, a complete *imago mundi*.[27] Every Indian sanctuary is based on the so-called *vāstumaṇḍala*, which the temple architect must know and master:

49 *View of Caṇḍarosaṇa and the surrounding deities in the mandala palace of Fig. 48.*

50 *Three-dimensional mandala in the Sumeru Temple in Chengde (Jehol, China), its base formed by a huge crossed vajra.*

> *From the stretching of the cord [with which the lines of the vāstumaṇḍala are drawn] ... every one of the movements is a rite and sustains, in its own sphere of effectiveness, the sacred building, to the same extent as the actual foundation supports its weight.*[28]

In drawing the basic lines of a Tantric Buddhist mandala these classical Indian instructions are still followed today (see p. 104).

The *vāstumaṇḍala* comprises a square divided into 64 or 81 (8 x 8 or 8 x 9) fields of equal size, which shows clear astronomical references. Thus the thirty-two outer fields represent the thirty-two *nakṣatras*, the deities symbolizing the lunar mansions or constellations that the moon passes through each month.[29] If along with these thirty-two deities we also include Brahmā enthroned in the middle, we get thirty-three deities, a figure already encountered in ancient Indian texts (*Api hymns* in the *Ṛg veda*),[30] as well as in Buddhist cosmography, namely in the form of the thirty-three gods on the cosmic mountain Meru.[31] The number thirty-two appears frequently in South(east) Asian historiography as the number of high regents of a kingdom; with the king that makes thirty-three, evidence that the earthly kingdom was seen as a reflection of the heaven of the thirty-three gods.[32]

51 *Grid of eight by eight squares superimposed on an elevation of the Kālacakra mandala palace.*

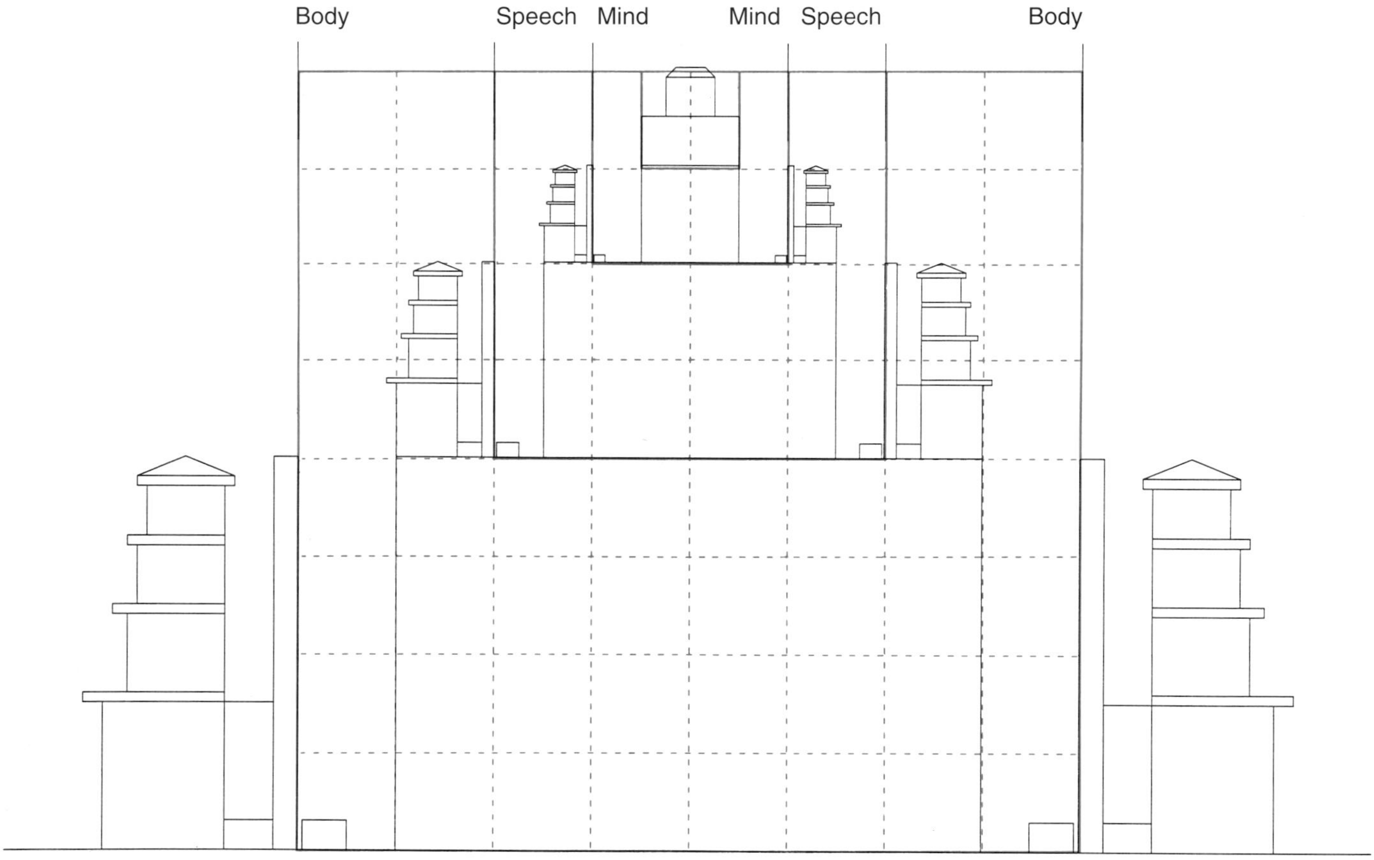

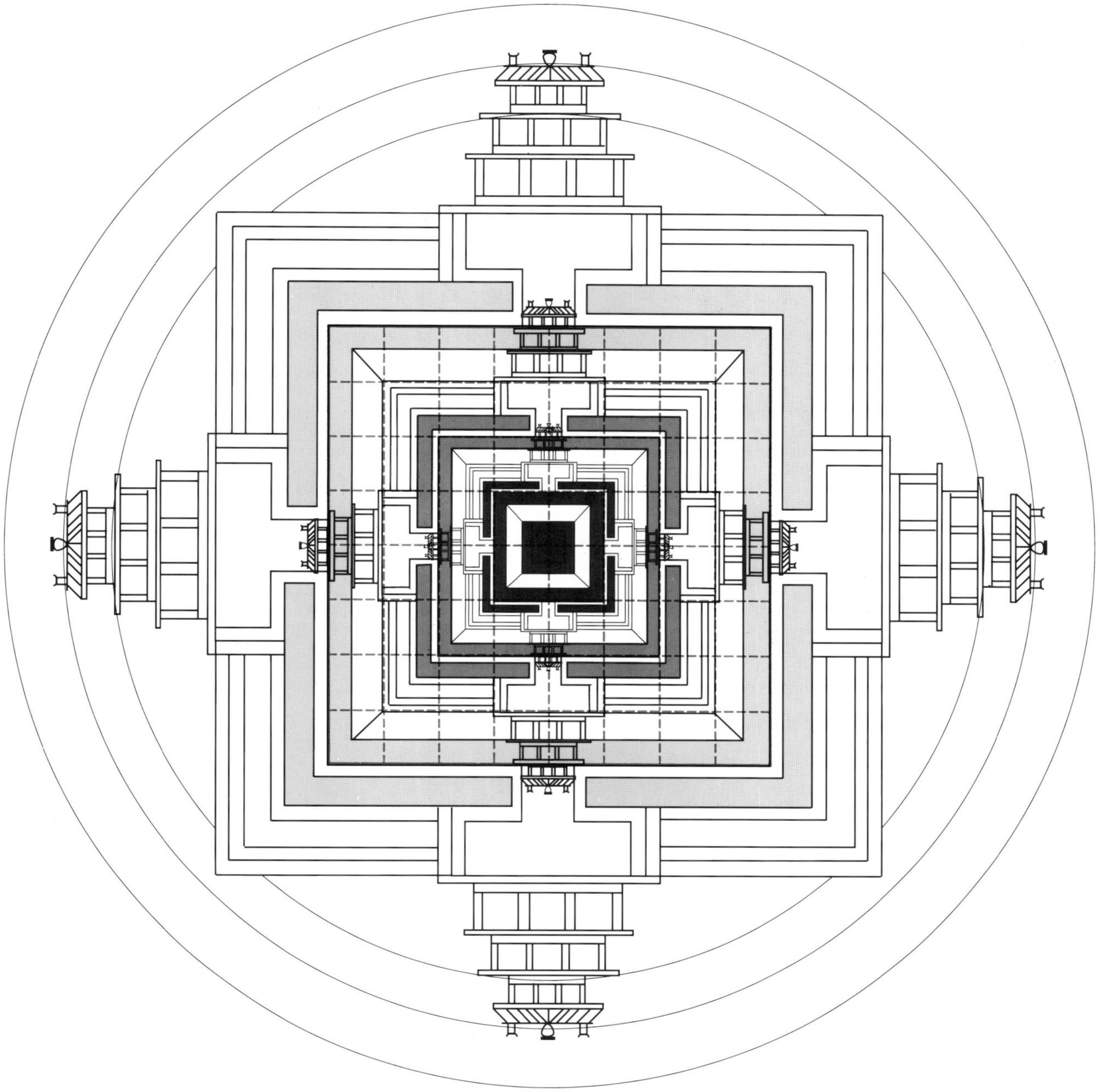

52 *Grid of eight by eight squares superimposed on a plan of the Kālacakra mandala palace.*

Ritual preparations

Just as in the actual mandala ritual the meditator approaches the divine centre from without via many intermediate steps, so too are the preparatory rites mainly aligned on this sacred centre. That is to say, the ritual events proceed in concentric sequences of movement about the centre of the mandala surface (the mandala table), the future seat of the principal deity. Besides, other Buddhist and popular religious rites also show sequences of movement typical of the mandala ritual. Examples that come to mind are the dances (mostly structured in circles) in the monasteries of Tantric Buddhism, the so-called *brgya bzhi* ritual,[33] or the ritual in which a lost soul is brought back.[34]

The ground ritual

If a mandala is to be created, first a clean, pleasant place must be chosen, such as a garden, a mountain or a palace, or else a hitherto unclean place must be ritually purified. First of all the colour and composition of the ground are checked. If for instance bones or potsherds are found, the mandala ritual cannot be put into effect in this place.[35] If purification of the place is necessary, earth must be cleared away in accordance with certain ritual instructions. For this the monks first draw on the ground a square grid of lines, subdivided into many small squares, and in it the 'lord of the soil' in the form of a snake, his position within the grid depending on the date and the season.[36] Starting from particular points, and following exactly the rules laid down, the person in charge identifies the areas in the grid where he must begin removing earth.[37]

Reciting the *Perfection of Wisdom in Eight Thousand Verses* can replace this ritual of testing the ground.

Then the ruler of the place, the local spirits and gods, Buddhas and Bodhisattvas, as well as – in the ritual of the Kālacakra and Saṃvara mandalas[38] – the earth goddess (*sa yi lha mo*), must be persuaded by means of words and offerings to consent to the construction of a mandala and release the ground for the ritual.

After the preparation of the ground, the square mandala table is set up (the surface or board on which the mandala is sprinkled). A complicated process of purification begins, the so-called 'purifying of the ground'. As wrathful emanations of Kālacakra (Vajravega), the monks draw the hindering spirits with hooks, bind them, put them in chains, and finally 'nail' them down in the ten directions of the mandala – the four cardinal and four intermediate directions and vertically above and below – with ritual daggers (*phur bu*) which the 'gnosis beings' (*jñānasattva*)[39] have previously been made to enter. This is done by repeated circumambulation of the mandala surface so that the practitioners, by their movement in space, form a 'mandala in action', a 'dynamic mandala'. Setting up the ten daggers on the table creates a first 'protective circle' or mandala (Plate 25, Fig. 53).

Then the *vajra*-master proceeds to the centre of the mandala table and emanates from himself ten wrathful deities, which descend into the ten daggers. The gnosis beings are called and become inseparable with the wrathful deities. As so often in Tantric rituals, the aim is twofold: on the one hand the deities with their terrifying appearance protect the ritual daggers and thus the place of the ritual events (like the protective circle established in imagination later, see p. 108f); on the other hand they act against inner enemies or hindrances within the practitioners themselves: against false ideas about reality and false craving that arises from ignorance. Another line of interpretation is this: although the wrathful deities appear in a certain form, they are fundamentally empty – a circumstance of which the practitioner must be aware, because all illusions, ultimately even that of the mandala, must be conquered and thus overcome by understanding emptiness.

Now the *vajra*-master encircles the table and on it strews mustard seed and ashes; he sprinkles water and coats the surface with the five products of a cow: butter, yoghurt, milk, urine and dung. These should if possible come from a holy,

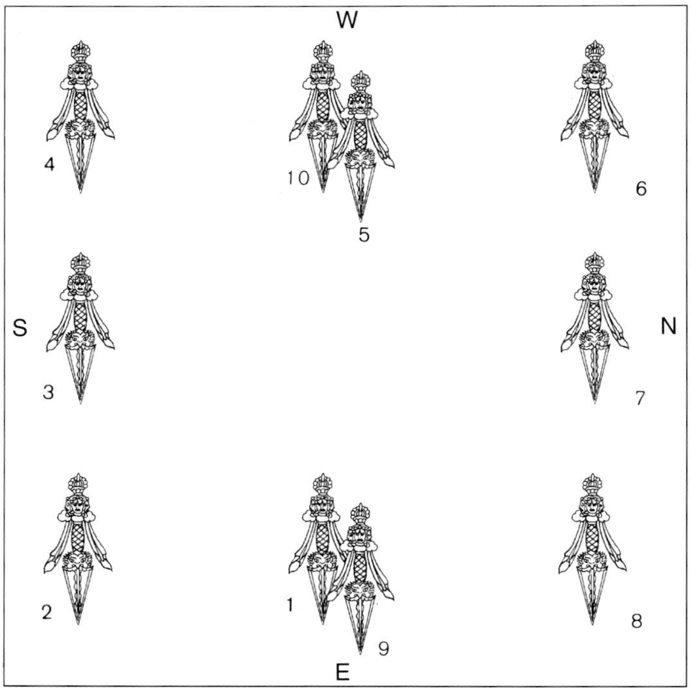

53 *Table surface with the ten ritual daggers. The numbers indicate the sequence of 'nailing' the daggers.*

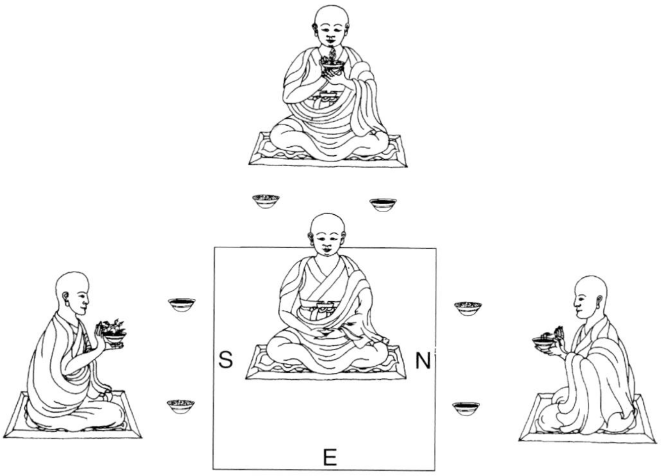

54 *Offering to the twelve 'offering goddesses'. Usually the offerings rest on the table surface.*

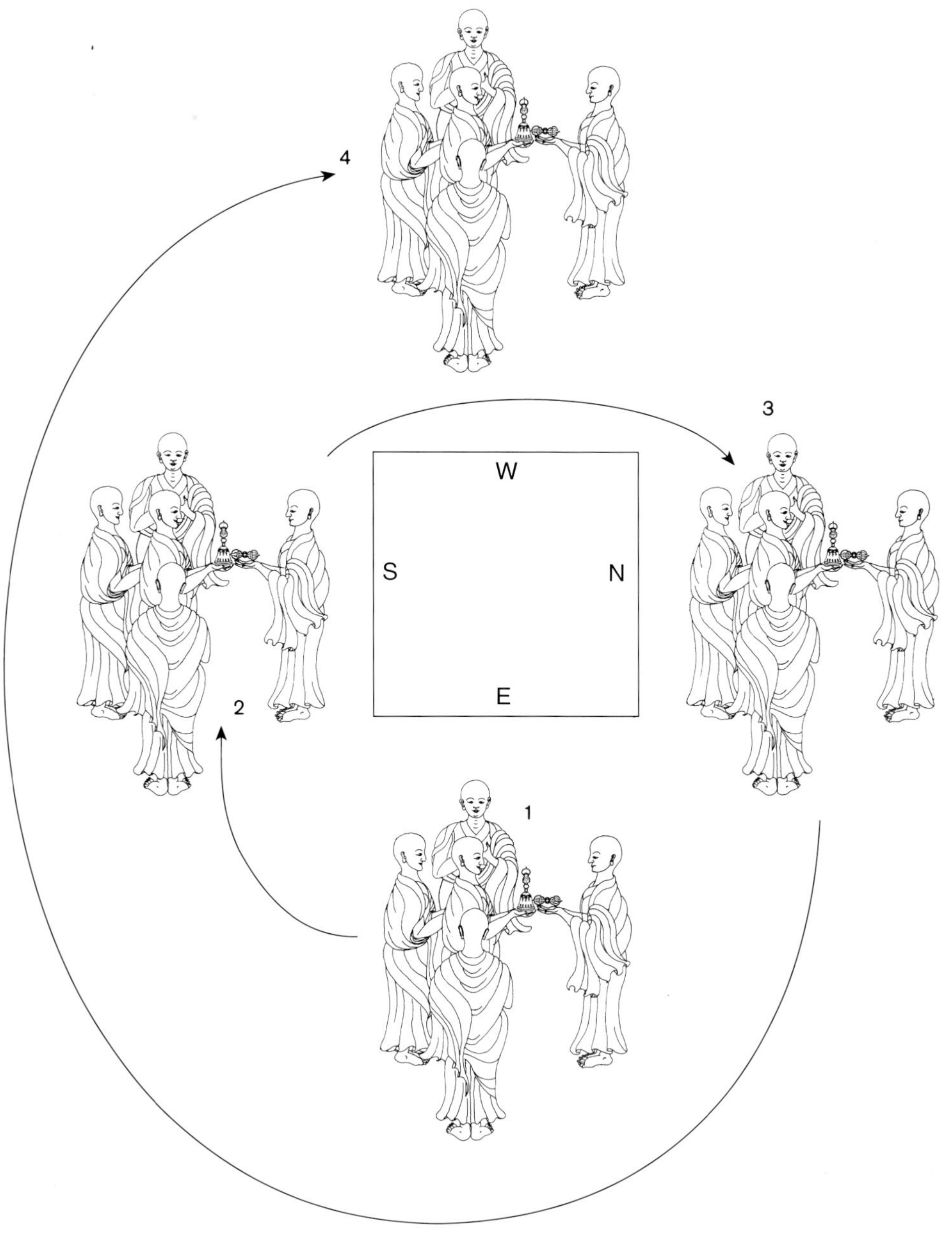

55 Ceremony of 'facing-together'. The numbers indicate the sequence.

red cow that has been fed beforehand on medicinal herbs so that everything it produces is beneficial.

Finally all the participants in the ground ritual step to the four sides of the mandala table, touch the surface with their fingertips and visualize every particle of the surface as a tiny *vajra*. In this way the ground is completely cleaned of any impurity possibly still clinging to it. Offerings and flowers are given, then the earth goddess is invoked once again and her permission requested. A meditation on the emptiness of all existence follows.

When the place of the mandala ritual and its surroundings have been purified, the 'claiming of the ground' follows. The *vajra*-master sits in the centre of the mandala surface, his face turned towards the east. He visualizes the protective circle and then the entire mandala and says to himself, "I shall draw a mandala in this place just as I have imagined it."[40] Following an offering to the twelve goddesses (Fig. 54), four monks standing on the four sides of the mandala table offer an outer mandala one after the other (Plate 24; see p. 24f); finally, in the imagination, the mandala is raised up in the air.

In the following phase the *vajra*-master and four monks 'enact' a mandala: after prostrations and meditative transformation into the wrathful aspect of Kālacakra (Vajravega), the *vajra*-master in the northeast corner orders the hindering spirits to quit the place.[41] Then in the east four monks, with the *vajra*-master in the middle, adopt certain postures.[42] The *vajra*-master turns towards each of the four monks, one after the other, and reciting the *mantra*, touches each monk's *vajra* with his own bell. Each monk in turn touches the

SW	W wheel Vairocana	NW
S jewel Ratnasambhava	C vajra Akṣobhya	N lotus Amitābha
SE	E sword Amoghasiddhi	NE

Table 7 The five directions and the Buddhas (Buddha 'families') assigned to them with their emblems in the Kālacakra tradition.[44]

master's *vajra* with his bell. Then with slow steps the monks betake themselves to the south side of the mandala table, then the north, and finally the west,[43] repeating in each place the ceremony of 'facing-together' (Fig. 55).

Each of the five directions of the mandala is assigned a Tathāgata-Buddha, or rather a Buddha 'family', an affiliation that is expressed by an emblem (Table 7).

The next stage is 'assuming the postures', when the surface of the table is 'marked' – purely symbolically – with the five emblems: the *vajra*-master blesses his feet by visualizing the five different symbols (*vajra*, sword, jewel, wheel and lotus) on the soles of his feet, each one in one of the five directions, touching the soles of his feet with the relevant *mudrā*, and assuming the relevant posture (Fig.56).

The 'blessing of the ground by stamping the feet' follows. The participants imagine that a three-pointed *vajra* appears on the soles of their feet, from which emanate wrathful deities. These protect the place, whilst annihilating all hindering powers and transforming each particle under their feet into a *vajra*, so that the ground takes on the nature of diamond.

After the renewed establishment of a protective circle, as a conclusion to the ground ritual the mandala surface is purified again. Once more mustard seed is cast, and the ritual table circled with incense.

Finally, the monks perform the 'expulsion of all hindrances'. They visualize countless wrathful deities emanating from the feet in order to dispel hindrances. This, like the entire dance, is done with the motivation of compassion.

56 The vajra-master marks the five directions with the five emblems.

57 *Ritual vase (bum pa) for the mandala ritual, North China. The neck of the vase bears a meander ornament on the bulge and simple arabesques below it. Eight kirtimukhas (demon-masks) distributed round the body of the vase disgorge strings of pearls with bell, shell, tassle, rosette, sun and moon pendants.*

Ritual vases – the five substances

Large flasks or vases made of gold, silver, iron, crystal, hardwood or clay (Fig. 57) are used in the mandala ritual.[45] They serve as seats for the mandala deities. If possible, each important deity has its own vase set on the border of the table after production of the mandala;[46] it is, however, possible to make do with fewer vases, for instance one for each direction. At a minimum, according to mKhas-grub rJe, one must use two flasks, an 'all-victorious flask' (*vijayakalaśa*) for the initiations and a 'working' or 'ritual flask' (*karmakalaśa*) with liquid used to sprinkle the mandala, the offerings and the participants in the ritual.[47] The flasks must be purified inside with incense and outside with mustard seed and saffron water, they must be filled with various ingredients[48] and – like a deity – wrapped in brocade. A coloured strip of cloth and a symbol identify which Tathāgata-Buddha (and hence which direction) is assigned to each flask.

Colour plates 23-47

23–44 *These plates show the individual steps in the Kālacakra mandala ritual. Please refer to the text, pages 75ff, for a detailed explanation.*

45 *Kālacakra mandala sprinkled from coloured powder. Its base measured 200 x 200 cm (79 x 79 in). A few details amplifying the detailed description on pages 68ff, 97ff, and 110ff: white disc at lower right corner of palace (northeast) = moon; red (half-)disc at upper left corner (southwest) = sun (in the course of the year, this configuration of the sun and full moon corresponds exactly to midwinter); semi-circles left and right of outer east gate (body realm) = air element; triangles beside outer south gate = fire element; squares beside outer west gate = earth element; circles beside outer north gate = water element (these elements form the seats of the eight nāga kings, who are represented only by dots). The letters that can be seen on the same platforms symbolize the thirty-six offering goddesses of the body realm; the six carts drawn by animals (four in the four gates, and two more above and below in the white ring) serve as carriages for the twelve wrathful deities of the same realm.*

46 *Painted version of the Kālacakra mandala, but with different proportions. Here most of the deities are reproduced in their bodily manifestation forms. An interpretation is provided in the enlarged detail on p. 98, the diagram with key numbers facing it (p. 99), and the accompanying explanations (see pp. 100–101).*

47 *Painting with Kālacakra and Viśvamātṛ in the centre. For further interpretation refer to the diagram with key numbers on p. 97 and the accompanying explanations (see pp. 100ff).*

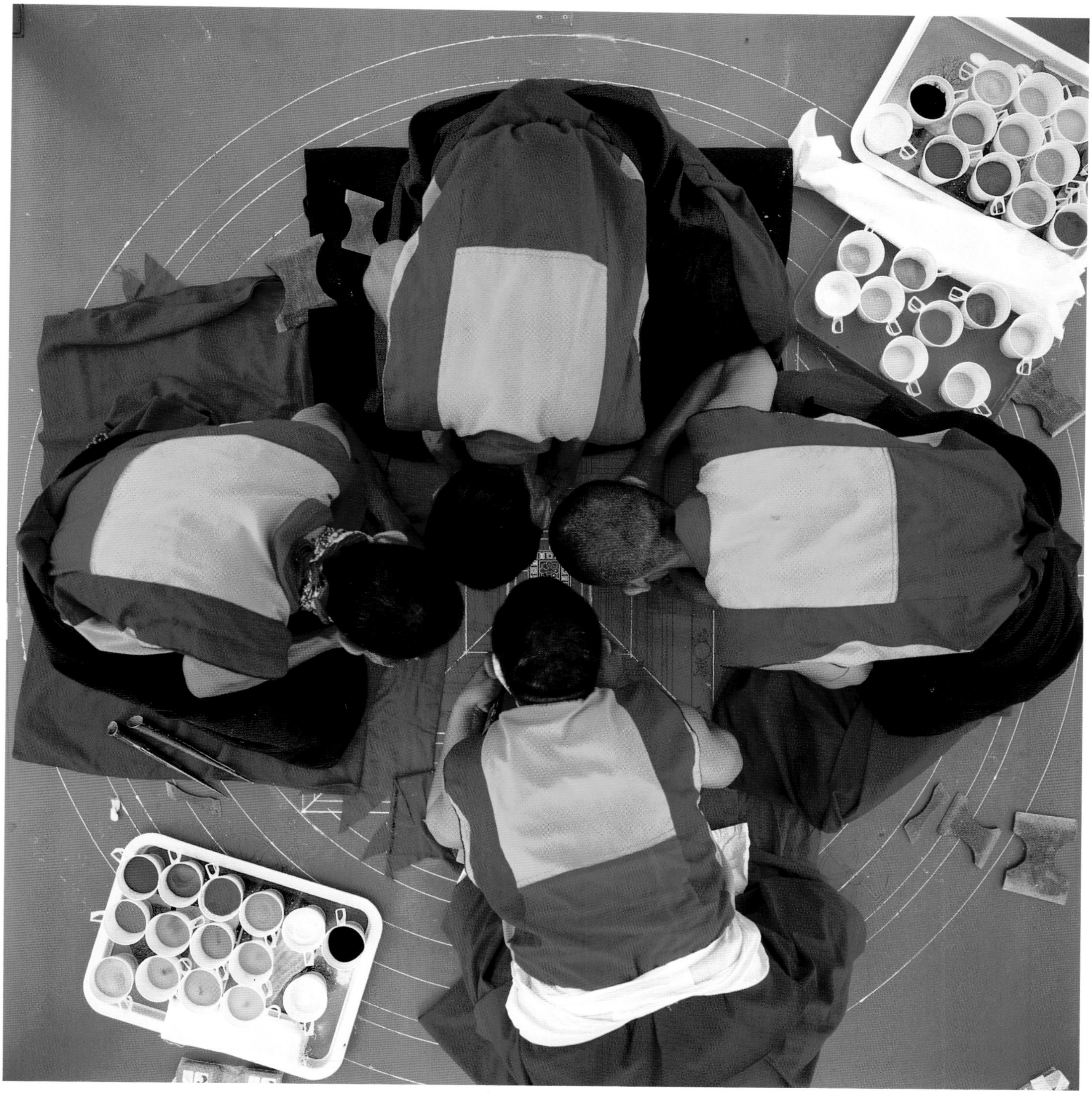

23 *Four monks during the sprinkling of a Kālacakra mandala*

24 *Preparations: presenting a grain offering to Kālacakra in the person of H.H. the Dalai Lama*

25 *H.H. the Dalai Lama nailing down and thus exorcizing hindering spirits*

26 *Blessing the ground by means of a round dance about the mandala surface*

27 *Certain phases of the preparatory ritual are accompanied with religious music*

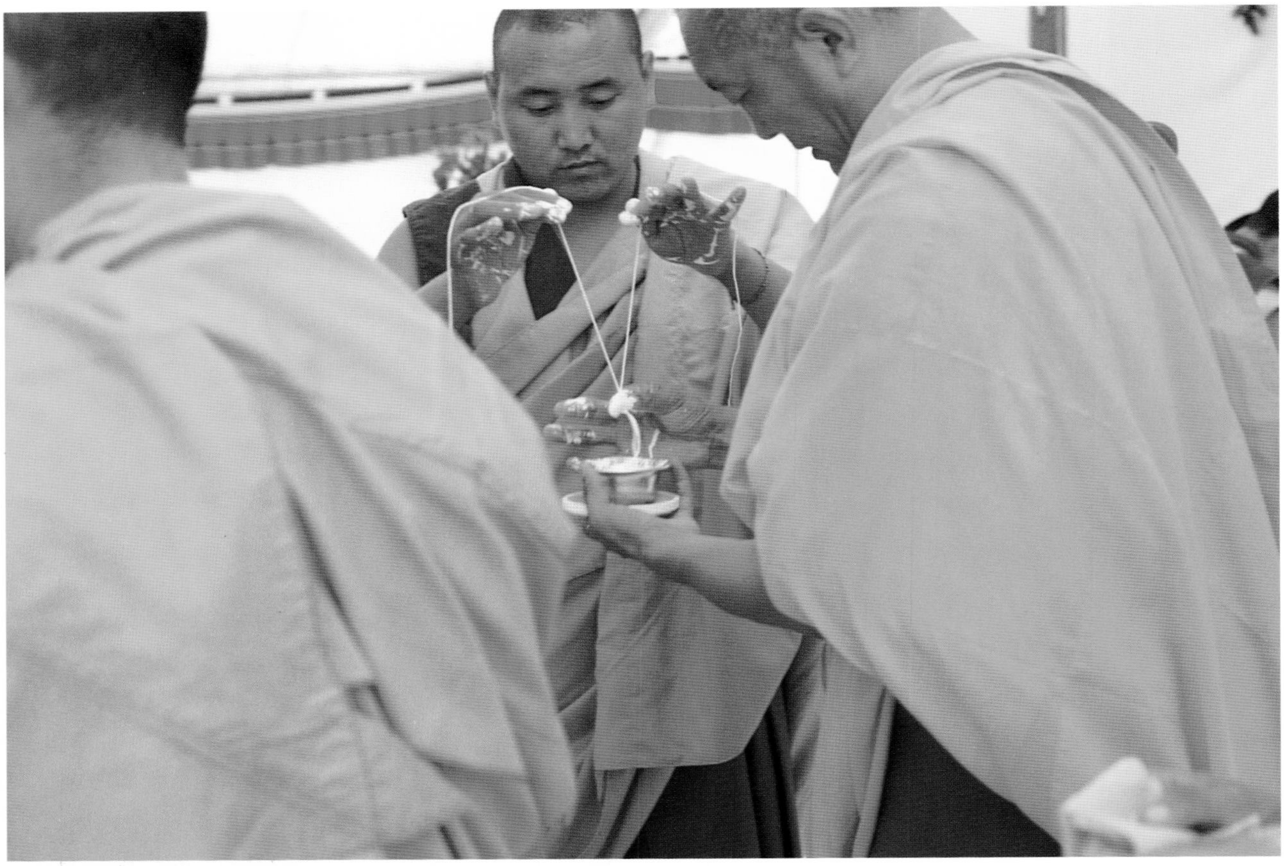

28 *Drawing the basic lines: chalking the 'wet cord' …*

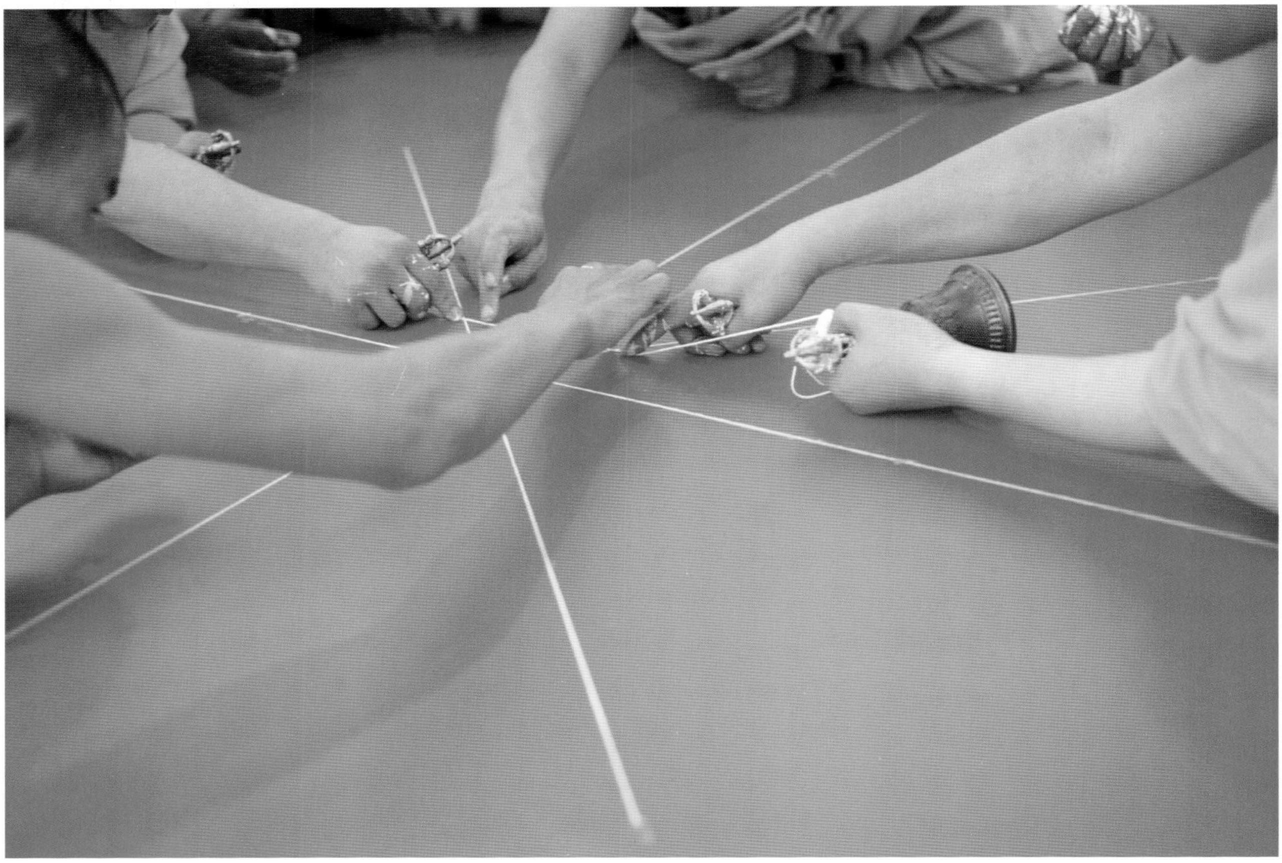

29 *… with which the eight most important lines are marked out.*

30 *Bringing to life: as the corresponding seed-syllable is recited, each grain becomes the symbol of a deity*

31 *Colouring: implements used for sprinkling the coloured powder*

32 *Sprinkling the mind realm*

33 *H.H. the Dalai Lama colouring the east wall of the mind realm*

34 *Colour bag, colour bowls and page from a handbook*

35 *Sprinkling the body realm*

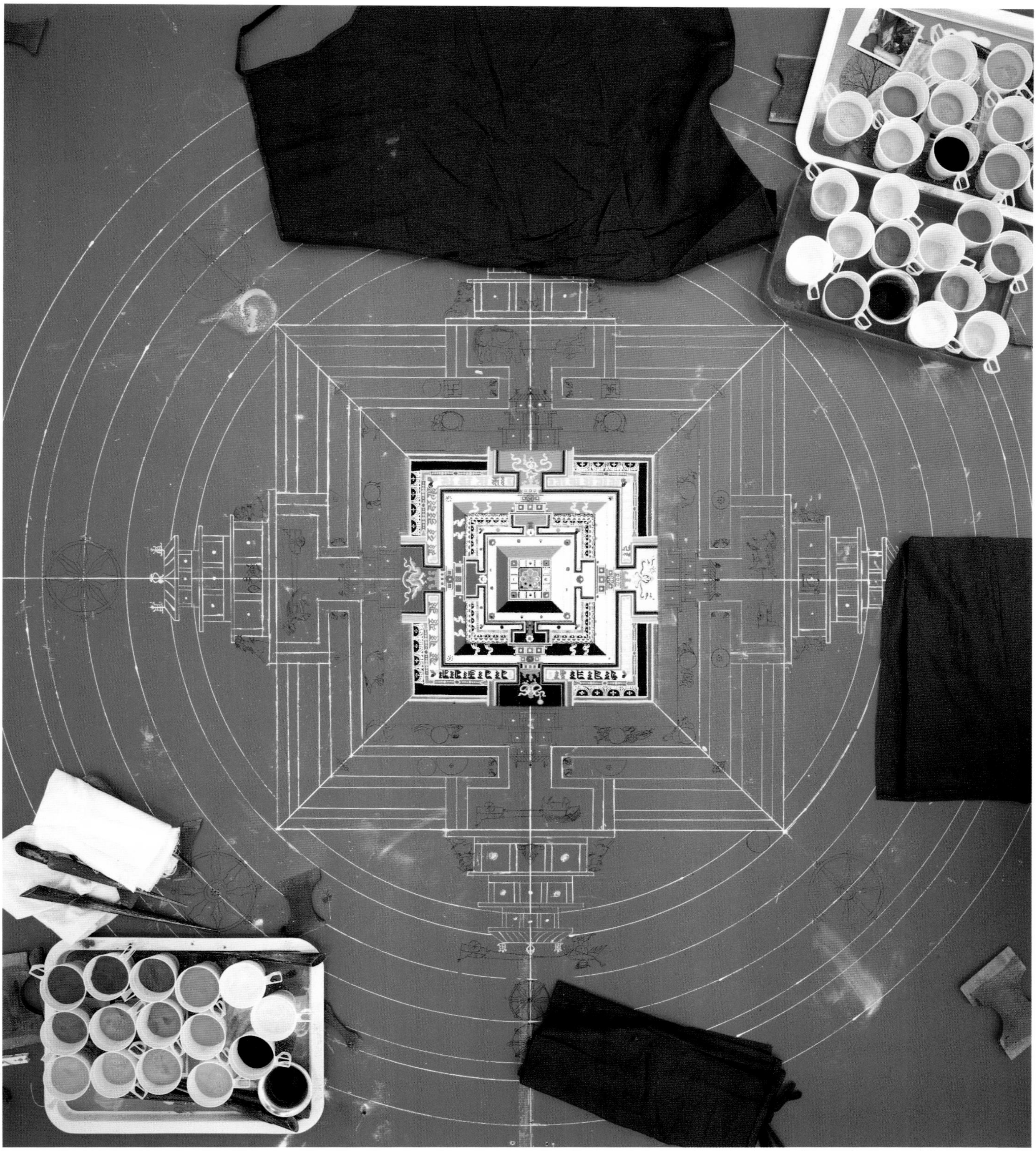

36 *Mind and speech realms almost complete*

37 *Initiations: entering the mandala blindfolded*

38 *Monk taking part in the initiations*

39 *Presentation of the five-lobed crowns …*

40 *… which symbolize the candidates' five aggregates and the five male Tathāgatas of the mandala.*

41 *Dismantling the mandala: wiping together the coloured powder …*

42 *… which is put in a vase dressed like a deity …*

43 *… and at the end of the ceremony is poured by H.H. the Dalai Lama into a nearby river …*

44 *… where it forms one last mandala.*

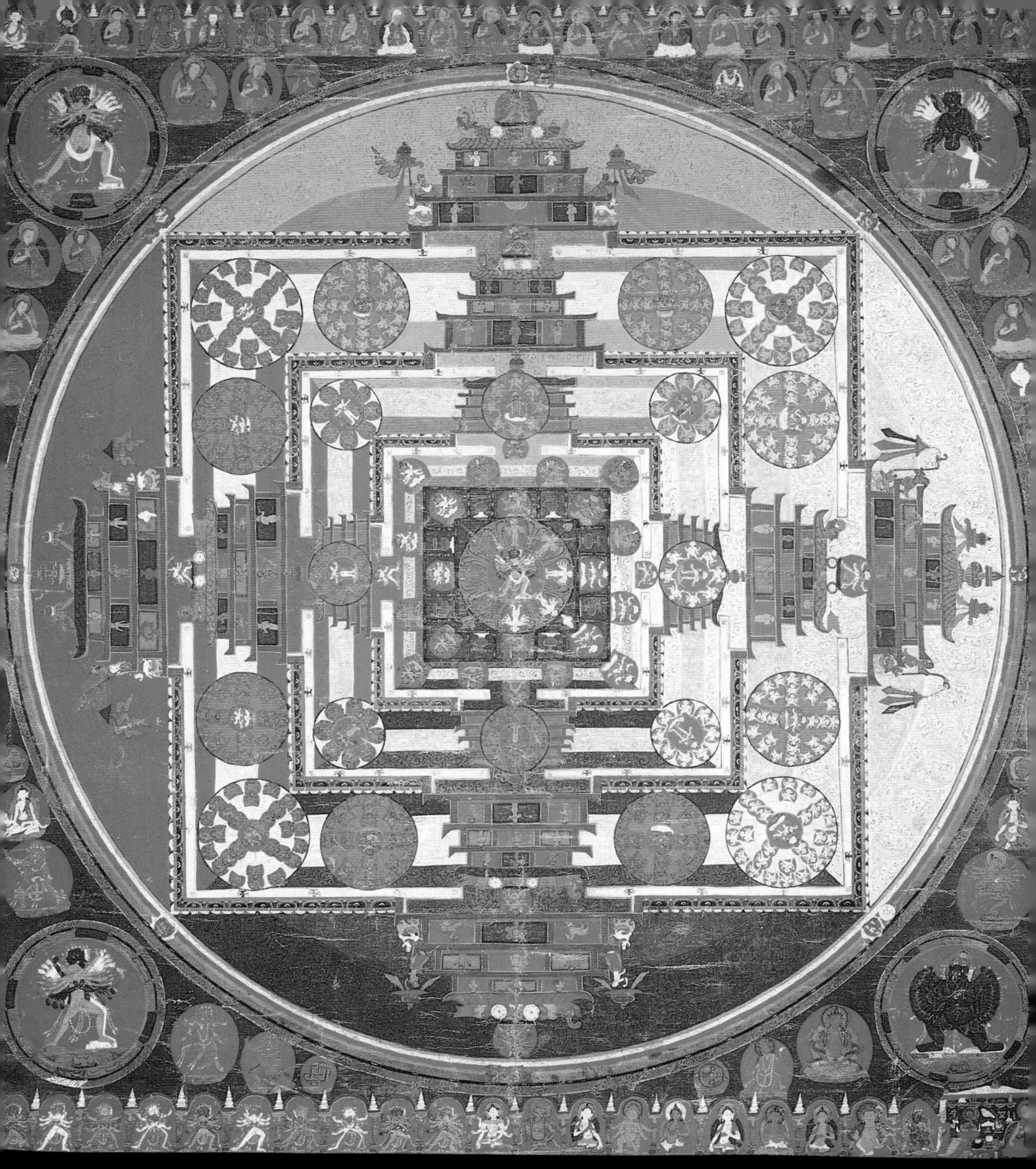

46 Painted Kālacakra mandala with the bodies of the deities depicted

47 *Scroll painting of Kālacakra, his partner Viśvamātr and important deities of the Kālacakra Tantra*

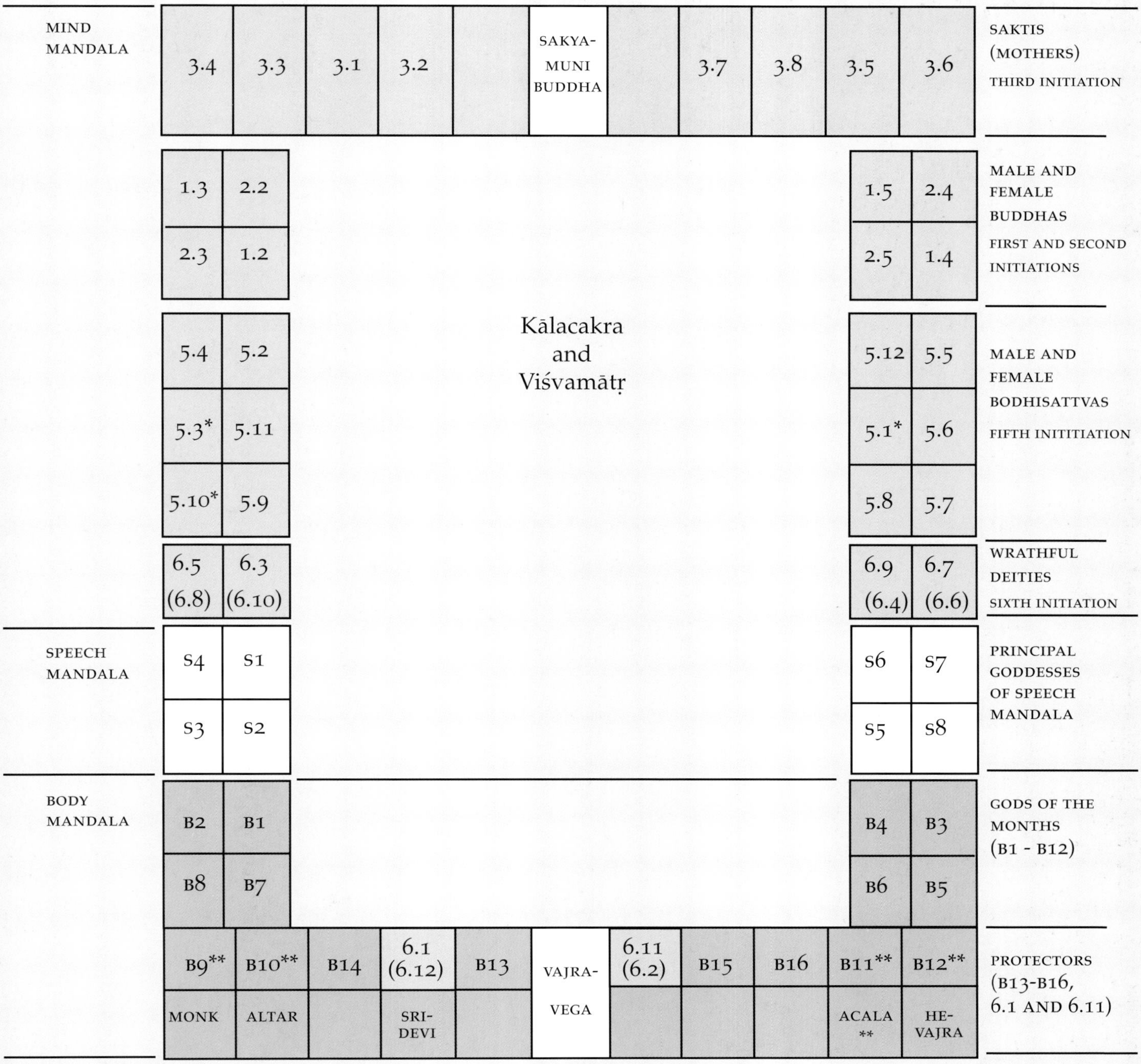

* Incorrectly painted

** Not identifiable (as with figures in unlabelled cells).The two in the top row may be kings of Shambhala.

Key to deities in Plate 47

Central region of Plate 46

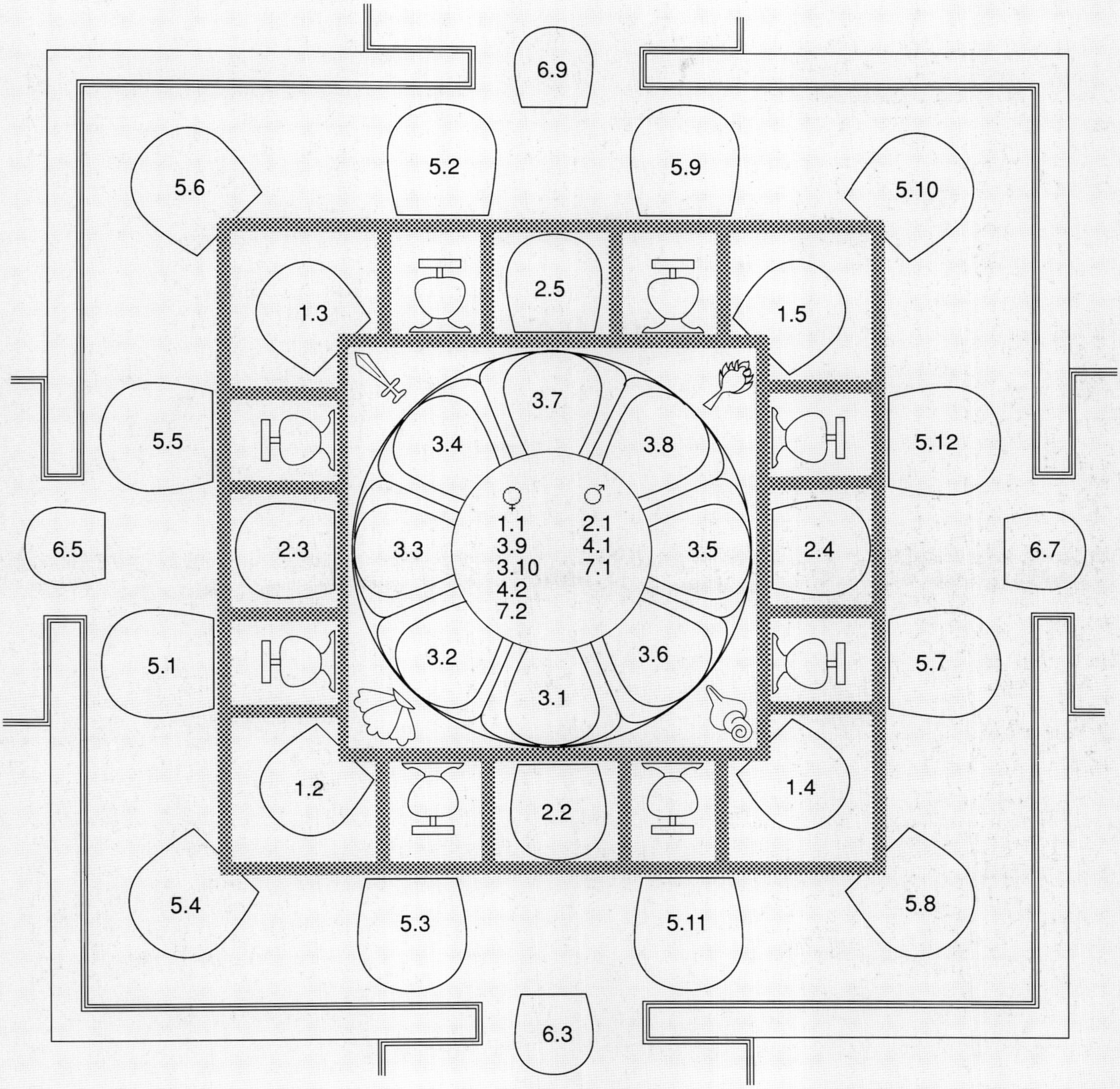

Key to deities in central region of Plate 46

The Deities of Plates 46 and 47 and their correlations

The most important deities visualized in the Seven Basic Initiations

The figures correspond to those in Tables 1, 2, 3, 4 and 5; in addition they identify the individual deities of Plates 46 and 47

	Deities	Seed → syllable	Emblem of deity	Position in the mandala	Purifies in human being
First Initiation (Tables 1, 16)					**Elements**
1.1	green Vajradhātvīśvarī + blue Vajrasattva (one with Viśvamātṛ)	Ā	vajra	centre	space
1.2	black Tārā + yellow Vairocana	Ī	sword	SE	air
1.3	red Pāṇḍarā + white Amitābha	Ṝ	jewel	SW	fire
1.4	white Māmakī + red Ratnasambhava	Ū	lotus	NE	water
1.5	yellow Locanā + black Amoghasiddhi	Ḹ	wheel	NW	earth
Second Initiation (Tables 1, 16)					**Aggregates**
2.1	green Akṣobhya + blue Prajñāpāramitā (one with Kālacakra)	A	vajra	centre	consciousness
2.2	black Amoghasiddhi + yellow Locanā	I	sword	E	mental factors
2.3	red Ratnasambhava + white Māmakī	Ṛ	jewel	S	feelings
2.4	white Amitābha + red Pāṇḍarā	U	lotus	N	perceptions
2.5	yellow Vairocana + black Tārā	Ḷ	wheel	W	forms
Third Initiation (Tables 2, 16)					**Winds**
3.1	black Kṛṣṇadīptā	A	censer	E	fire-accompanying wind
3.2	black Dhūmā	HA	black fan	SE	tortoise wind
3.3	red Raktadīptā	AḤ	butter lamp	S	upward-moving wind
3.4	red Marīcī	HAḤ	red fan	SW	lizard (*kṛkala*) wind
3.5	white Śvetadīptā[1]	AṂ	food	N	pervading wind
3.6	white Khadyotā	HAṂ	white fan	NE	*devadatta* wind
3.7	yellow Pītadīptā[1]	Ā	conch	W	serpent (*nāga*) wind
3.8	yellow Pratīpā	HĀ	yellow fan	NW	*dhanaṃjaya* wind
3.9	green Vajradhātvīśvarī (one with Viśvamātṛ)	HOḤ	vajra	centre above	life-holding wind
3.10	blue Viśvamātṛ (identical with Viśvamātṛ in the centre of the mandala)	PHREṂ	knife	centre below	downward-emptying wind

	Deities	Seed syllable →	Emblem of deity	Position in the mandala	Purifies in human being
Fourth Initiation					**Two main channels**
4.1	blue Kālacakra + Viśvamātṛ	HŪṂ	vajra	centre	right channel
4.2	yellow Viśvamātṛ + Kālacakra	PHREṂ	knife	centre	left channel
Fifth Initiation (Tables 4, 16)					**Senses**[2]
5.1	green Vajrapāṇi + blue Śabdavajrā	A	vajra	centre[3] above	sense of hearing
5.2	green Dharmadhātuvajrā + blue Samantabhadra	Ā	vajra	centre[3] above	other phenomena
5.3	black Khagarbha + yellow Gandhavajrā	E	sword	E	sense of smell
5.4	black Sparśavajrā + yellow Sarvanivaraṇaviṣkambhin	AI	sword	SE	tangible objects
5.5	red Kṣitigarbha + white Rūpavajrā	AR	jewel	S	sense of vision
5.6	red Rasavajrā + white Lokeśvara	ĀR	jewel	SW	tastes
5.7	white Lokeśvara + red Rasavajrā	O	lotus	N	sense of taste
5.8	white Rūpavajrā + red Kṣitigarbha	AU	lotus	NE	visible forms
5.9	yellow Sarvanivaraṇaviṣkambhin + black Sparśavajrā	AL	wheel	W	sense of touch
5.10	yellow Gandhavajrā + black Khagarbha	ĀL	wheel	NW	smells
5.11	blue Samantabhadra + green Dharmadhātuvajrā	AṂ	vajra	centre[2] below	mental sense
5.12	blue Śabdavajrā + green Vajrapāṇi	AḤ	vajra	centre[2] below	sounds
Sixth Initiation (Tables 5, 16)					**Action faculties and activities**
6.1	green Uṣṇīṣacakravartin + blue Atinīlā[3]	HA	vajra	centre above	faculty of urination
6.2	green Raudrākṣī + blue Sumbharāja[4]	HĀ	vajra	centre above	ejaculating
6.3	black Vighnāntaka + yellow Stambhakī	YA	sword	E	mouth faculty
6.4	black Atibalā + yellow Yamāntaka	YĀ	sword	SE	defecating
6.5	red Prajñāntaka + white Māmakī	RA	jewel	S	arm faculty
6.6	red Jambhakī + white Padmāntaka	RĀ	jewel	SW	going
6.7	white Padmāntaka + red Jambhakī	VA	lotus	N	leg faculty
6.8	white Māmakī + red Prajñāntaka	VĀ	lotus	NE	taking
6.9	yellow Yamāntaka + black Atibalā	LA	wheel	W	faculty of defecation
6.10	yellow Stambhakī + black Vighnāntaka	LĀ	wheel	NW	speaking
6.11	blue Sumbharāja + green Raudrākṣī[4]	HAṂ	vajra	centre below	supreme faculty / faculty of ejaculation
6.12	blue Atinīlā + green Uṣṇīṣacakravartin[3]	HAḤ	vajra	centre below	urinating
Seventh Initiation					
7.1	blue Vajrasattva + green Dharmadhātvīśvarī (on Kālacakra's head in the mandala)	HAṂ	vajra	centre	aggregate of deep awareness
7.2	blue Prajñāpāramitā + green Akṣobhya (one with Viśvamātṛ and Kālacakra)	KṢAḤ	vajra	centre	element of deep awareness

Other significant deities

These deities play no role in the Seven Basic Initiations
except for the four last-named protectors (6.1, 6.12 and 6.11, 6.2)
The letters and figures refer to the diagram for Plate 47 on p. 97

8 goddesses of the Speech Realm and their partners (in brackets, their positions in the mandala)

S1	black Carcikā + yellow Indra (E)
S2	black Vaiṣṇavī + yellow Brahmā (SE)
S3	red Vārāhī + white Rudra (S)
S4	red Kaumārī + white Gaṇeśa (SW)
S5	yellow Aindrī + black Nairṛti (W)
S6	yellow Brahmāṇī + black Viṣṇu (NW)
S7	white Raudrī + red Yama (N)
S8	white Lakṣmī + red Kārttikeya (NE)

Deities of the Body Realm (in brackets, their positions in the mandala)

12 gods of the months:

B1	black Nairṛti + yellow Jvaladanalamukhī Rākṣasī (E)
B2	black Vāyu + yellow Pracaṇḍā (SE)
B3	red Agni + white Varuṇā (S)
B4	red Ṣaṇmukha (Skandakumāra) + white Lakṣmī (SW)
B5	white Samudra (Varuṇa) + red Vārāhī (N)
B6	white Gaṇeśa + red Kaumārī (NE)
B7	yellow Śakra (Indra) + black Vāyavī (W)
B8	yellow Brahmā + black Vidyut (NW)

B9–B12 cannot be identified with certainty as their colours do not agree with those mentioned in the available sources; however, they are probably Rudra + Gaurī (N), Kubera + Kauberī (W), Viṣṇu + Śrī (E), Yama + Kālī (Yamī) (S)

12 protectors:

B13	black Nīladaṇḍa + yellow Mārīcī (E)
B14	red Ṭakkirāja + white Cundā (S)
B15	yellow Mahābala + black Vajraśṛṅkhalā (W)
B16	white Acala + red Bhṛkuṭī (N)
6.1 (6.12)	green Uṣṇīṣacakravartin + blue Atinīlā (above)
6.11 (6.2)	blue Sumbharāja + green Raudrākṣī (below)

Notes:

1 Palden Yeshe here differs from Sopa 1985(a), Tenzin Gyatso 1985, etc. According to him, Pītadīptā and Pratīpā are in the north and Śvetadīptā and Khadyotā in the west; see Palden Yeshe, n.d. (Ger.): 16, 24.

2 These Bodhisattvas are related to the centre, but in the mandala they are depicted to the left (as seen from the centre) of the entrances in the mind realm.

3 Uṣṇīṣacakravartin and Atinīlā dwell in the centre above the mind mandala, but their exact position is unclear.

4 Sumbharāja and Raudrākṣī 'dwell' not in the mind mandala like the other initiating deities, but in the body mandala, on a black underground cart drawn by eight-legged lions.

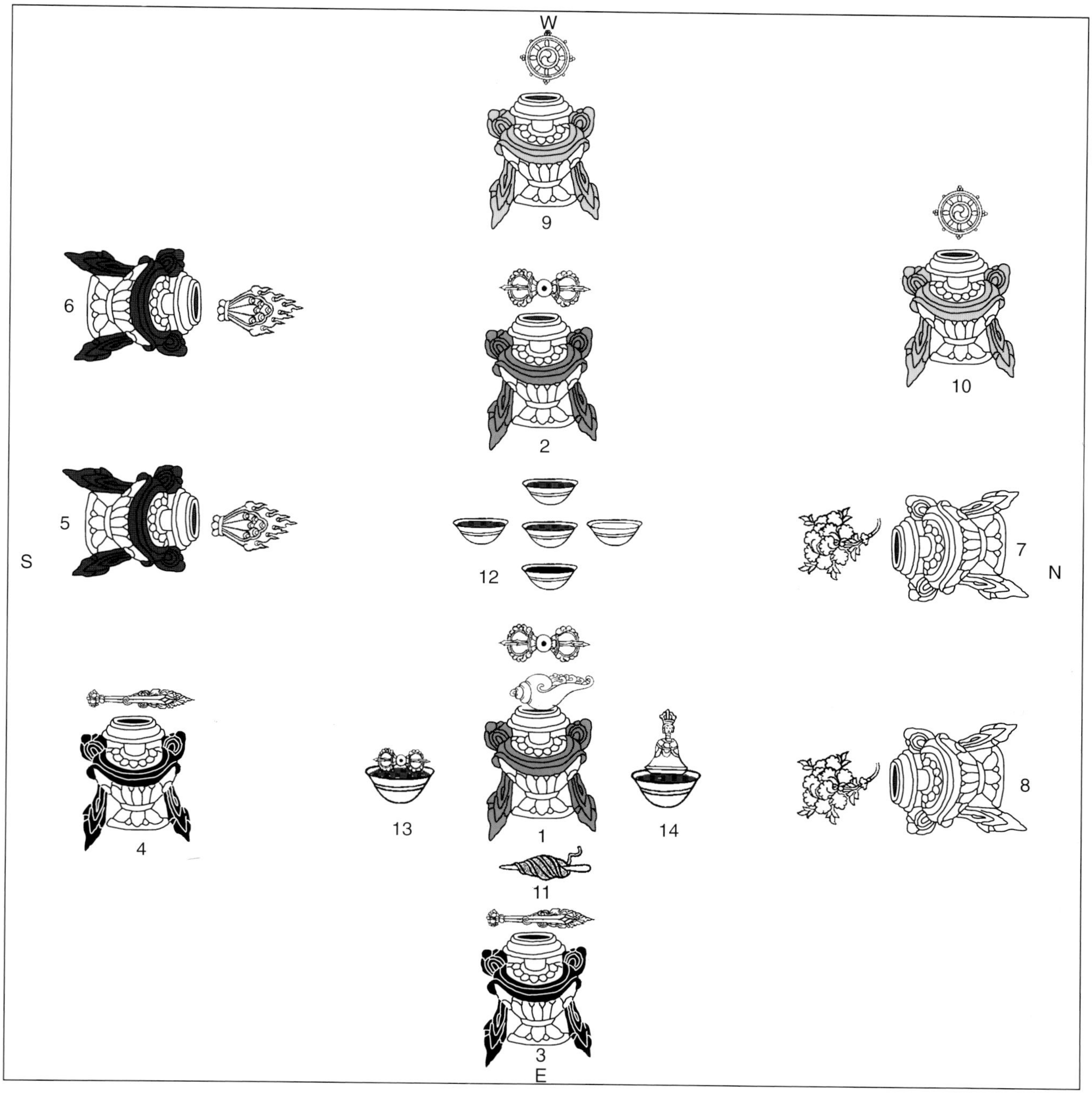

58 *Mandala-style arrangement of the five substances: (1–10) vases – [(1) is the 'all-victorious green vase' (above), (2) the 'victorious blue vase' (below)]; (11) chalk cord; (12) coloured powders – in the five basic colours, arranged mandala-fashion: black in the east, marked with the seed-syllable* I; *red in the south, marked with* Ṛ; *yellow in the west, marked with* Ḷ; *white in the north, marked with* U; *green in the centre, marked with* A; *(13) vajra; (14) bell. The numbers indicate the order in which the substances are set out.*

The flasks, each holding a flower or branch, do not as a rule have a place in the finished mandala. Before marking out the diagram, however, the monks stand them for a short time in the relevant places on the table surface, to prepare them for the ritual together with other substances; their arrangement forms a mandala in the process (Fig. 58). Beforehand, the *vajra*-master requests the deities to enter into the flasks:[49] he touches his heart with one end of a five-coloured cord, while the other end is wound round a *vajra* that lies on a conch shell on top of the 'all-victorious flask'. In other words, the master – and hence Kālacakra – uses the cord to send the deities into the flasks, which are visualized as empty. Afterwards they will be carried around the table (Fig. 59) and set out according to the deity each contains (Fig. 58).

The conch shell holds water from all ten flasks and thus the essence of all the deities. After the five substances (flasks, chalk-cord, coloured powders, *vajra* and bell) have been prepared and the adepts have cast off desire, the *guru* purifies the body, speech and mind of his disciples with this consecrated water.

59 *Procession with the ten vases. The vajra-master goes in front with incense, and the vases are carried behind him in the following sequence of colours: green, blue, and two each of black, red, white and yellow.*

Drawing the mandala lines

Mandalas cannot be drawn and painted freehand, but are based – like all Tibetan religious statues or paintings – on a basic grid of lines.[50]

The preparation of the chalk lines begins by fixing the centre of the mandala and drawing the eight major lines: the east–west and north–south Brahmā-lines (axes), the south-east–northwest and southwest–northeast diagonals, and the inner wall lines of the mind mandala in the order east, north, west and south.[51] The basic measurement or unit in the Kālacakra mandala is taken to be the width of the entrance to the mind mandala, a measurement that depends on the length of the side of the mandala table. Eight such basic units correspond to the length of the wall of the mind mandala, sixteen basic units correspond to that of the speech mandala and thirty-two to the horizontal extent of the body mandala.

A white cord coated with moistened chalk, the 'wet cord', is used for drawing the principal lines.[52] By stretching this out just above the surface of the table and plucking it delicately, a straight white line, the 'working line' (*las thig* = *karmasūtra*) can be applied (Plates 28, 29).[53]

When this has been done, the preparation of the deities follows: a monk purifies their seats with saffron water, and the *vajra*-master sets down a grain of barley on the relevant place for each deity and recites a *mantra* for each (Plate 30). In this way the monks generate the entire mandala and the deities within it.

Now the mandala previously created in imagination and raised up in the air is called forth for a short time and merged into a single mandala with the one laid out on the table. As soon as the monks have made offering to the deities and requested their empowerment, in meditation they again raise the mandala into the air.

Actual construction of the mandala

The actual construction of the mandala follows as the last phase of ritual preparation. It begins with the snapping of the 'dry cord' or 'wisdom thread', which imparts the 'gnosis lines' (*ye thig* = *jñānasūtra*).[54] With the snapping sound the deities and their consorts are invoked and dissolved into the string. This cord is twisted from five different coloured threads, the five colours of which symbolize the wisdom knowledge of each of the five Tathāgata-Buddhas:[55] green for Akṣobhya, black for Amoghasiddhi, red for Ratnasambhava, white for Amitābha and yellow for Vairocana.[56] These gnosis beings and their partners are invited to become non-dual with the strand that symbolizes them, and thus one with the whole twisted cord. The cord, brought to life with deities in this way, is laid over the east–west Brahmā-line and is 'copied' by plucking. This process is repeated for all the other lines: first for the seven remaining basic lines, then for the other lines. Finally the deities are requested to leave the place again.

At this point the colouring of the mandala begins. The *vajra*-master sprinkles the first line, the east wall of the mind mandala (Plate 33); then four monks slowly make the whole mandala take shape, starting from the centre. The tools used for sprinkling are fine, tubular funnels (Plate 31), from which the coloured powder – in the case of the Kālacakra mandala created at Rikon, silicon dioxide (quartz)[57] – trickles out as their rough edge is rubbed. The colours and shapes are precisely stipulated. As a visual aid, the monks in charge use 'handbooks' in which are depicted the most important figures and ornaments (Plate 34).

As already mentioned, the deities in a mandala do not necessarily have to be depicted in their bodily manifestation form. mKhas-grub rJe mentions three styles of representation: the 'pledge seal' (*samayamudrā* or *samayamaṇḍala*) of mind, in which only the emblems of the relevant deities are painted (Plate 10); the 'law seal' (*dharmamudrā*) of speech,

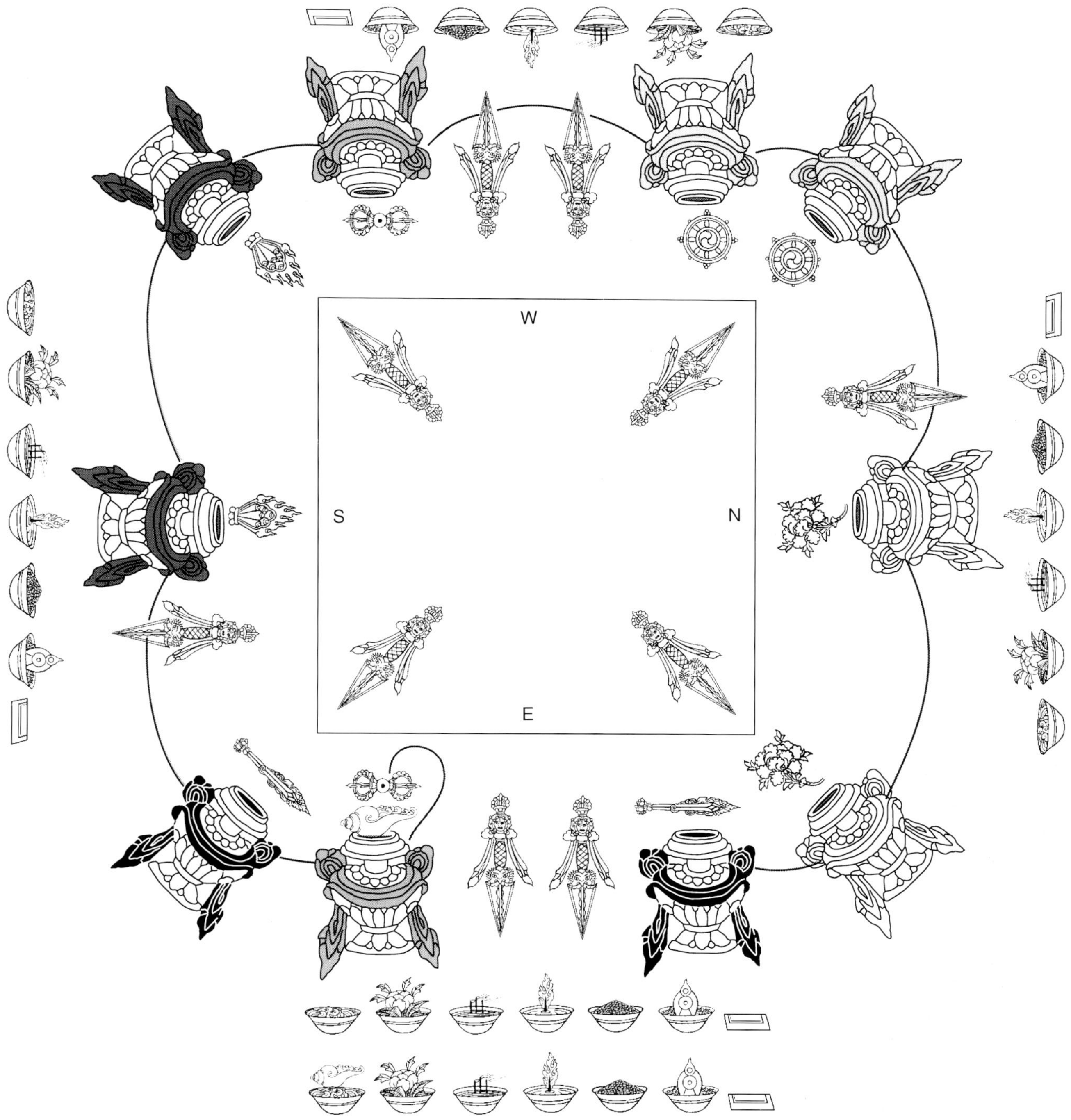

60 Vases and offerings arranged around the completed mandala.

in which the seed-syllable of each deity is placed; and the 'great seal' (*mahāmudrā*) of body, in which the complete form of the deity is drawn (Plates 11, 46), or a statue of the deity is set in the appropriate place.[58]

In conclusion, after some eight days of preparation, the *vajra*-master purifies the corners of the mandala table with saffron water and decorates them with flowers. The vases are ceremonially carried round the table – again forming a 'dynamic mandala' – and arranged round the table together with offerings for the twelve offering goddesses. In the process the vases and the deities they contain must of course be assigned to the correct sides of the mandala (Fig. 60).

Meditative preparation for the mandala ritual

Like all complex Tantric practices, the ritual of the Kālacakra mandala requires meditative as well as ritual preparations, which gradually and very purposefully bestow positive *karma* on the disciples. That these preparations are brought again and again into relation with later phases of the *sādhana*[59] and indeed anticipate later steps is only natural, seeing that according to the *Kālacakra Tantra* everything is mutually interwoven and on different levels analogous structures exist and analogous processes occur.

In the *Kālacakra Tantra* 'energy stockpiles' from two accumulations are spoken of: the building up of positive *karma* during the preliminaries, and the meditation on the 'four doors to liberation'.[60] The former is a condition for the successful commencement of the second step, which in turn constitutes a precondition for beginning the so-called 'generation stage'. The meditative practices consist above all of making inner and outer offerings – including the mandala offering (see p. 24), self-protection (see p. 108), and protection of the place of the ritual (see p. 108ff).

Inner offering

In the 'inner offering', after he has fundamentally purified himself, the meditator presents himself as an offering. He or she offers the five fluids and five kinds of meat, which in turn symbolize the five aggregates and five elements of which the *yogin* consists.

61 *Drawing of skull-cup for the 'inner offering'.*

To make the inner offering, the *yogin* must himself become the deity Kālacakra. A green lotus serves as a base, on which lie a white moon, a red sun, a black Rāhu and a yellow Kālāgni disc. On top of this base arises the syllable HŪṂ, which transforms into a five-spoked, blue *vajra*, which in turn changes into a simple blue form of Kālacakra with one head, two arms and a female partner. After the recitation of the six syllables OṂ, ĀḤ, HŪṂ, HOḤ, HAṂ, KṢAḤ – the seed-syllables of the six Buddha 'families', each of which is related to one of the six chakras (Table 10) – there appear six *vajraḍākinīs* (female 'space-walkers'), who symbolize deep awareness, and clear away both external and internal hindrances. Internal hindrances include above all the false idea of a truly existing 'I' and, connected with that, 'grasping' at things.

After this purification the *yogin* performs another significant visualization, whose structure clearly conforms to that of the universe and the mandala. The five meats and five fluids are 'created':

> *In emptiness (śūnyatā) arises from the seed-syllable YAṂ a black, bow-shaped foundation of air, in both corners of which stands a banner;*
> *Above this arises from RAṂ a fire disc in the shape of a triangle;*
> *The seed-syllable ĀḤ transforms into a human head in each of the three corners of the fire triangle;*
> *From the syllable OṂ is formed a skull-cup, which rests on the three human skulls (Fig. 61). It is white outside, indicating method, and red inside, representing wisdom;*
> *In the centre of the skull the meditator imagines a red lotus flower with eight petals, each one marked with a seed-syllable; two further syllables appear in the centre of the lotus;*
> *The five seed-syllables with a short vowel transform into the various fluids ('nectars') and represent the five aggregates of which the yogin consists. The other five, with long vowels, each symbolize a kind of meat, portraying the practitioner's five elements.*

The schematic representation (Table 8) shows the characteristic mandala arrangement of the inner offering; in each direction there is a particular syllable and the deity emerging from it, as well as the bodily fluid and aggregate, or else the meat and element, related to this deity. The relationship between inner offering, person, and Kālacakra mandala results from the identity of the emanated deities with the female and male Buddhas residing in the centre of the mandala.

The meditator now lets light radiate from the HŪṂ syllable in his heart, which sets in motion the air, the foundation of the whole visualization. Because of this the fire flares.

	navel chakra lotus	
Ṛ horse flesh (1.3) fire element goddess Pāṇḍarā throat chakra jewel	L̥ excrement (2.5) forms aggregate Buddha Vairocana	L̥̄ elephant flesh (1.5) earth element goddess Locanā
R blood (2.3) feelings aggregate Buddha Ratnasambhava	Ā human flesh (1.1) space element goddess Vajradhātviśvari **bell** **---crown chakra---** **vajra** A semen (2.1) consciousness aggregate Buddha Akṣobhya	U urine (2.4) perceptions aggregate Buddha Amitābha brow chakra lotus
Ī dog flesh (1.2) air element goddess Tārā heart chakra sword	I bone marrow (2.2) mental factors aggregate Buddha Amoghasiddhi	Ū cow flesh (1.4) water element goddess Māmaki

Table 8 Mandala-style arrangement of the inner offering,[61] and the male and female Buddhas visualized with it. The first number indicates the mandala initiation in which the substance in question is purified, the second, the position in the sequence of purifications within the relevant initiation.

The ten substances (five elements and five aggregates), as well as a white *vajra* that floats down from above and first touches the substances, melt – until finally the entire contents of the skull-cup resemble a white moon.

This purification anticipates or 'ripens' a later yoga practice: stirring the air disc corresponds to the ability of the *yogin* to attain control over the energy winds in his channels. The energy winds thus restrained enable the development of inner heat in the navel chakra; in the inner offering this heat corresponds to the flaring up of the fire. The *vajra* that touches the substances and dissolves into them also has its correspondence in the completion stage: there the inner heat (*gtum mo*), which rises in the central channel up to the crown, melts the white, male *bodhicitta*-drops, which then 'flow' into the navel chakra, just as in the inner offering the white *vajra* (= white *bodhicitta*-drops) slide into the skull-cup (= navel chakra) and dissolves there. Just as the offering fire melts and boils all the old impure substances and fluids in the skull-cup – in the end letting them take on the pure colour of the moon, so is the meditator liberated in the completion stage from all mental defilements and disturbances. The impure fluids and meats of the inner offering symbolize not only the actual aggregates and elements to be purified, but all the unfavourable mental attitudes. A similar process is known to take place in the course of dying, when the white *bodhicitta* from the crown moves into the heart chakra to enter there the 'drop that is indestructible during the lifetime' (see p. 59).

But to return to the inner offering: in a second part of this visualization process the point is to purify again the substances that have melted and mixed together, to increase them and give them the radiance and immaculacy that are fundamentally theirs. This is effected in four steps (Table 9) – each correlated with a seed-syllable, colour, and direction – which thereby form a mandala. This second part of the inner offering should also be seen in analogy with the later completion phase, in which it corresponds to the complete purification of the four drops from all stains – an action that in the final phase of the completion stage leads to the blissful deep realization of emptiness.

	Place of visualization	**Generation of seed syllable**	**Transformation of syllable into planet**	**Buddha aspect from which planet's rays bring nectar of deep awareness**	**Effect of nectar on substances in skull-cup**	**Direction in the mandala**
1	left palm →	OṂ →	white moon →	*vajra* body of all Buddhas →	purified	N
2	right palm →	ĀḤ →	red sun →	*vajra* speech of all Buddhas →	marvellously increased	S
3	both palms →	HŪṂ →	black Rāhu →	*vajra* mind of all Buddhas →	radiant/ luminous	E
4	in centre of both palms →	HOḤ →	yellow Kālāgni →	*vajra* wisdom (deep awareness) of all Buddhas →	completely undefiled	W

Table 9 Second phase of the inner offering. Numbers 1–4 indicate the sequence of the steps in the visualization.

Outer offerings

A blue goddess (Vicitramātṛ) and a blue god (Vajrasattva) enter the bell and *vajra* and consecrate them. The so-called 'outer offerings' are then purified by means of the six seed-syllables OṂ, ĀḤ, HŪṂ, HOḤ, HAṂ, KṢAḤ.[62] After that the meditator mentally emanates out of emptiness perfectly pure crystal vessels, which contain various outer offerings: water for drinking, washing the feet, sprinkling the body and rinsing the mouth; twelve offerings each offered by a goddess,[63] and flowers, incense, light, food and music as symbols of the five sense organs.

In the longer version of the ritual an outer mandala-offering is also made to the *guru* (*bla ma*), the central deity Kālacakra, and the Three Jewels (Buddha, teaching and community of monks); furthermore the Buddha Vajrasattva is then invoked and requested to wipe away and forgive all sins and unkept vows, and to become one with the body, speech and mind of the disciple.

The 'protective circle practice' precedes the 'seven-limb basic practice', in which the meditator acquires more merits: he prostrates before Kālacakra; lets various letters emanate into his heart; admits infringements of the precepts; rejoices in the meritorious deeds of others; asks the Buddhas to transmit the teaching; requests them to abstain from liberation for the time being for the sake of all living beings, and at the same time to assist the meditator to help others gain enlightenment. There follows the promise to develop in the future the altruistic thought of enlightenment (*bodhicitta*), give up egoism, and practise the ten perfections (*pāramitā*) and the four principal virtues: love, compassion, sympathetic-joy and equanimity. The meditator thus concludes the phase of gathering the accumulation of merits with the promise that he will attain the 'four doors to liberation' – i.e., emptiness, signlessness, wishlessness and non-action.

Protection of self and of place

In a further visualization, the meditator purifies his own body, speech, mind and deep awareness by imagining a moon dragged three times through his body from top to bottom, which peels his body from head to foot like a snake shedding its skin. This makes the body as white as the moon disc. Thereupon the meditator generates seed-syllables on the six chakras, which transform into Tathāgata-Buddhas – in this way each chakra establishes a connection with a Tathāgata 'family' and can be assigned one of the directions in the mandala (Table 10).

After this purification by means of the Tathāgata-Buddhas, in which evil is dispelled, the meditator transforms his body into a diamond body, by mentally emanating *vajras*, first to the six energy centres, then to the elbow, wrist, hip, knee, ankle, finger and toe joints, and to the ears, nostrils, eyes, tongue and glottis, genitals, palms, soles and anus. From these *vajras* radiates in all directions a spherical 'mandala' with enormously powerful light: green upwards, blue downwards, black to the east, red to the south, white to the north and yellow to the west. In these rays are burnt up all hindrances and demons that harm living beings.

The visualization that follows next – for the protection of the place in which the mandala ritual will be carried out – deserves particular attention, inasmuch as in this visualization a mandala that resembles the actual Kālacakra mandala is already fashioned.

Above a space mandala arises an air mandala, and above that a fire, a water and an earth mandala, which join together in a single disc, in the centre of which stands a palace. The meditator visualizes himself in the wrathful form of Kālacakra (Vajravega), standing on a lotus in the centre of the palace. Vajravega is blue in colour, has three necks, four heads and twenty-four hands, and is clad in snake and bone

	Chakra in which visualization takes place		Disc visualized as base		Seed syllable visualized		Transformation of seed syllable into Buddha	Direction in the mandala
1	brow chakra	→	white moon disc	→	OṂ	→	Amitābha	→ N
2	throat chakra	→	red sun disc	→	ĀḤ	→	Ratnasambhava	→ S
3	heart chakra	→	black Rāhu disc	→	HŪṂ	→	Amoghasiddhi	→ E
4	navel chakra	→	yellow Kālāgni disc	→	HOḤ	→	Vairocana	→ W
5	crown chakra	→	green space disc	→	HAṂ	→	Akṣobhya	→ C above
6	sexual chakra	→	blue disc of deep awareness	→	KṢAḤ	→	Vajrasattva	→ C below

Table 10 Correlations between chakras and Tathāgata-Buddhas. Numbers 1–6 indicate the sequence of the steps in the visualization.

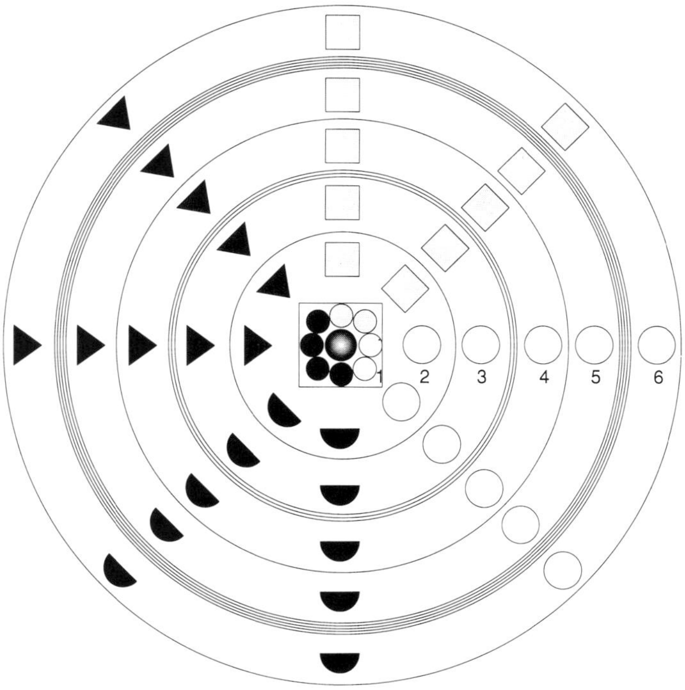

62 *Mandala of the protective deities.*

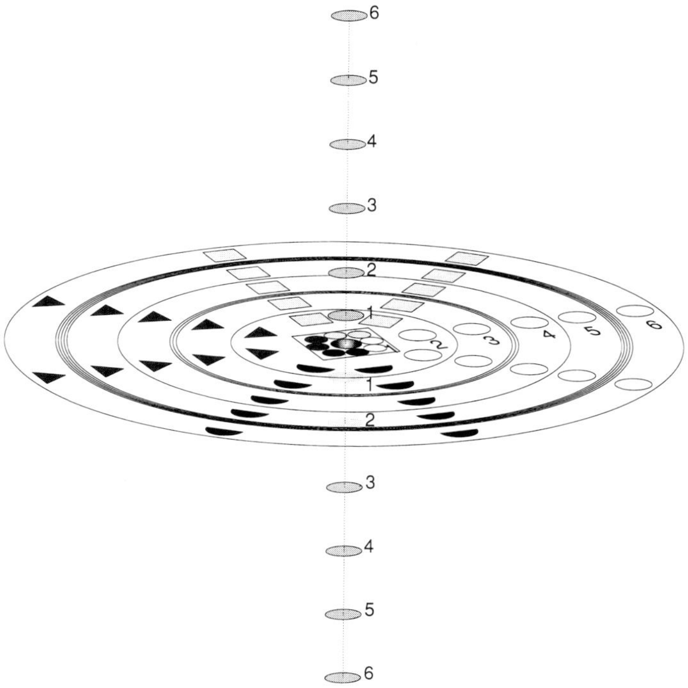

63 *Mandala of protective deities (Fig. 62), in three dimensions.*

ornaments and a tiger-skin loincloth. In the form of Vajravega, the meditator generates sixty protective deities in the heart chakra, which leave the body in a certain order through the ears, nostrils, eyes, mouth, urethra, anus, and an opening in the crown, and arrange themselves in a mandala in six concentric circles (Figs 62, 63). Each group of deities purifies one of the six elements, and two groups each guard the body, speech and mind realms (Table 11).

Still in the form of Vajravega, the meditator then fetches with hooks beings who have already attained perfect wisdom (gnosis beings); each unites with one of the sixty protective deities so that gnosis being and protective deity become of a single taste. In this state specific deities grant the eleven initiations. After several steps the six groups of protective deities each penetrate into one of the meditator's six chakras and there transform into seed-syllables (Table 11).

	Deities	**Element the deities purify**	**Realm the deities guard**	**Chakra the deities reach**	**Seed syllable they transform into in the chakra**
1	10 wrathful protectors[64]	deep awareness	mind realm	sexual chakra	→ HAṂ
2	10 gods of the elements	space	mind realm	crown chakra	→ OṂ
3	10 protectors of the directions[65]	air	speech realm	brow chakra	→ I
4	10 gods of the planets[66]	fire	speech realm	throat chakra	→ Ṛ
5	10 *nāga* kings[67]	water	body realm	heart chakra	→ U
6	10 elementals[68]	earth	body realm	navel chakra	→ Ḷ

Table 11 The sixty deities of the protective circle mandala, and their correlations. Numbers 1-6 indicate the sequence in which the deities are generated and transformed in the chakras.

Generation stage

As already mentioned, in Anuttarayoga Tantra, to which the *Kālacakra Tantra* also belongs, a distinction is made between the stages of generation and of completion. The generation stage is divided into four: generation of the 'supreme victorious mandala', 'supreme victorious activity', the 'yoga of the drops', and the 'subtle yoga'[69] – stages that correlate with phases of human development.

First stage: the supreme victorious mandala (dkyil 'khor rgyal mchog)

As described above (p. 69), the meditator generates a cosmos within himself: from the syllables YAṂ, RAṂ, VAṂ and LAṂ come the four element discs of air, fire, water and earth. Upon these rises Mount Meru.[70] Right at the top, in the middle of the mountain, from the syllable KṢAḤ grows a lotus flower, on the corolla of which appear three planets: white moon, red sun, and black Rāhu with yellow Kālāgni, these last counting as one. All these separate elements unite to form the ten interlocking letters and characters (Fig. 66), from which a cosmos arises once more. On top, from the syllable HŪṂ is formed a *vajra* tent and inside it, from BHRUṂ, a palace of enormous brilliance, the diamond palace. Each realm of the palace – whether body, speech or mind mandala (see p. 69ff) – is enclosed on the outside by a luminous, shining wall (Figs 44, 45). Along both the inside and the outside run platforms, upon which, in the course of the visualization, the individual deities take their seats (in the mind mandala they occupy an 'upper floor' as well; Figs 45, 64).

The mandala deities are begotten like human beings, develop like embryos and foetuses, and are 'born' analogously to human children. The interpretative explanation: the palace on Mount Meru is produced instead of the lotus flower, which symbolizes a female sex organ; while the *vajra* tent, enclosing the entire realm, corresponds to the male sex organ, and the three planets to the three principal wind channels.[71] In the further course of the meditation a white moon disc marked with thirty-two vowels, a red sun disc beneath (with eighty consonants), and a white HŪṂ riding on a black HI, unite in the centre of a lotus in the palace, which represents the womb.[72] From this mixture arises the syllable HAṂ, and from that the victorious Kālacakra; from the syllable PHREṂ[73] emanates a chopping-knife, and from that Kālacakra's female partner, Viśvamātṛ (Table 12).

The following correlations also bear witness to the analogy between the generation of the central divine couple and that of a human being: the moon disc corresponds to the white *bodhicitta*-drop (from the father), the sun to the red *bodhicitta*-drop (from the mother), the white HŪṂ to the 'clear light' consciousness, and the black HI syllable to the wind that serves as the vehicle of that consciousness. The moon and other elements of the visualization each symbolize a type of profound wisdom ('gnosis'), one of the Tathagata-Buddhas, and one of the five aggregates of the *yogin*, showing once more that according to Tantric conceptions the seed of Buddhahood lies dormant in every being. As in the case of the development of a person, in which the ten winds arise very early on, from Kālacakra and Viśvamātṛ emanate first of all the ten goddesses (*Śakti*: *nus ma*), who gather round the central divine couple.[74]

Step of visualization	**Corresponding wisdom**	**Tāthagata-Buddha and direction in the mandala**		**Aggregate of the yogin**
moon and 32 vowels	mirror-like wisdom	Vairocana	(W)	forms
plus sun and 80 consonants	wisdom of equality (of all things)	Ratnasambhava	(S)	feelings
plus consciousness and HŪṂ	discriminating wisdom[75]	Amitābha	(N)	perceptions
plus wind and HI	(all-)accomplishing wisdom[76]	Amoghasiddhi	(E)	mental factors
all together transform ↓ HAṂ ↓ Kālacakra	wisdom of reality (of all things)	Akṣobhya	(C)	consciousness

Table 12 Stages in the generation of Kālacakra and correspondences of individual elements of the visualization.

The remaining deities of the Kālacakra mandala develop in a complicated process after the birth of these ten Śakti goddessess.[77] These correspond to the aggregates, elements, sense powers, sense objects, action faculties and activities, in short to the 'components' of a person (Table 6); they develop analogously to the human foetus.[78] Attracted by the sounds of pleasure coming from the central divine couple, these deities find their way into the meditator who has taken on the form of Kālacakra, and there merge with the aggregates, elements, etc. Riding on rays of light, they get into the body of Viśvamātṛ, and back via the crown aperture into the body of the meditator.

In the crown the deities mix with the white *bodhicitta* – a drop that dissolves in the 'fire of great passion' (*gtum mo*), flows down in the central channel, and via the sexual organ enters the partner Viśvamātṛ. The drop then transforms into the various seed-syllables, these into the emblems, and these in turn into the 720 other deities of the Kālacakra mandala.[79] Only then, after this sojourn in the womb, do the deities take the seats they are entitled to in the mandala, a process that suggests simply the conclusion of development in the womb, but not birth itself. The following deities are emanated into the mandala in the same way.

A first group of seventy deities to be emanated belongs to the mind level of the mandala (Fig. 64). The generation of these deities is analogous to the first five months of the development of the embryo or foetus. The meditator emanates the central couple, Kālacakra and Viśvamātṛ, the ten Śaktis, and the vases and corner insignia; this corresponds to the embryonic phase, i.e. the first three months in which, according to the Tantric Buddhist view, the principal channels and the ten winds along with the six chakras are formed.

The first twelve deities are related to the twelve shifts of the breath (see p. 55ff), but also – in the outer wheel of time, that is the universe – to the twelve signs of the zodiac, and thus to the twelve wind-tracks around Mount Meru (see p. 22ff).

The generation of the five male and five female Buddhas (also called 'mothers'), who symbolize and purify the aggregates and elements, is analogous to foetal development in the fourth month (the embryo becomes the foetus).

To the fifth month, during which the six senses develop, corresponds the emanation of the twelve male and twelve female Bodhisattvas, who represent and purify the six senses and their objects, and of the twelve wrathful deities, who represent and purify the action faculties and activities.

64 *Assignment of the 722 deities of the Kālacakra mandala to the respective realms of the palace.*

The 70 deities of the mind mandala
'Sub-mandala' of great bliss:
2 principal deities: Kālacakra + Viśvamātṛ
10 Śakti goddesses

'Sub-mandala' of deep awareness:
6 male Tathāgata-Buddhas (only 5 play a part in the initiation; they have female partners, not counted here[80])
6 'mothers' or female Buddhas (only 5 play a part in the initiation; they have male partners, not counted here[81])

24 Bodhisattvas (12 male, 12 female)
10 wrathful deities (5 male, 5 female; another 2 are located in the body mandala)
12 offering goddesses, on platforms outside wall of mind mandala

The 116 deities of the speech mandala
80 deities (8 *yoginīs*, each with male partner and 8 surrounding goddesses)
36 goddesses of desire, on platforms outside the speech mandala

The 536 deities of the body mandala
360 deities of the days (12 gods of the months, each with partner and 28 surrounding goddesses)
12 wrathful deities (6 couples), in carts
20 *nāgas* (10 serpent kings with fierce consorts)
36 goddesses of non-desire, on platforms outside the body mandala
108 deities in the 10 charnel grounds outside the palace (10 very fierce goddesses with *nāga* consorts; 88 main elementals)

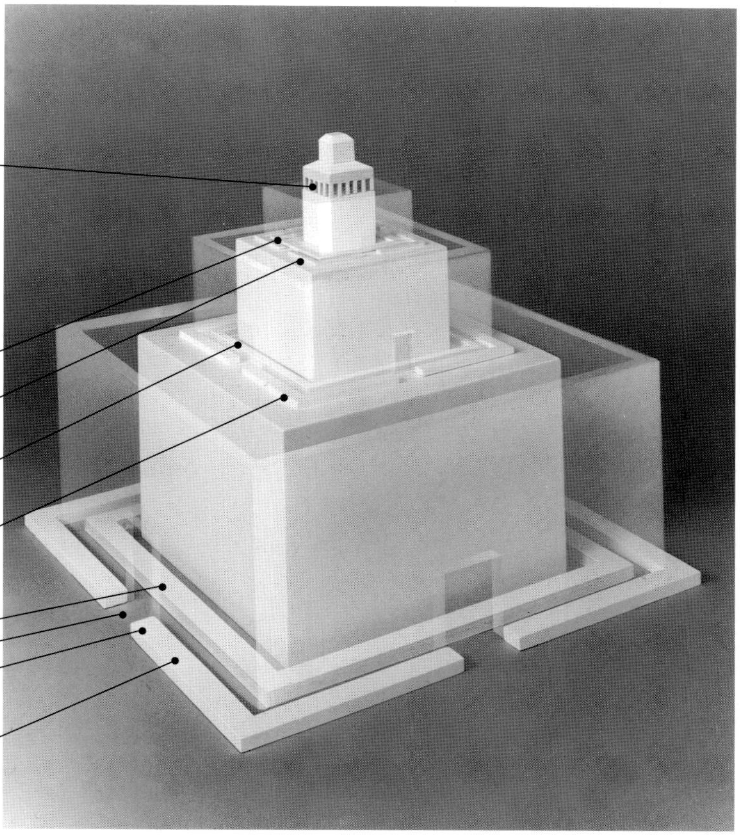

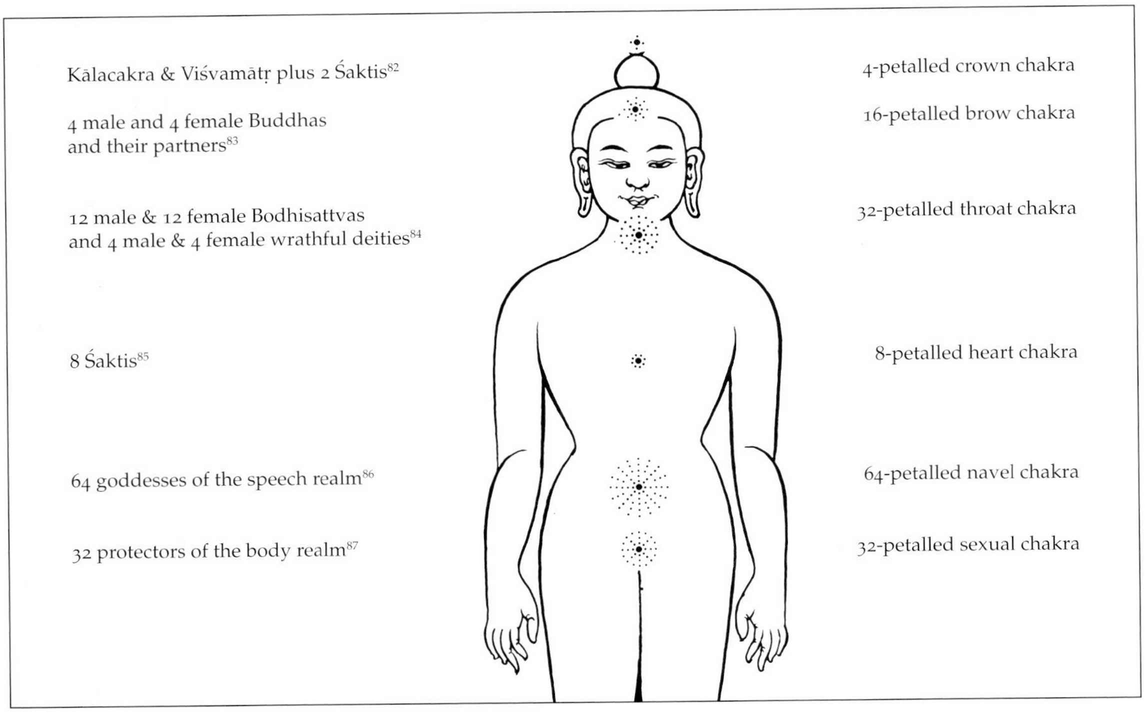

65 *Assignment of the most important mandala deities to particular chakras.*

	Elements in universe	**Elements in 'mother'**	**Syllables**	**Colours**
11	great bliss/ deep awareness	(central energy channel?)[89]	fine, wavy line (*nāda*) at top	green or black
10	sun	right energy channel	dot = *anusvāra* (Ṃ of HAṂ)[90]	red,yellow or white[91]
9	moon	left energy channel	crescent = *visarga* (Ḥ of KṢAḤ)[90]	white or red[91]
8	gods	(central energy channel?)[89]	HA(Ṃ)	dark blue
7	lotus (on Meru)	womb	KṢA(Ḥ)	green
6	Meru	sexual chakra[92]	MA[93]	white, yellow, red & black
5	earth	navel chakra	LA	yellow
4	water	heart chakra	VA	white
3	fire	throat chakra	RA	red
2	air	brow chakra	YA	black
1	space	crown chakra	vowel A, which 'gives life' to all consonants(not shown)	

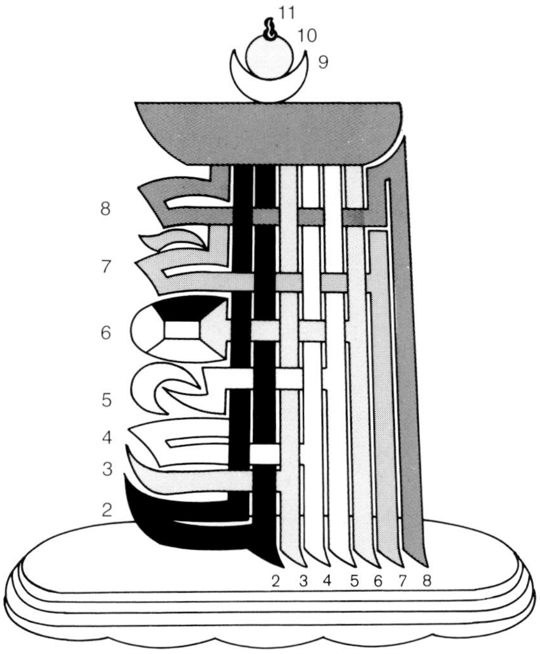

66 *The 'tenfold mighty one' (daśākāro vaśī; rnam bcu dbang ldan) – seven 'mighty' interwoven letters and three additional signs – in relation to the elements (universe) and chakras (person).*[88]

The generation of the eighty deities of the speech mandala, or speech level of the mandala, is analogous to foetal development in the sixth and seventh months.

In accordance with the construction of the mandala palace, there follows on the lowest level of the palace the emanation of the deities of the body mandala: the 360 gods of the days, who symbolize and purify the 360 days of a year in the outer wheel of time, and the 360 bones and joints in the inner wheel of time; as well as the six wrathful couples, who represent the twelve apertures of the human body.[94] This stage of development corresponds to the eighth month in the development of a foetus, in which it takes on its final form.

In the last phase are formed the ten *nāga* couples and the ten ladies of the charnel ground, who take their seats outside the palace walls of the mandala and are responsible for purifying the remaining energy channels. Then, during the ninth month a foetus develops pores, hair and skin.

Finally, in the tenth month,[95] arise the twelve offering goddesses, who establish themselves on the platform outside the mind mandala, and the 'thirty-six ladies of desire', who stay outside the speech mandala and are responsible for the desire to act (for example to speak, move, spit or scratch), as well as the 'thirty-six ladies of non-desire' (outside the body mandala), who cause the wish to act to be absent. These emanations are still linked to the development of an embryo inasmuch as they are the last, but also indispensable preconditions for birth.[96]

Mandala deities and human constituents

Every constituent of a human being is connected with a certain direction, an emblem, and so forth, but it is also true that each individual deity in the mandala is assigned to a particular part of the person, for which it stands and which it purifies in the course of the mandala ritual (Table 6; see also p.100ff).

The correspondences between mandala deities and the human body also include analogies between the most important deities of the three mandala realms and the energy centres (Fig. 65).[97]

Finally the comparison in Figure 66 explains the analogies or correlations between the universe, the person – here a woman – and the so-called 'tenfold mighty one'. The seven letters, three additional signs and fine line form as a whole the root *mantra* of the Kālacakra mandala ritual, a symbol for the outer, inner and other Kālacakra.[98]

Second stage: the supreme victorious activity (las kyi rgyal mchog)

The deities in the meditatively generated mandala have not yet awoken to life, but have simply developed like a foetus in a womb. According to the Kālacakra tradition, just as in the birth of a human being, so too in the mandala meditation there now follows the phase of awakening: the four female Buddhas Māmakī, Pāṇḍara(vāsinī), Tārā and Locanā, each embodying a profound wisdom, awaken Kālacakra and Viśvamātṛ with their melodious songs and by taking their places in certain chakras – just as they bring about the birth of a child with their songs (Table 13).

Again the eight Śaktis arise round the divine couple Kālacakra and Viśvamātṛ, arranged mandala-fashion like the winds in the human body, with which they are in fact identical (see p. 55 and Table 6);[99] and much as described before, the deities of the mandala are again generated in the womb of Viśvamātṛ and then 'born'.[100]

In the *sādhana* there now follows a phase that seems complicated, but becomes intelligible when related to the birth process. From the syllable HŪṂ in the meditator's heart emanates Vajravega, the wrathful form of Kālacakra. Grinning and gnashing his teeth, Vajravega stands on a cart drawn by a mythical creature: he thrusts a hook into Kālacakra's navel, ties his hands, threatens him with weapons and drags him in front of the meditator, in whose heart he finally dissolves.

Here, in coded form, a central yoga practice is described, which gains importance in the final phase of the *sādhana* and inverts an important birth event: the winds of deep

SW	W wheel earth element goddess Locanā embodying mirror-like wisdom (4) HOḤ in navel chakra[101] (bliss drop)	NW
S jewel fire element goddess Pāṇḍarā embodying wisdom of equality (of all things) (2) ĀḤ in throat chakra (speech drop)	C	N lotus water element goddess Māmakī embodying discriminating wisdom (1) OṂ in brow chakra (body drop)
SE	E sword air element goddess Tārā embodying all-accomplishing wisdom (3) HŪṂ in heart chakra (mind drop)	NE

Table 13 The four female Buddhas (goddesses) who awaken life with their songs, and their correlations. These are four of the five female Buddhas who perform the first initiation (Table 16). Numbers 1–4 give the sequence of the visualizations.

awareness, which during birth leave the body and bind their objects (see p. 57f), are calmed by the tying of Kālacakra's hands and then returned to the central channel at the level of the navel chakra – i.e. the point at which they left the central channel at the moment of birth. Thus each of the winds of consciousness (mental, visual, auditory, tactile, gustatory, olfactory) is returned to the central channel.

After the binding of the winds of consciousness, the deities are ready to receive the eleven initiations in the course of which they are purified together with the constituents of the meditator.

According to Tibetan tradition, the initiations are described before the mandala meditation. Here we depart from this sequence because the initiations are related to phases in the life of a growing child and consistently follow the previous events, which demonstrate striking analogies with the generation and birth of a child.

The seven basic initiations

The complicated Tantric ritual practice is carried out with a gradual procedure, to which different categories of initiations, or empowerments (*abhiṣeka; dbang bskur*) also belong: the seven initiations of entering like a child, in which phases of childhood are imitated, the four high and the four very high initiations.[102] Below we present the first group of initiations.

After particular vows have been made, and the curtain veiling the mandala has been removed, the candidate for initiation, dressed as a deity, is ready to enter the mandala in visualization. As his eyes are bound at first (Plate 37, 'entering the mandala blindfolded'), the *vajra*-master (at the same time the emanation of the principal deity of the mandala) leads him like a small child.[103] Vows to the five Tathāgata-Buddhas, the meditative transformation of the disciple's six elements into the six female Buddhas, and the setting of the seed-syllables of the six male Buddhas in the chakras[104] are followed by a visualization in the course of which all Buddhas existing anywhere penetrate and dissolve into the disciple. Once again he must make numerous vows; only then should he enter the mandala with his *guru* by the east gate and circumambulate the body mandala three times. Back in front of the east gate, he transforms himself into Akṣobhya, then into Amoghasiddhi. Following a complex ceremonial sequence, he then wanders through the mandala, in the process taking successively the form of each of the six Tathāgata-Buddhas.

Next follow two 'prognostic actions', whose outcome tells the *vajra*-master how he should lead the disciple in question into the mandala. As soon as the blindfold is removed from his eyes, for a short time a colour appears to him, which gives the master information of the kind of Buddha-activity (*'phrin las bzhi*: calming, increasing, subduing, controlling) this disciple should practise. Then one disciple, acting on behalf of all the others, throws a flower onto the mandala itself, or onto a diagram symbolizing it. From the position of the flower the *vajra*-master sees which Tathāgata-Buddha the disciple has a special inner relationship with.[105]

Already the previous evening the disciples had been asked to lay *kuśa* grass under their mattress and pillow, to analyse attentively the dreams coming in the fourth watch of the night – around dawn, and according to the type of dream prepare themselves appropriately for the important moments of the initiations and appraise themselves of the possible success or failure of the initiations.[106]

When these preparations are concluded, the candidate can finally take off the blindfold and behold the entire mandala in all its splendour. The initiations purify the disciple systematically and gradually so that he eventually becomes a 'suitable vessel for Tantric practice'.[107] Because of that the principal deity and other deities empower him to practise different meditations, which all help him to experience the inherent mind of clear light, and at the same time to open him to the sorrows of all living beings. The initiations are consequently steps on the path to Buddhahood.

It would be wrong to suppose that purification takes place solely through consecrated external substances. The basis is formed rather by powers and substances that every being carries within itself. The purification of body, speech and mind is carried out in two initiations each, while in the seventh initiation 'deep awareness' ('great bliss' and 'understanding of emptiness') is purified. The tetrad of body, speech, mind and deep awareness is related to the four drops in the brow, throat, heart and navel chakras (see p. 56), therefore these four drops are purified for the first time by the initiations – a purification that will be continued in later phases of the *sādhana*.

During the seven initiations the disciple accordingly experiences a 'birth' four times in visualization: at the beginning of the first, third, fifth and seventh initiations, in fact in front of each of the four faces of Kālacakra in turn, and thus always in a new direction, another quadrant of the mandala (Table 14). In each of the four spiritual births, the disciple mentally enters via the mouth of the *vajra*-master – who has transformed himself into Kālacakra – into the body of the deity, passes through it and by way of Kālacakra's penis (*vajra*) reaches the vagina (*padma*) of the goddess Viśvamātṛ, where he dissolves into a drop of emptiness. Out of the emptiness (*śūnyatā*) arises a syllable, which turns into one of four symbols – and this in turn into a six-armed deity and its female partner. The deity represents a Tathāgata-Buddha and thereby an aspect of Kālacakra.

Initiation birth precedes	Direction	Seed syllable	→	Symbol	→	Deity	= Buddha
First	N	OṂ	→	lotus	→	*vajra* body deity	white Amitābha + red Pāṇḍaravāsinī
Third	S	ĀḤ	→	jewel	→	*vajra* speech deity	red Ratnasambhava + white Māmakī
Fifth	E	HŪṂ	→	sword	→	*vajra* mind deity	black Amoghasiddhi + yellow Locanā
Seventh	W	HOḤ	→	wheel	→	*vajra* deep awareness deity	yellow Vairocana + black Tārā

Table 14 Seed-syllables emanated from emptiness, then symbols, and finally Tathāgatas. These are the 'births' that the yogin experiences in the first, third, fifth and seventh initiations.

As the initiatory deities come and unite with him, the fire of great desire (*gtum mo*) ignites in Kālacakra's heart: the white *bodhicitta* in his crown melts, flows down through the central channel and then finds its way into Viśvamātṛ's womb. The meditator, abiding in Viśvamātṛ's womb, thus receives an internal initiation and is 'born' as a Tathāgata-Buddha and set on the initiation seat.[108] In a corresponding way before the third, fifth, and seventh initiations the *yogin* again becomes one of the Tathāgata-Buddhas.

The four steps are related to the drops of the four states (see p. 56f), one of which is purified in each initiation stage: in the first and second initiations the drop in the brow chakra, in the third and fourth the drop in the throat chakra, in the fifth and sixth the one in the heart chakra and in the seventh the one in the navel chakra (Table 15).

SW	seventh initiation HOḤ **navel chakra** bliss drop	NW
third and fourth initiations ĀḤ **throat chakra** speech drop	Kālacakra and Viśvamātṛ	first and second initiations OṂ **brow chakra** body drop
SE	fifth and sixth initiations HŪṂ **heart chakra** mind drop	NE

Table 15 The seven basic initiations and their relation to the directions in the mandala and the four drops in the corresponding chakras of the person.

For each of the seven initiations a special 'initiation substance' is needed, which purifies a group of the disciple's constituents on the one hand, and on the other a particular group of mandala deities. Thus water, the substance of the first initiation, purifies the disciple's five elements and the five female Tathāgatas of the mandala; the five-lobed crown (Plates 39, 40) purifies the five aggregates and the five male Tathāgatas, and so on (Table 16).

In demanding visualizations the initiation candidate has to mix each of the thirty-six most important components of his being with the corresponding portion of the initiation substances, so that a certain seed-syllable arises. From it emanates the symbol of the relevant direction (sword in the east, jewel in the south, etc.) and from that one of the thirty-six deities of the mind realm. In this way the correlation between the thirty-six constituents of the person and the thirty-six mandala deities is again made plain. A representative example, one of the thirty-six visualizations, may illustrate:

> *The five elements of the student and the water in the vase*[109] *turn into emptiness. From within emptiness the space element of your body and the upper and lower portions of water, mixed with the water of the conch,*[110] *appear as two*[111] *seed-syllables Ā, which transform into two vajras, from which are generated two green Vajradhātviśvarīs, with three faces ... and six arms ..., embraced by Vajrasattva.*[112]

After the goddess (female Buddha) has been initiated herself and has entered the external initiation substance – in the case of the first initiation, water – she bestows initiation

Initiation		External substance used for initiation	Purification of and transformation into	Corresponding event in human development
From the syllable O± arises a **lotus** and from that **white Amitābha** with consort; in the form of Amitābha, **the body** is purified (and thence the 'body drop' or 'waking state drop' in the brow chakra) in the **north** before Kālacakra's white, peaceful face:				
FIRST	water initiation	water	5 elements → 5 female Tathāgatas	bathing of a newborn baby
SECOND	crown initiation	5-lobed crown	5 aggregates → 5 male Tathāgatas	first cutting of the hair[114]
From the syllable ĀḤ arises a jewel and from that **red Ratnasambhava** with consort; in the form of Ratnasambhava **the speech** is purified (and thence the 'speech drop' or 'dream state drop' in the throat chakra) in the **south** before Kālacakra's red, ecstatic face:				
THIRD	crown ribbon initiation	10 parts of the crown ribbon	10 winds and channels → 10 Śakti goddesses	ear-piercing and first adornment
FOURTH	*vajra* and bell initiation	*vajra* and bell	left channel → Kālacakra right channel → Viśvamātṛ	speaking the first word[115]
From the syllable HŪ± arises a **sword** and from that **black Amoghasiddhi** with consort; in the form of Amoghasiddhi the **mind** is purified (and thence the 'mind drop' or 'deep sleep state drop' in the heart chakra) in the **east** before Kālacakra's black, wrathful face:				
FIFTH	(*vajra*-)conduct initiation	thumb-ring[116]	6 sense powers → 6 male Bodhisattvas 6 sense objects → 6 female Bodhisattvas	child's first enjoyment of sense objects
SIXTH	name initiation	bracelet	6 action faculties → 6 male wrathful deities 6 actions → 6 female wrathful deities	naming
From the syllable HOḤ arises a **wheel** and from that **yellow Vairocana** with consort; in the form of Vairocana, **great bliss/ deep awareness** is purified (and thence the 'bliss' or 'ecstacy drop' in the navel chakra) in the **west** before Kālacakra's yellow face established in meditation:				
SEVENTH	permission initiation			
7.1	the actual initiation	5 hand-symbols: vajra, sword, jewel, lotus and wheel	deep awareness → Vairocana	child's first reading lesson[117]
7.2	giving of mantras and 3 substances	eye medicine mirror bow and arrow	Prepares for conceptual realization of emptiness Helps realization of the illusoriness of all things Helps direct realization of emptiness in meditation[118]	
7.3	master's initiation	*vajra* bell	aggregate of deep awareness → Vajrasattva (Kālacakra) element of deep awareness → Prajñāpāramitā (Viśvamātṛ)	

Table 16 The seven basic initiations, their course and correlations.[113]

on the disciple: she touches his crown, shoulders, upper arms, thighs and hips with the relevant substance. Touching the internal substance (one of the thirty-six constituents) with the external initiation substance leads, besides purification, to great bliss and understanding of emptiness.

The transformation of any constituent into a deity takes place in one of the six chakras – thus, for instance, the space element becomes Vajradhātviśvari in the crown chakra.

Step by step, the disciple visualizes all the important groups – the grosser ones to begin with, then the more subtle ones – in the form of goddesses and gods, who eventually enter the disciple's body via the relevant chakras. The four-stage purification and transformation of the body sows the seeds for a later phase of the mandala ritual, in which the qualities of the respective deities are attained – all the aspects of supreme Buddhahood.

Corresponding to the position of the initiation deities in the mandala, each individual initiation is closely related to a particular level of the mind mandala. Thus the first and second initiations take place in the intermediate region, the third and fourth in the centre, and the fifth and sixth on the border of the mind mandala, while the last, the seventh initiation, like the fourth, is connected with the centre (comparison of Tables 1, 2, 4, 5 and 6 with the description of the mandala deities, p. 100-102ff, makes clear the analogies between the individual deities in the mandala palace and the inner mandala).

The seven initiations are in addition related to essential stages in childhood (Table 16), parallels that confirm once again that the entire mandala ritual must be understood as a 'natural' process, whose regularities and rules are universal but still have to be knowingly and consciously experienced.

Third and fourth stages of the generation stage

The two last phases of the generation stage include yoga practices that because of their complexity can only be described in summary. They have parallels with a human being's passage to adulthood on the attainment of sexual maturity.

In the third stage, 'the yoga of the drops', the so-called 'four joys' are experienced by means of the descent of the white *bodhicitta*-drop. First of all the disciple must transform himself into Kālacakra and visualize seed-syllables in his own and Viśvamātṛ's energy centres in the following sequence: OṂ in the brow chakra, ĀḤ in the throat chakra, HŪṂ in the heart chakra, HOḤ in the navel chakra, HAṂ in the sexual chakra, and long HĀ in the crown chakra. In addition the sexual organs of Kālacakra and Viśvamātṛ are blocked with the syllables PHAṬ and AḤ respectively, so that the white *bodhicitta*-drop cannot leave the body.

Either through meditation, or by the power of the embrace of the two Buddhas, the downward-emptying wind kindles the inner heat (*gtum mo*) in the navel centre, whose heat rises up the central channel and melts the white *bodhicitta*-drop above, which then flows downward in the central channel. Each time the drop passes one of the chakras, the meditator experiences a state of joy – in the end, simultaneous joy, the simultaneous experience of bliss and emptiness.

In the fourth part of the generation stage, the 'subtle yoga' (*phra mo'i rnal 'byor*), the four joys are experienced again, this time while the *bodhicitta*-drop from below rises into the crown chakra. Even though the joys in subtle yoga have the character of bliss and knowledge of emptiness, in this phase not all impurities have yet been eliminated, and emptiness is not yet perceived directly and completely. This is achieved – at least in Anuttarayoga Tantra – only in the completion stage.

Subtle yoga should enable the adept to see the mandala in full vividness for four hours, and in addition to visualize the mandala with all 722 deities in a tiny drop in the upper opening of the central channel, between the eyebrows. This four-hour vision should moreover be so clear that the *yogin* can see even the whites of the individual deities' eyes.

Subtle yoga is concluded with recitation of the *mantras* of all the deities assembled in the mandala, making offerings, and the complete dissolution of each of the various groups of deities into an energy centre (chakra) or a part of the body:

> *Kālacakra and his partner Viśvamātṛ melt into a 5-spoked*[119] *vajra in the yogin's crown chakra; the Śaktis into a 9-spoked vajra in the heart chakra; the male and female Tathāgata-Buddhas into a 17-spoked vajra in the brow; the male and female Bodhisattvas and wrathful deities into a 33-spoked vajra in the throat chakra; the deities of the speech mandala into a 65-spoked vajra in the navel and the protectors of the body mandala into a 33-spoked vajra in the sexual chakra. The twelve great Hindu gods become vajras in the organs of action and the serpent spirits (nāga) and element gods vajras in the limbs and fingers.*

Finally the meditator dissolves into emptiness and is regenerated as a 'simple' Kālacakra with one head and two arms, a manifestation he should try to maintain all day long. And as the practices began with the wish that all beings may be granted liberation through one's own efforts, so this important part of the mandala ritual, the *sādhana*, ends likewise with the altruistic wish that the merits accumulated through the ritual and meditation may be of use for the spiritual development of all sentient beings.

From now on, the person undertaking the practices attempts to live all day – when eating, sleeping, getting up, working and so forth – what he experiences in meditation, and to aim at the final goal, the completion stage.

Completion stage

The four yogas of the generation stage ripen the practitioner and prepare his stream of consciousness in advance for the completion stage, which leads to the attainment of perfect Buddhahood in the form of Kālacakra and his partner. This stage too involves complex visualizations, which can only be properly understood and carried out under the guidance of a spiritual teacher. Because of this, and also because the practices can be performed away from the actual Kālacakra mandala, we content ourselves below with a brief account of the most important stages.

The ultimate goal of Tantric practices is to attain the four perfectly pure and complete aspects of a Buddha – here of Kālacakra and Viśvamātṛ. To achieve this, the four drops must be purified and transformed, an undertaking that begins in the generation stage and is gradually brought to completion in the 'six yogas' as follows: the body drop in the crown chakra turns into the 'manifestation of empty forms' (*nirmāṇakāya* state),[120] the speech drop in the throat chakra into 'sound of emptiness' (*saṃbhogakāya* state),[121] the mind drop in the heart chakra into 'non-conceptual supreme wisdom' (*dharmakāya* or *jñānadharmakāya* state), and the drop of deep awareness[122] in the navel chakra into 'immutable great bliss' (*svabhāvakāya* state).[123]

The goal of the first yoga, 'withdrawal of the senses' (*so sor bsdud pa*), is to stop the activity of the wind energies of the six sense organs and direct the winds into the central channel, practices that can only be successful if certain rules are observed, concerning the right time of day, posture and point of gaze.[124]

Correct performance of the practices leads to ten manifestations or signs of empty forms, four gross and six subtle,[125] which a dying person also perceives on entering death. The first sign is like (thin) smoke, the second like a mirage, the third like fine glowing embers sometimes emitting sparks ('fireflies'), and the fourth is likened to a steadily burning butter lamp. The subtle signs are described as follows: a fire vision or glow (yellow and related to the planet Kālāgni); a pale white like the light of the full moon in the autumn sky or the moon just appearing on the horizon; a refined red like sunlight pervading the sky in the morning; a heavy darkness like that of a starless sky after nightfall (sign of the planet Rāhu); the natural colour of the sky when it is free of either sun and moonlight or darkness.[126] The sixth sign is a blue drop, in which appears last a hair-thin black line (*nāda*), and within this is seen minutely small the empty form of Kālacakra and his partner – a manifestation on which the meditator has to concentrate for as long as possible.

Only now is the adept ready for the second yoga, 'concentration' or 'contemplation' (*bsam gtan*). He is meant to perfect this ability by himself becoming the tiny divine couple at the upper end of the central wind channel and attaining the so-called 'five certainties'.[127]

In the third yoga, 'wind control' or 'vitality-stopping' (*srog rtsol*), the meditator makes the tamed winds from the left and right flow into the central channel, and brings them into the navel chakra, at the same time blocking the openings of the two side channels. The winds, especially the life-holding and downward-emptying winds, are united in the navel chakra by two techniques: *vajra*-recitation (or *vajra* breathing) and vase-breathing. In the first, the meditator makes use of a special breathing technique that teaches him to concentrate the energies in the navel chakra, or in a more advanced stage, in the heart chakra.[128] In the vase-type meditation[129] and breathing, the winds from the upper and lower regions of the body are brought through the central channel into the navel chakra and united there with the drop of sexual ecstasy and also with the mind and empty body of the meditator. As Nāropa expressed it, "the energies above and those below are brought together and kissed with the mind".[130]

In the fourth yoga, 'retention' (*'dzin pa*), the gathered winds are held continuously in the central channel[131] and prepared for the fifth yoga.

During the fifth yoga, 'mindfulness' (*rjes dran*), the meditator imagines that he himself is Kālacakra, and unites with the five female Tathāgatas and the ten Śaktis. This uniting can be performed with an actual partner (*karmamudrā*), with a visualized one (*jñānamudrā*), or with the empty body of Viśvamātṛ (*mahāmudrā*), depending on whether the practitioner has dull, medium, or sharp mental ability.[132] Through this actual or merely imaginary union, the fire of inner heat (*gtum mo*, also 'fire of great desire') is kindled, which melts the white *bodhicitta*-drop in the crown chakra. As a result the drop flows down the central channel, so that the four great states of bliss are experienced, and remains fixed on the tip of the *vajra* (penis). At the same time the red *bodhicitta*-drop moves up tothe crown chakra, where it must be left until exceedingly great immutable bliss arises.[133] This too is analogous to an event at the moment of death: the white *bodhicitta* flows down and leaves the body there, while the red *bodhicitta* rises and leaves the body through the nostrils. It is, however, crucial in the fifth yoga to prevent this flowing out, in other words both white and red *bodhicitta* are 'held' (as described in *Thought and action by analogy*, see p. 63).

In the sixth yoga stage, 'meditative stabilization' or 'concentration' (*ting nge 'dzin*), the *yogin* continues the transfer of the white, male and red, female drops. This is done in twelve steps, in each of which 1,800 white drops reach the bottom and 1,800 reach the top – so that in the end 21,600 white and 21,600 red drops are stacked one above the other in the central channel. While the drops move up and down the 21,600 karmic winds dissolve – the same winds that flow through the human body in the course of a day and serve as a vehicle for all kinds of consciousnesses. The practitioner thus purifies himself step by step of all defilements and eventually attains Buddhahood.[134]

Through the power of piling up the white and red constituents,
Twenty-one thousand six hundred in number,
Up and down throughout the central channel,
May the material constituents of my body be consumed
as iron is by mercury!

May the 21,600 immutable Great Blisses
realizing Emptiness
Cease that number of karmic winds,
Quickly purify obstructive predispositions,
And I attain a Conqueror's exalted body!

May I easily achieve these wishes
Without hindrance, becoming a supreme captain
Releasing transmigrators through this supreme path
Into the supreme land of jewels of a Conqueror!

In short, through whatever collections of wholesome virtue,
As illustrated by this, have been accumulated,
May I quickly take birth in Shambhala, the treasury of jewels,
And complete the stages of the path in Highest Yoga Tantra![135]

Once Buddhahood is attained, aids such as depictions of deities, ritual objects, and indeed the mandala itself, are no longer necessary. They can be destroyed. In the case of the Kālacakra mandala, the coloured powder from which it was sprinkled is wiped together carefully (Plate 41) and poured into a river (Plate 43), where it forms one final mandala – when the powder trickling into the water makes concentric circles, which soon vanish in the infinity of water droplets (Plate 44).

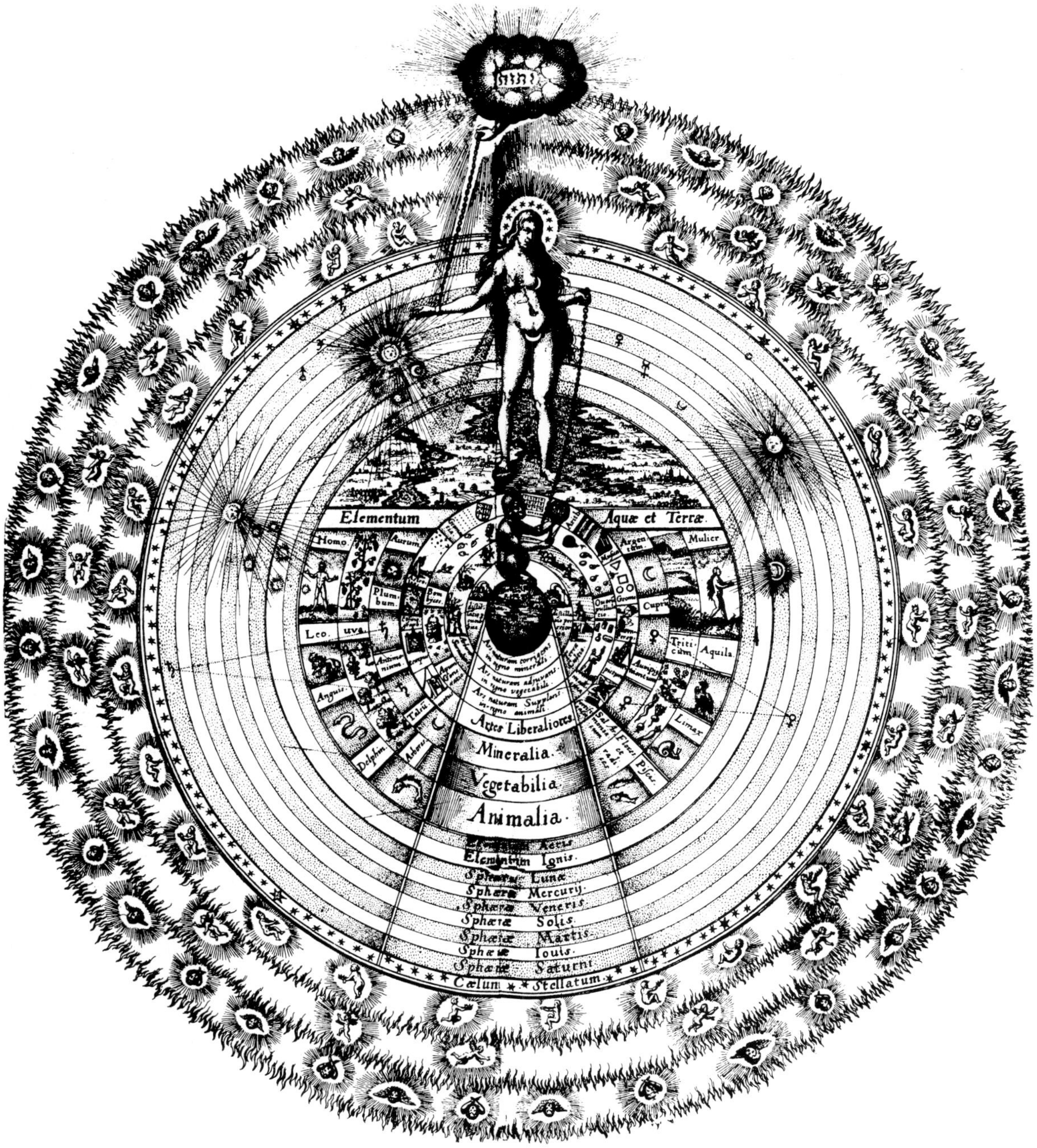

67 *The mandala as archetypal symbol of unity: copper engraving by J.-Th de Bry (Oppenmeimii 1617) in which man (microcosm) and macroscosm form a mandala-like structure.*

The Mandala and the West

Symbol of unity and divinity

Attempts have been made to establish the original source of the mandala and its spread over great distances from a clearly defined region of origin. Thus for example, Schuyler Cammann finds that mandalas were already known in Dunhuang in northwest China. Their basic structure shows similarities to representations on the backs of mirrors of the Han period (209–2 BC, 25–220 CE).[1] The typical T-markings of these mirrors, which render the four gates of the 'Middle Kingdom' in the centre of the world (i.e. China), are above all reminiscent, says Cammann, of the four T-shaped entrances of a mandala palace.

According to present-day understanding, however, it is a most questionable undertaking to draw the conclusion, based on individual matching elements, that mandalas and *yantras* go back to Chinese cosmic diagrams of the Han period – not least because mandala representations are known not only in Tibet but all over the Indian sucontinent. If one followed Cammann, all these mandala representations would also have to go back to the Han tradition, which as a matter of cultural history is well-nigh impossible.

Yet Camman is not alone with his theory. Siegbert Hummel, who refers to Cammann's work, likewise conjectures that the mandala diagram arose not in India but in Tibet, or in neighbouring China, in 'pre-lamaist' times. Hummel goes still farther back in time than Camman, when he establishes that in some prehistoric sites from the Tibetan megalithic can be found the forerunners of present-day 'lamaist' mandalas.[2] According to Hummel it is therefore perfectly justifiable to regard the mandala and the gnosis associated with it as a megalithic legacy, and to look for the mandala principle prevailing in Tibet in prehistoric traditions in Tibet itself.[3] These hypotheses, built on little reliable material, lead no further; in the end, mandala-like shapes and rituals can be established in many places in the world.

In this connection, one contribution of the Swiss depth psychologist Carl Gustav Jung (1875–1961) is the fruitful hypothesis that circle and quaternity are symbols deeply rooted in the human soul that can emerge in different places without implying any direct diffusion.[4] Jung showed himself very open-minded towards eastern teachings, and we have not least to thank him for the fact that the word 'mandala' is not entirely unknown in the West.

In spite of the valuable basic approach and the important introduction of the mandala into the European world of thought, a certain caution is called for regarding Jung's attempt to interpret *individual* elements of Tibetan mandalas. Thus, he interpreted the outermost fire circle of the mandala – for him apparently synonymous with a *yantra* – as, "the fire of desire, from which proceed the torments of hell". He analysed the mandala palace as a 'monastery courtyard', equated the mandala without further ado with the concept of *yin* and *yang* – which comes from the Chinese world of thought, and even spoke in relation to Tibetan Buddhist mandalas of emanations of the (Hindu) Śiva.[5] We should not forget that Jung's knowledge of Tibetan Buddhism was strictly limited, not least because of the dearth of reliable publications and studies, which led almost inevitably to the misunderstandings and misinterpretations mentioned.

Jung nevertheless grasped intuitively a great deal of the deeper meaning of the mandala ritual, as is shown in these few lines from his interpretation of a Tibetan mandala:

> *The goal of contemplating the processes depicted in the mandala is that the yogin shall become inwardly aware of the deity; that is to say, through contemplation he recognizes himself as the deity and thus returns from the illusion of individual existence to the universal totality of the divine state.*[6]

This is an observation we can agree with, in accordance with the discussion in this book from the Tibetan Buddhist point of view, as long as by 'divine state' is meant not an image of the divine shaped by Christianity, but Buddhahood.

Why did Jung interpret mandalas as images of the divine? For him, mandalas were "real or natural symbols of unity, as they appear to us in dreams and visions", i.e.

"quaternities, or rather multiples of four, or squared circles".[7] These 'unifying symbols' or symbols of unity:

> *... are usually fourfold and consist of two intersecting pairs of opposites (e.g. right/left, up/down). These four points define a circle, which represents the simplest symbol of unity apart from the point, which is why it is the simplest image of the divine.*[8]

Thus Jung perceives central point, circle and quaternity as well-known symbols of the divine.

Archetypes?

Carl Gustav Jung also analysed the *function* of the mandala, the 'protective circle'. It seems to him "the traditional antidote for chaotic states of mind".[9] He was led to this realization not least by some of his patients, who in states of psychological dissociation or disorientation created mandalas and apparently used them as a centre to attain inner order, come to themselves and regain unity of the psyche, the so-called 'self'. Jung speaks of: "an *attempt at self-healing* on the part of nature, which does not spring from conscious reflection but from an instinctive impulse".[10]

But it should be made clear that the depth psychologist did not believe all mandala representations to be derived from chaotic or conflict-filled states. According to him, people all over the world draw, paint, carve in stone and build such 'spontaneous imaginative productions', namely, when they let them 'happen psychically', that is arise without consideration from within. Such mandalas arising from dreams and visions are to be found in Europe, says Jung, above all in medieval natural philosophy, which leant on ecclesiastical use of allegory based on sets of four (four evangelists, four rivers of heaven, four winds, etc.).[11]

Jung used his theory of archetypes to explain the fact that mandala-like structures – among which he also included the cross and other quaternity symbols[12] – are found worldwide. Archetypes were primeval images based on an "unconscious disposition of as it were universal distribution" (impersonal collective unconscious), a disposition capable in principle of producing the same, or very similar, symbols in all times and places. "The archetypes are rather like organs of the pre-rational psyche. They are perpetually passed on, identical forms and ideas without specific content."[13] According to Jung it is therefore the collective unconscious that brings forth the archetypal symbols of unity, such as the forms of mandalas.

Difficulty of comparison

Jung recognized that a mandala does not really have to be painted or drawn, but can also be danced – as some of his female patients did,[14] or executed and experienced in ritual, just as we have shown in the section on *Ritual preparations* (see p. 75ff). On the basis of an early Christian ritual described in the apocryphal Acts of John (*c.* third century), he exemplified the ritual circle process as follows:

> *... a mystical round dance that Christ arranged before his crucifixion. He ordered his disciples to take hold of each other's hands and form a circle. He himself stood in the middle. They moved in the circle while Christ sang the song of praise ...* [15]

What Jung wrote in his commentary on this Christian round dance could be used virtually unchanged as a commentary on a Buddhist 'mandala round dance' (see for instance Fig. 59):

> *From time immemorial the circle and centre has been a symbol of the divine, illustrating the unity of the incarnate god: the single point in the centre and the many of the circumference. Ritual circumambulation often leans consciously on the cosmic allegory of the rotating night sky, the 'round dance of the stars', an idea still contained in the old equation of the twelve Apostles with the constellations of the zodiac ... In every case the ceremonial round dance aims at and brings about the impression of the circle and centre as well as the moving of each point of the circumference into the centre. Psychologically this arrangement denotes a mandala and thereby a symbol of the self, on which are aligned not only the individual I, but at the same time many others of like mind or linked destiny.*[16]

For Jung, Christ standing in the centre was someone towering above the ordinary man and embracing unity, a symbol for the 'self' of every human being; the mandala round dance was an act of dawning of higher consciousness, understood as the connection established between the consciousness of the individual and the higher symbol of unity.[17]

The Swiss psychologist was aware that despite the 'archetypal origin' he assumed, there were differences between the various mandala forms. He pointed out a divergence between Christian and Buddhist mandalas, whose significance should not be underestimated: a Christian will never say in his contemplation, "I am Christ", but only, with Paul, that Christ lives in him. A Buddhist, however, meditates in the conviction that he can be and ultimately is Buddha.[18]

This raises the complicated topic of the comparability of different religious contents and concepts. As mentioned, Jung's commentary on the round dance of Christ resembles one on the Buddhist mandala ritual – with the exception of the last part, which speaks of the 'self' and the 'I' – terms that must obviously not be described indiscriminately as identical with Buddhist concepts of the same name. Is 'consciousness' in Buddhism to be understood the same way as with us? Does the ego in Buddhism correspond to the ego of Jung? Does Buddhism too recognize an 'unconscious', and if so, does the idea have anything in common with the unconscious of the Jungian school?

Question upon question, which cannot be answered here, all the more so since both Buddhism and Western thought have each developed a variety of psychological concepts. So the point of the final pages of this book is not to compare Jung's depth psychology in detail with the Tibetan Buddhist body of thought;[19] rather I should like to formulate a few basic ideas about the mandala ritual as a stimulus to independent study of the mandala 'phenomenon'.

Dangers and opportunities

A visualization – not only one of a mandala – is a typical 'centre ritual'. Even if Buddhism strives to dismantle, undo and dissolve the ego, the meditator stands at the centre of the ritual events. Visualization is thus a process of seeking and finding the centre, one's own centre. Does this mean that a visualization, and in particular a mandala visualization, is tantamount to an egocentric practice, an 'ego trip'?

This impression could in fact arise from a superficial evaluation of the process. But what actually happens in a supposedly egocentric visualization; or better, what ought to happen in it? The closer a meditation comes to the centre, the centre of the mandala and the centre of the deity whose form the meditator has assumed, the more it loses substance and concreteness, till in the end the emptiness of everything, even of the meditator himself, is recognized, including his own manifestation as a deity.

In addition, the whole course of the mandala ritual makes it clear that the goal of the diverse spiritual and meditative efforts cannot be one's own release alone. Rather, the goal is twofold: *one's own liberation for the benefit of all other living beings!*

Undeniably, however, there is a danger that visualization may lead not to a dissolution of the ego, but to its enhancement. After all, the person meditating feels himself to be a god or goddess; he says to himself again and again that he has divine qualities and is enlightened! This latent threat of egocentrism explains the urgency of the Buddhist warning that under no circumstances should one practise visualization thoughtlessly and unaccompanied by a spiritual teacher.

Through demanding yoga practices, destructive powers can also arise. In this connection Jung speaks of:

> *... the sphere of the chaotic personal unconscious, in which everything is found that one would willingly forget and that one would at all costs admit neither to oneself nor to another and would anyhow not take to be true.*[20]

Meditation too touches on these inexpressible matters ... Carried out correctly, the visualization process, as we have come to know it, certainly has an autosuggestive effect whose importance should not be underestimated. A visualization is not just about experiencing and recognizing emptiness, but is also about accepting the here and now, living together with other beings, who are indeed empty, devoid of any essence, but nevertheless need our support and affection. The meditator accepts his own being, admittedly having attained insight into his true nature and confidence in himself. According to one Buddhist spiritual master, the attitude that says one can do nothing, and that one has no inner power, is false. He says:

> *Buddha is in us: compassion, wisdom, power; you must realize this! Now! Don't doubt yourself! ... Instead of thinking, God or Buddha is up there, we think: I am God, I am Buddha. ... In this moment you identify yourself with divine qualities.*[21]

Concentrating on the one, the absolute centre, allows the isolated individual to experience unity – and with it security, confidence, power and bliss.

The role in this process of the person who leads and escorts the 'mandala-dancer' raises a problem. This concerns the phenomenon of 'transference' (to use a term from Western psychology), of becoming totally dependent on the *guru*. As pointed out, every student needs the leadership of such a *guru*, and it is necessary for him to imagine the *guru* as Buddha, in fact that *guru* and Buddha are one for him. This can result in unwelcome commitments, but Tibetan Buddhists – at least the far advanced among them – have also recognized this danger. Milarepa, for example, was once able to advise Gampopa: "Regard even your *guru* as an illusion!"[22]

Suffering microcosm – suffering macrocosm

We live in a time in which we are coming to sense ever more clearly how strongly we are bound up with the 'outside world', how much we are part of a living, life-supporting system contained in the so-called biosphere, which extends from the skin of our planet (if not beyond) to the depths of the earth and the ocean. Human beings threaten at least three of the elements mentioned repeatedly in the mandala ritual, namely earth, water and air. They are exploited, manipulated and polluted by us – and slowly, so-called modern civilization is starting to understand that by felling entire primeval forests, eradicating many plant and animal species, endangering genetic diversity, destroying the ozone layer, overusing the soil, nuclear and chemical contamination and so forth, it is polluting itself. In this situation, it is worth reflecting on the Tantric Buddhist idea that we are part of a cosmic whole, 'limbs' of this world. Of course when it is said that our arms and legs are the continents of the universe (see *Offering of the universe: the grain mandala*, p. 24f), we do not have to take it literally; rather such an allegorical mode of expression means: the world is us and we are the world; or in the words of Tantric Buddhism, "As it is without, so it is in the body".[23] When the world or a part of it is suffering, I too suffer; when I suffer, the world suffers. When I harm the world, I harm myself and other beings and components; when I exploit them, I exploit myself!

We have encountered in various aspects the fundamental wisdom of Tantric Buddhism, according to which structures and events recur endlessly from the expanse of the macrocosm to the minuteness of the microcosm and everything appears as a copy of another copy ...,[24] in other words, we have discovered that the person and all other beings are not part of the cosmos but contain this cosmos within themselves – in such a way that they are constructed similarly to the macrocosm and the same processes take place within them as in the world around them. This is a view also formulated by early Christian theologians, such as Origen (*c.* 185–253):

> *Understand that you have within yourself herds of oxen, ... flocks of sheep and herds of goats ... Understand that in you are even the birds of the sky. And marvel not if we say that these are within you, but understand that you yourself are another little world and have within you the sun, moon and stars.*[25]

Such a view implies the recognition that outside and inside, object and subject represent pairs of opposites constructed by the person, which lead to confusion and wrong conduct and which must therefore be overcome.

The worldview of Tantric Buddhism denies the possibility of tackling impurities and faults selectively, postulating instead holistic action that takes into account mutual interrelations and the right to existence of the whole of nature. Thus, according to Tantric teachings, the person who wishes to purify himself must keep in view not just himself but all the other living beings, and even include the entire cosmos in his efforts. Mandala meditation is an aid that makes it easier to discern far-reaching interconnections, while time after time reminding one of the 'divinity' or Buddhahood that underlies everything – more than that, allowing one to actually experience it. How different this is from the numerous 'rites of violation' of our technologically-oriented and consumerist world, and the attitude that the universe – with man as the centre – belongs only to us and is our rightful property.

Notes

Chapter One
Introduction: Approaching the Mystery
(Pages 9–13)

1 Vira & Chandra 1961–72, Parts 12–15; bSod-nams rgya-mtsho & Tachikawa 1983, 1989, 1991.

2 e.g., Wayman 1982/83.

3 The far more common colour sequence is: east = white or blue; south = yellow; west = red; north = green.

4 Tibetan authors have fiercely debated the typical characteristics of the Tantric path, and how they differ from those of the Sūtra path. Thus it is asserted that the Tantrayāna is marked by a large repertoire of methods, which allow the different characters of individual practitioners to be taken into account. The view is also held that the Tantric path offers a quicker and simpler way to liberation or is open only to 'highly developed' people; on this, see Doboom Tulku 1988.

5 e.g., Mullin 1988: 276.

6 Here the difficulty of generalizations becomes apparent. Vergati (1986: 39ff) shows, for example, that among the Newars in Nepal the production and use of mandalas is an essential part of important life-cycle rituals (ritual marriage of a young girl before puberty [Newārī: *ihi*]; ritual on reaching seventy-seven years, seven months and seven days; also Newar new year ritual and ritual at the time of a long drought). These are obviously not primarily a matter of visualization .

In South Indian Śaivite ritual also, where a mandala is used, visualization does not play the same dominant role as it does in Tibetan Buddhism; nor are mandalas used for initiations (Brunner 1986: 28ff).

In Tibetan Buddhism mandalas are also used for the achievement of worldly ends, e.g. to attain health, fame or children (Macdonald 1962: 146ff).

In Sanskrit, apparently, no convincing philological explanation of the term 'mandala' is to be found: "In modern usage the semantic content, apart from ritualistic use, coincides principally with circle or ring, anything round" (Mode 1987: 929).

In old Nepal, 'mandala' was also used as a term for large administrative units, especially states or provinces (principalities, etc.); thus the expression *Nepāla-maṇḍala* is found in Licchavi inscriptions of the seventh and eighth centuries (Slusser 1982: 9, 86).

7 Tharchin 1987: 78.

8 mKhas-grub rJe in Lessing & Wayman 1978: 271; see also Mullin 1985a: 151.

9 Lo Bue 1987: 795.

10 e.g., Anne Chayet 1985; Boerschmann 1925, Figs. 1, 2, 17.

11 Stein 1921, Plates Vol. CIII; Vol. II: 974f, Nos 00186, 00187; another early mandala was found in the roof of the Qianxun Pagoda, Chongsheng Temple, in Dali, Yunnan – this is a Vajradhātu mandala from the 12th century, in which the seed-syllables and names of all the deities of the mandala are mentioned (Lutz 1991).

12 In Śaivite mandalas also this area schematically depicts a temple and is called the 'house' (*bhāvana*) of Śiva; in accordance with *Śāradātilaka*, after Brunner (1986: 25). The palace does not necessarily have to be square. There exist a few mandalas with a round palace (bSod-nams rgya-mtsho & Tachikawa 1989: 98).

13 According to Béguin, mandalas with figures are 'body mandalas'; those with the deities' seed-syllables 'speech mandalas'; and those with only the emblems 'mind mandalas' (Béguin 1981: 18, see also p. 104f).

14 In earlier times, probably only the creation of mandalas in coloured powder was known; not until later were mandalas also painted on a permanent support, as a rule on cloth. In this way they could be stored away and used repeatedly. Contemporary Śaivite material from South India likewise leads one to suppose that the basic concept of the mandala allowed for merely *momentary* use.

15 These statements refer to South Indian Śaivism; on this see Brunner 1986: 19. Among the Newars the *yantra* always represents the goddess (Taleju), and the use of *yantras* is more esoteric than that of mandalas. However, the function of *yantra* and mandala among the Newars appears to be the same: the aim is to create a place in which the invoked deities may dwell for a certain time (Vergati 1986: 44f).

Chapter Two
The Centre of the Buddhist Wheel of the Teaching: Basic Ideas
(Pages 15–17)

1 Other possible translations are given in brackets.

2 In the first class of Tantras, great weight is attached to external rites, for instance ritual purification. In the second, equal weight is given to outer activities and inner yoga. In the third class, inner yoga practices dominate, while in Anuttarayoga Tantra inner yoga stands unambiguously in first place.

3 The translation of the word *śunyatā* is not simple. Alex Wayman has argued that when translating the term in English, 'voidness' is preferable to 'emptiness' (Wayman 1978b: 72); in German there is no corresponding distinction. [The present translator, like many others, prefers 'emptiness', and is convinced neither by Wayman, nor by Guenther (1972: n. 4 to Chapter V) who rejects both alternatives (MW)].

4 Hopkins 1983: 36.

5 Tenzin Gyatso 1985: 412.

6 Maitreya (in Hopkins 1985: 14).

7 On this point Buddhism is often incorrectly understood, e.g. by Max Weber, who imputed to it a 'specifically asocial character' and claimed the Buddhist ethic was one of inaction, unconcerned with the welfare of one's neighbour (Weber 1988: II, 230).

8 According to Tenzin Gyatso (1985: 396); see also Thurman (1987: 12). Elsewhere in the *Kālacakra Guru Yoga* it says one should hold the wish to attain Buddhahood even at the cost of one's own life (Tenzin Gyatso 1985: 389).

9 Dhargyey 1985: 122f.

10 Dhargyey 1985: 127.

11 See n. 9; Tsang Nyön Heruka 1982: 92.

12 Tenzin Gyatso 1985: 391.

13 Jamyang 1981: 4.

14 Mullin 1982: 53.

Chapter Three
Outer Mandala: The Cosmos
(Pages 18–50)

1 La Vallée Poussin 1923–31: II, 139.

2 La Vallée Poussin 1923–31: II, 142. According to other traditions the south face of Meru is yellow.

3 Schabert 1990: 23f.

4 Not, as one sometimes reads in Western literature, below Mount Meru (La Vallée Poussin 1923–31: II, 148ff).

5 This model deviates in certain respects from other Western redrawings. In the reconstruction of Keilhauer & Keilhauer (1980), Meru stands on a hemisphere, the seven mountain walls are each as high as their respective distances from Mount Meru, and the hells are beneath Mount Meru – details that do not agree with *Abhidharmakośa.*

6 From Snellgrove 1967: Fig. XXI.

7 This is equivalent to 9 miles according to the Kālacakra tradition, from which the parable comes. According to the *Abhidharmakośa*, it is half this, i.e. 7.5 km. The parable is taken from Newman (1987: 499).

8 This has a height of 1,600,000 *yojanas* and shows an almost infinite diameter.

9 Kalu Rinpoche, 1986: 66–7.

10 Schuh (1973: 48f) gives another, differing, description: "The earth is represented as a hemisphere of radius 200,000 *yojanas* ... built up of four shells each 50,000 *yojanas* thick. These four shells ... are composed materially of each of one of the four elements ..." And later: "The resulting vertical extension of the world ... suggests the conclusion that one started with a complete sphere as the form of the world."

The sole publication in which both Buddhist pictures of the cosmos are reproduced accurately and to scale is that of Iwata & Sugiura (1989). While the Japanese depiction of the *Abhidharmakośa* universe largely agrees with that in the present volume, several data relating to the Kālacakra cosmos in that publication have been misintepreted and misdrawn: the discs of the different elements lie on top of one another, not nested inside one another, and the Mount Meru standing on the earth disc is significantly higher than is shown in the Japanese publication. This depiction also omits the very important planetary tracks, which enclose Meru like an umbrella.

11 The function of the twelve wind-tracks is not yet sufficiently well understood. According to one view, the twelve wind-circles transport only the sun (Imaeda 1987: 630, and A. Berzin, personal communication). The circles are evidently also related to the 27 lunar mansions: twelve touching segments of the twelve circles form a kind of ellipse that is divided into 108 (= 12 x 9) equal sectors, each four of which make one of the 27 lunar mansions (*nakṣatra*). Schuh (1973: 59) thinks the twelve signs of the zodiac were perhaps imagined as a boat, circling on the tracks around the world mountain, the wind as mover prescribing the direction in the sense of a clockwise rotation. In this connection, motion in latitude could be thought of as quite individually variable, as with sailing boats (see also n. 2 to Ch. 4).

12 Olschak & Wangyal (1972) and Gerner (1987: 46) incorrectly claim these representations show the origin of the world.

13 Gar-je K'am-trül Rinpoche (1978: 4); Schuh (1973: 45); Huang Mingxin (1987); Berzin (undated).

14 According to another tradition the geometric shapes do not represent the continents but are simply markings on them, the continents themselves being larger. If one takes the outer circle (Figs. 11, 12) and subdivides it into twelve segments, a continent has, according to this tradition, the size of half a segment.

Names of the joyless realms, or hells, after Berzin; Newman (1987) has 'gravel water' instead of 'thorns'.

15 Lessing 1976; Schubert 1954; Tharchin 1987: 61ff; Wayman 1973: 101ff; Kalu Rinpoche 1991: 83.

16 According to Tharchin 1987: 78; see also Evans-Wentz 1958: 324f.

17 In the *Dharmamaṇḍala Sūtra* also the human body is seen as a mandala, with the trunk as the centre and the arms and legs in the four cardinal directions (Lo Bue 1987: 789, 795).

18 These perhaps symbolize the eight seas (Schubert 1954).

19 Schubert (1954) speculates that these ultimately represent the eight mountain ranges around Meru. In outer mandalas in which the elements described here are reproduced in three dimensions, the eight goddesses may be represented by the eight lucky symbols. There are also groups of twelve or sixteen offering goddesses.

20 Possibly symbolizing the eclipse planets or lunar nodes Rāhu and Ketu.

21 This interpretation agrees with that of Mus, who reached this conclusion by quite a different route (Mus 1933: II, 114). In Sri Lanka, according to Mus (1933: 360), the *harmikā* is called the 'citadel of the gods'.

22 Mus 1933: II, 245. The dome is also called 'egg' (*aṇḍa*), recalling the egg-shaped Hindu universe.

23 Mus 1933: II, 248.

24 Govinda (1976); Mus (1933); Snodgrass (1988); Tucci (1988a, I), etc.

25 Govinda (1966: 219); Lauf (1972: 140); Essen & Thingo (1989: 45).

26 Tucci 1988a.

27 Tucci (1988a: 41f); Govinda (1976: 55–63); see also the Tibetan version of the *Vinayakṣudrakavastu* of the Mūlasarvāstivādins, in Roth (1980: 183ff); *Kriyāsaṃgraha* in Bénisti (1960: 89ff). On the Japanese tradition of correlations between *stūpa* levels and elements see Saso (1991: 123ff).

28 The five elements – in the Kālacakra tradition, from bottom to top: space, air, fire, water, earth – also contain the seven joyless worlds, the homes of the *nāgas* and the *asuras*.

The quite widespread interpretation, according to which the lowest level of the *stūpa* represents earth and the uppermost space, leaves unanswered the question of whether this 'cosmos' in the form of a *stūpa* stands as it were on its head. For the cosmos – in both the *Abhidharmakośa* and the Kālacakra traditions – consists of lighter parts below and heavier above. Govinda's attempt (1971) to demonstrate that early *stūpas* with their big domes already represented the five elements does not seem plausible to me, as on this interpretation the dome must be equated with the water element. Mus (1933) and we too in this book show, however, that the dome represents something else, namely the vault of the heavens, which extends over earth and water.

Because the Tibetan *stūpa* is set on a prominent plinth and its heavenly realm is elongated, no doubt the original analogies must have fallen into oblivion and given way to secondary explanations (Fig. 21).

29 Irwin 1980: 20ff.

30 Stein 1962: 170.

31 The dagger-shaped form of Meru stands out even more sharply if the invisible cosmos-head above the mountain is interpreted as a hilt. Obviously this interpretation of Meru as earth-dagger still needs to be corroborated with additional data; for the time being it must be viewed merely as a hypothesis.

32 Irwin 1980.

33 Irwin (1980: 16); Mus (1933: II, 362) also holds the opinion that the *yūpa* recalls the cosmic tree, the pillar that separates heaven and earth, the giant, the mountain, the cosmic arrow or lance, in a word, the world axis.

34 e.g., in the *stūpa* of Swayambunath, Nepal, as came to light during repairs, according to Mus (1933: II, 361).

35 For instance in Vedic India, in ancient China, in Germanic mythology, and in the mythologies of central and northern Asia (Eliade 1958: 52ff).

36 Strictly it ought to be the centre of the southern continent, Jambudvīpa, but sometimes the *bodhi* tree, and with it Bodhgayā, appears to be regarded as the centre of the entire world.

37 See the Tibetan depictions of the 'wheel of life'. See also Norbu & Turnbull 1972: 22–3.

38 Already in ancient India the cosmic axis could take four by and large interchangeable forms, namely those of mountain, pillar, tree and giant, of which Buddhism has taken over at least the mountain and the tree (Mus 1933: II, 117).

39 Also in Mus 1933.

40 Additional similar *stūpas* are found in Bhutan, Western Tibet (Tholing; Gerner 1987: 55), and Central Tibet (Sungkhar; Gerner 1987: 61).

41 According to the construction plans for a *stūpa* in Rikon, Switzerland, translated by Amy Heller.

42 Gyalzur & Verwey 1983: 179.

43 Tucci 1988a: 17; *tshangs thig* really means 'purity line'. The same term is used for the central axis of the 'mighty ten stacked syllables' (*daśākāro vaśī*, Fig. 66; and for the north–south and east–west axes of any mandala).

44 Tucci 1988a: 47ff.

45 Bénisti 1960: 97ff; Mus 1933: II, 105ff, 213ff; see also the interesting remarks and drawings in Saso 1991: 122ff, 139, 149, etc. According to Saso, in the lotus meditation of Tendai Buddhism a *stūpa* is formed in the body of the person meditating in the lotus posture: square, yellow earth beneath the stomach, round, white water disc above the navel, triangular, red fire in the heart area, crescent-shaped, dark blue air in the throat area and leaf-shaped, green space in the head chakra.

Then this *stūpa* is transformed into Vajrasattva. According to Saso (1991: 203) the meditator visualizes that a large *stūpa* filling the entire cosmos dwindles to the size of the body and all Buddhas enter it, becoming part of the body.

46 *Sang hyang Kamahayanikan* (cited in Mus 1933: II, 214). Two eyes are often painted on each of the four sides of the *harmikā* of a Nepalese *stūpa*. The Tathāgata (Buddha) Vairocana, seated in the centre, is looking with one of his four faces in each of the four directions (Plate 3).

47 Govinda 1986: 7.

48 Mus 1933: II, 102.

49 Heine-Geldern 1982: 72.

50 Gar-je K'am-trül Rinpoche 1978: 7. Shambhala is one of the 'hidden countries' (*bas yul*), which only those with faith and right motivation can find. Khenbalung, another *bas yul* in the Himalaya, also shows a mandala structure: there four paths lead to the four gates, one in each of the four cardinal directions. The centre is formed by a mountain surrounded by (four?) lakes, of the colours of the mandala (Diemberger & Schicklgruber, n.d.: 13ff; Bernbaum 1980).

51 Gutschow 1982: 50ff. Gutschow (23ff) also shows that shrines or temples dedicated to the twenty-four mother goddesses enclose the city of Kathmandu (in three concentric circles of eight), forming – at least in imagination – a mandala. It is interesting that to each temple in this imaginary mandala is assigned a *mantra*, a part of the body, an energy channel (*nāḍī*), a deity and so on – an idea similar to one we shall meet in the Kālacakra mandala. During the ritual visit to the twenty-four shrines over a period of twelve months (two shrines each month) the faithful meditate on each of the twenty-four parts of the body.

52 For Kirtipur, see Herdick 1988. The city, which appears to be based on idealized Indian treatises, is symmetrically divided into six or twelve districts. Kirtipur, like ancient Burmese towns also (Aung 1987), shows twelve gates, which are connected to the twelve districts. For China, see Ledderose 1980: 238; Eck 1987.

53 Heine-Geldern 1982; Aung 1987.

54 Heine-Geldern 1982; Eck 1987.

55 Schabert 1990: 15.

56 Schabert 1990: 20ff; Herodotus I, 28. Further examples of mandala-style city layouts are Nicosia (Cyprus) and Palmanova (Italy).

We know from India and Thailand that besides individual buildings, whole complexes of buildings, cities, or even considerably larger territories could constitute a mandala-style cosmogram. Thus the four Indian places of pilgrimage Badrinath (in the north), Rameshvaram (south), Purī (east) and Dvārakā (west) form the vertices of a sacred area embracing the greater part of India, which the pilgrim circumambulates or travels round like a mandala or temple (Eck 1987; Fischer *et al.* 1987).

57 Grünwedel (1915: 73) speaks of 96 million.

58 According to Gar-je K'am-trül Rinpoche (1978), the city is called 'Ma-la-ya'; according to Grünwedel (1915: 73) this is the name of the park lying to the south of the royal palace.

59 According to another source, the Kālacakra mandala is to the south of the city in a sandalwood grove, which has lakes in its eastern and western parts (Newman 1985: 55; see also Schubert 1953).

60 After Amy Heller's translation of the Tibetan caption. The blockprint and caption are reproduced in Snellgrove 1967: Fig. XXII.

Chapter Four
Inner Mandala: The Person
(Pages 51–59)

1 Tucci 1961: 87, 108–9.

2 An exact assignment of the winds on which the planets 'ride' and the most important winds in the person is not easy to carry out. Usually the teaching is of ten principal winds in the person but, as Serkong Rinpoche explained in a teaching in Madison, apparently there also exists a presentation of twelve winds in the person.

In the Kālacakra system there are ten planets, in five pairs: moon and sun; Rāhu and Kālāgni; Mercury and Mars; Venus and Jupiter; Ketu and Saturn (Newman 1987: 433; Kongtrul 1995: 158).

Around Mount Meru run twelve circular wind-tracks, which are no doubt to be interpreted in the first place as signs of the zodiac, but perhaps also as planets. I am indebted to Reinhard Herdick of Munich for the remark that the twelve tracks can be connected with the sun or moon as follows: if we divide the year into twelve sections and observe the track of the sun (or moon) in each section, we discover that the sun (moon) covers different tracks, supposedly of varying length, of which two are the same in the twelve months, so that we get 6 x 2 tracks. Indeed, the twelve wind-tracks can be split up into two 'sets' of six colours each (Plate 4, left).

Even if the twelve wind-tracks around Mount Meru should indicate the twelve solar months of the zodiac (= exact division of the ecliptic into twelve sections), they can also be related to the planets, as assigments of the planets to the signs of the zodiac are well-known (e.g., Majupuria & Gupta 1981: 18; see also Wayman 1973: 158).

3 e.g., Éliade 1957: 76ff.

4 Kramrisch 1946: 57ff. There is a diagram of the *vāstupuruṣa* in Becker-Ritterspach (1982: Fig. 10). According to one tradition the spine of the deity appears to coincide with the central axis of the temple, the mouth with the main gateway, the head

with the dome (Kramrisch 1946: Vol. 1, 71; Vol 2, 359). It is, however, questionable whether this actually refers to the *vāstupuruṣa*, as this appears to lie flat on the ground.

In Western architecture, Vitruvius' theory of proportions and the anthropometric architecture of the Renaissance, both sought the harmony of a building in agreement with human proportions (e.g., Schabert 1990: 40–49).

5 According to Heine-Geldern (1982: 9), in Thailand each monastery represents a small diagram of the structure of the world too.

6 According to Tenzin Gyatso (1985: 277–8, etc.), 'pristine mind (bliss)'.

7 Certain joints also seem to belong together: left elbow and right knee (and vice versa), left wrist and right hip (and vice versa), and left shoulder and right ankle (and vice versa).

8 According to one source there are 80,000 channels (Tenzin Gyatso 1985: 298). Genesis of the 72,000 winds: initially there arise four channels in the centre and four outer ones surrounding them, making eight channels. The four outer channels, each assigned to a cardinal direction, divide again. These eight outer channels (which are connected with the heart chakra) each divide again into three channels, producing 24 finely branching channels. Adding the twelve channel-cords (four central plus eight outer) to the base makes 36, a number that seems to correlate with the 36 deities of the 'seven basic initiations' and the 36 principal components of a person that have to be purified. Division of all 36 channels (or division into three, of each of the 24 channels) generates 72 channels, each of which splits up into a thousand extremely fine channels, producing 72,000 channels (partly after Dhargyey 1985: 104; see also Lati Rinpoche & Hopkins 1990: 93).

9 Other Sanskrit names: *caṇḍālī*, *avadhūti* or *susumnā*.

10 Other Sanskrit names: *lalanā* or *iḍā*.

11 Other Sanskrit names: *rasanā* or *piṅgalā*.

12 Markel 1990; see also n. 2, above. In the nine-planet system, the eclipse planets are Rāhu and Ketu ('comet'), but the introduction of the tenth planet, Kālāgni, as second eclipse planet frees Ketu to resume its original role as comet.

A description of the *nāḍīs* may be found in Chang (1963: 56 [1982: 170–71]), which also mentions some variations.

13 In India the word *cakra* possesses several meanings: wheel, discus, potter's wheel, circle (Mode 1987: 925).

14 e.g., Mullin 1985a: 164.

15 Mullin 1985a: 163ff.

16 One partner symbolizes 'method' or the path (e.g., the white deities), the other 'wisdom' (e.g., the red deities).

17 The sketch reveals another possible explanation for the apparently not quite consistent course of the mandala ritual. If we compare for example the spatial arrangement of the aggregates or elements with the order in which they are purified in the relevant initiations (Table 1), the following sequence can be established: east, south, *north*, west (instead of *west*, north) – an order we shall come across time and again. With the help of Fig. 35 this sequence can be better understood: corresponding to the Kālacakra cosmos (see p. 22), each initiation begins with the first element, space (green = centre), and goes by way of the second element, air (black = east), to fire (red = south), water (white = north), and thence the fifth element, earth (yellow = west).

18 In this connection *bodhicitta* means 'drop' (*bindu*; *thig le*) rather than altruistic 'thought of enlightenment' (see p. 16). Every person possesses white (male) and red (female) *bodhicitta*-drops, whose distribution in the body and role in the concluding yoga practices will be explained later.

19 Names after German edition of Lati Rinpoche & Hopkins (1990: 94). Dhargyey's details differ sharply as far as the crown and throat are concerned. He mentions explicitly only five chakras, which he characterizes as follows (Dhargyey 1985: 114ff):

crown – four colours (white, red, green, black), triangular centre, 32 channels
throat – red, round centre, 16 channels
heart – white, triangular centre, 8 channels
navel – four colours (white, red, green, black), round centre, 64 channels
sexual organ – red, triangular centre, 32 channels

Similar details in Lati Rinpoche & Hopkins (1990: 94); Wayman (1973: 174). There is also an account of the chakras in Chang (1963: 57 [1982: 171]), with some deviations.

20 This is generally referred to as the chakra in the private parts; in this publication the term 'sexual chakra' is used.

21 According to Mullin (1985a: 164) there are eight lotus petals in the centre of the sexual organs, and thirty-two at the anus.

22 Lati Rinpoche & Hopkins 1990: 95, and Dhargyey 1985: 117.

23 Five of these winds correspond to the five principal winds in other Tantric systems, but the remaining five winds of the Kālacakra system are not identical with the so-called five secondary winds of other schools (see also n. 2, above), though they have the same names as those of Hindu yoga and Vedānta. The idea that the human body has winds flowing through it is well known to Hinduism. Thus in the *Chāndogya Upaniṣad* (II, 13) there is a teaching of five winds, which can be related to the five directions, five channels, sense organs, deities, and five elements – sun, moon, fire, rain, wind (Mus 1933: II, 441–50). On the correspondence between wind and breath, see also Mus 1933: 144ff.

24 According to Dhargyey 1985: 119f, and Tenzin Gyatso 1985: 291; see also Mullin 1985a: 165, who renders some names differently.

25 *Kṛkala* or *kṛkara* is translated into Tibetan as *rtsangs pa*, 'lizard', 'chameleon'. *Nāga* may mean either a snake or a creature that is half-snake, half-human. *Dhanaṃjaya* literally means 'wealth-conquering' and *devadatta* 'god-given', both well-known as

personal names. 'Fire-accompanying' or fire-inhabiting wind (Lati Rinpoche & Hopkins 1990: 19).

26 In the central channel above the heart chakra.

27 In the central channel below the heart chakra.

28 Acording to Mullin (1985a: 163), 'male fluids'. Data on the fluids according to Hopkins (1985: 113). A certain similarity with the liquids of the inner offering (see p. 106f) should not be overlooked; there, however, urine is found in the north and bone marrow in the east.

Gnoli and Orofino (1994: 272) present a different diagram that does not match the text of the First Dalai Lama as used here. According to Gnoli and Orofino, the left channel (moon) forks to the centre (excrement) below the navel chakra; the right channel (sun) forks to the left (urine), and the middle channel (Rāhu), to the right (semen).

29 The term *Śakti* is scarcely used in Tibetan Buddhism (see p. 134, n. 77).

30 See Newman 1987: 520ff; Gnoli & Orofino 1994: 270ff; Schuh 1973: 65ff. 'Breath' translates the Tibetan *dbugs*. We have used the expression 'shift of the breath' to translate the Tibetan term *'pho ba*. There are 12 *'pho ba* in a (solar) day (Skt. *dina*, Tib. *nyin zhag*). One *'pho ba* is equal to 1,800 breaths, or 5 *nāḍi* (or *daṇḍa* or *ghaṭi*). One *nāḍī* (*chu tshod* in Tibetan) is equal to 360 breaths, or 24 minutes. There are 60 *nāḍī* in a day, and 1,800 (i.e. 30 x 60) *nāḍi* in a month. A month may also be divided into 5 'mandalas' of 360 *nāḍī*.

31 See n. 2, above; a Tibetan text that establishes a correlation between the signs of the zodiac and the human winds (with different names to the ones given here) is found in Wayman (1973: 157ff).

32 According to Hopkins 1985: 114ff; Tenzin Gyatso 1985: 308ff.

33 On this see Dhargyey 1985: 121ff; Tenzin Gyatso 1985: 260ff; Sopa 1985b: 148; Mullin 1985a: 166.

34 After Dhargyey (1985: 121ff) and Mullin (1985a: 167). According to Tenzin Gyatso (1985: 260), this drop is found in the crown chakra.

35 While the winds of the lower half of the body come together in the navel chakra.

36 The lower in the sexual chakra.

37 The lower in the sexual chakra; according to Hopkins (1985: 121), in the middle of the uppermost part of the sexual organ.

38 According to Dhargyey (1985: 121ff), in the crown chakra, while the winds of the lower half of the body remain in the sexual chakra; according to Hopkins (1985: 121), on the tip of the sexual organ.

39 The four stages or states are also related to the four Buddha bodies: *nirmāṇakāya* ('manifestation body'), *saṃbhogakāya* ('enjoyment body'), *dharmakāya* ('absolute truth body'), and *sahajakāya* ('innate body'), also known as *svābhāvikakāya* ('self-existent or nature body') (see also p. 135, nn. 120–3).

40 In the mandala the Bodhisattvas connected with these characteristics are not depicted in the centre, but on the left (looking out from the centre) of each of the four entrances of the mind mandala. However, it is clear from the symbol assigned to them – the *vajra* – that these elements belong to the centre.

41 It is striking that a sense and sense object not belonging together are placed side by side. This arrangement corresponds exactly with that of the Bodhisattvas in the mind realm of the Kālacakra mandala, which mediate the fifth initiation. In fact, the two components – whose combined value comes to 13 – always belong together, e.g. sense of sight (5) in the south and forms (8) in the northeast.

42 According to Hopkins 1985: 115ff; Tenzin Gyatso 1985: 318ff; in this scheme too, activity & action faculty which do not actually belong together are placed side by side, corresponding to the deployment of the twelve wrathful deities that give the sixth initiation. Once again, the two components whose combined count makes 13 belong together, e.g. mouth faculty (3) in the east and speech (10) in the northwest.

43 According to the Tantric Buddhist conception, consciousness 'rides' on wind; the two are mutually dependent, just as a man who can see but cannot walk and a blind man who can walk but cannot see, depend on one another if they want to pick a fruit from a tree in the distance. Example after Dhargyey (1985: 129).

44 However, traces of the two *bodhicittas*, the male, white and the female, red, also exist in the remaining chakras. The chief location of the white *bodhicitta* is the crown, of the red the navel. In the heart chakra the white and red *bodhicitta* balance one another; see also Mullin 1985a: 166.

45 There are five songs: each goddess first sings a song alone, then all four together sing a fifth song.

46 The four goddesses are related to the four elements air, fire, water and earth, but also to the four chakras, as well as the four types of deep wisdom (Table 13).

47 According to the Kālacakra tradition – and contrary to other Tantric schools – after birth certain winds also flow through the central wind or energy channel: the winds of the element of deep awareness. These number 675 per day, i.e. 56 $^{1}/_{4}$ in each of the twelve shifts of the breath.

48 In Tantric Buddhism *sādhana* (*sgrub thabs*) is a kind of meditation in which the meditator 'invokes' a deity and identifies him or herself with it. In Anuttarayoga Tantra this refers to the stage in which the mandala and its deities are generated (according to Jackson 1985b: 120).

49 In fact two side channels and one central channel each in the upper and the lower parts of the trunk = six channels (cf. Fig. 35).

50 According to dGe-'dun grub (in Mullin 1985a: 180; see also p. 134 n. 126, p. 135 n. 131). Dhargyey (1985: 83) and Mullin (1985b: 119) deviate somewhat. According to Deti Rinpoche: "The water element of the body weakens the fire. Separated from the fire, earth sinks into water. Water is dried up by wind.

Wind absorbs into consciousness. Consciousness dissolves into space."

According to Mullin, and also Chang (1963: 103ff [1982: 232ff]), each dissolution of an element is followed by a vision, corresponding to the four gross after-death visions: mirage, smoke, embers, butter lamp (see p. 118).

51 According to Dhargyey (1985: 91) within the 'drop that is indestructible during the lifetime' there exists another, 'forever indestructible drop'. This drop is "indestructible throughout this life, through death, through the intermediate period, through the full duration of one's existence in the cycle of existence, and right on through to one's attainment of Enlightenment and, following that, as an Enlightened Being" – an idea that stands in a relation of some tension with the Buddhist teaching of the transitoriness of all things.

52 Dhargyey 1985: 91.

53 These visions are similar to those in the 'six yogas' (see p. 118f).

54 In this way a *yogin* unifies the 'mother clear light' (= clear light of death) and the 'son clear light' (clear light attained through meditation).

Chapter Five
The Other Mandala: The Tantric Method
(Pages 61–119)

1 Although each of the centres and each of the ten winds is closely related to one of the six aggregates, according to the *Kālacakra Tantra* the dissolution of the winds takes place in all the centres, regardless of the specific correlations.

2 In other Anuttarayoga Tantras (e.g. *Guhyasamāja*), three 'bases' – death, intermediate state and birth – must be purified, whereas in Kālacakra the intermediate state is dropped. These traditions also differ in their meditative path, which regards the intermediate state as an important part: the 'effective clear light' and the so-called 'illusory body', the body assumed by a deceased being in the intermediate state, should be united, as only this allows direct perception of emptiness. In these traditions too the winds are guided into the central channel, but they are dissolved in the heart chakra into a drop the size of a mustard seed. After the 'pure illusory body' created by the *yogin* has finally fused with the 'effective clear light', the last impurities disappear and the 'three Buddha bodies' (*kāya*) can be attained.

3 Jackson 1985a: 30. According to Dhargyey (1985: 151) and Mullin (1985a: 182f), a *yogin* of dull mental ability consummates the union first of all in the form of a *karmamudrā*; a *yogin* of middling ability in the form of a *jñānamudrā*; and a sharp-minded one directly in the form of a *mahāmudrā* (see also n. 132, below).

4 According to Dhargyey 1985: 30, 152.

5 Tenzin Gyatso 1985: 248.

6 e.g., Hopkins 1985: 27.

7 For this purpose the deity can be imagined sitting in a palace (Tenzin Gyatso 1981: 117).

8 According to Tenzin Gyatso 1981: 19–20, and Tsongkapa 1981: 115–38.

9 Tenzin Gyatso 1985: 386, n. 9.

10 The following description is after Tenzin Gyatso 1981: 21–4, and Tsongkapa 1981: 103–14.

11 Tenzin Gyatso 1981: 22.

12 Tenzin Gyatso 1985: 401–2; see also Dhargyey 1985: 58ff.

13 See also Schöne 1983.

14 Tucci 1980: 63–4.

15 Mircea Eliade, in *History of Religions*, Vol. 11: 'Spirit, Light and Seed'.

16 Such mandalas of coloured powder are called *rajomaṇḍala* (*rdul tshon gyi dkyil 'khor*). According to Macdonald (1962: 104) the fine powder is made from rice. In the Kālacakra mandala sprinkled at Rikon, Switzerland, in Autumn 1985, silicon dioxide (quartz) was used, practically free of solid inclusions. Examined under the microscope, the quartz grains were all very angular and sharp-edged, which suggests that the quartz minerals were ground. Investigation of three test colours revealed: the white sand was without added colouring, i.e. consisted of the basic quartz substance (SiO_2); the black colour was caused by a fine, black powder, probably soot, adhering to the surface of the quartz; and the red colour was created similarly with organic pigments (Investigation of the Eidgenössischen Materialprufungs- und Forschungsanstalt ['Swiss Materials Testing and Research Institute'], Dübendorf, No. 134 432, Dr H. Vonmont).

The analysis of material used to make a Yamāntaka (Vajrabhairava) mandala at the Linden-Museum in Stuttgart showed that calcium sulphate dihydrate was used (analysis report by Landesmuseum für Technik und Arbeit, Mannheim, 6.1.1995). The mandala was made in December 1992 by six monks from the Tse Chok Ling monastery, Dharamsala.

17 Although the expression 'Tathāgata-Buddha' is redundant, since Tathāgata always implies Buddha, we use it in this book to make it easier for the reader to remember the meaning of the term. A Tathāgata unites in himself the collections of gnosis (insight into 'suchness', or 'thusness' (*tathatā*)) and merit; through gnosis he has 'gone' (*gata*) to the single taste of 'thusness'; through merit he has 'come' (*āgata*) back from 'thusness' to cyclic existence with the 'form body'. Therefore he is called Tathāgata, 'the thus-gone', 'the thus-come'; after mKhas-grub rJe (Wayman 1973: 45).

18 This text reveals a departure from the Kālacakra universe already described: definite geometric shapes are ascribed to the element discs, which do not agree with the (visible)

Kālacakra universe, as there the elements clearly form gigantic round discs (Plates 6, 8; Figs 12, 43; see also Plate 9 for colours and form of discs.

19 Palden Yeshe, n.d.: translation adapted from (Eng.) p. 5 , (Ger.) p. 10 .

20 Palden Yeshe, n.d.: after (Eng.) p. 5 , (Ger.) p. 11.

21 The mind mandala on top is subdivided into mandalas of 'deep awareness' and 'great bliss'.

22 Dhargyey 1985: 57.

23 I was helped in this by Messrs Rottermann and Glauser of the Rocad company, Bern. Peter Nebel converted the computer drawings produced by them into models. In the meantime some of the computer drawings were used to create a computer animation (see Brauen and Hassler 1997). Some of the drawings are reproduced in Brauen 1994.

24 Berzin, n.d.; Serkong Rinpoche 1982.

25 Palden Yeshe, n.d.: after (Eng.) pp. 5–6 , (Ger.) pp. 11–12.

26 Evans-Wentz (1957); Fremantle & Trungpa (1975); Thurman (1994); in German also Dargyay (1977).

27 Eliade 1937: 196; Eliade 1958: 64; Kramrisch 1946.

28 Kramrisch 1946: 39. Tibetan temples (*lha khang*) also often display the mandala principle. Besides wall paintings with depictions of mandalas, the architectural plan of the temple is often determined by the mandala structure. One thinks of the Jokhang in Lhasa (see p. 49; Fig. 28) or the monastic precinct of Samye (p. 31; Figs 25, 26). The central temple of the Chos 'khor monastery in Tabo also forms a mandala, similar to the Sarvavid-Vairocana mandala, as Shashibala (1989) has shown. Also worth mentioning in this connection is Pule Si in Jehol (Chengde, China), whose main hall, the Xuguang Ge, forms a mandala and encloses a three-dimensional Saṃvara mandala (Chayet 1985: 39ff).

29 More accurately, the rulers of the twenty-eight lunar constellations plus four rulers of the planets, "who rule over the equinoxial and solstitial points referred to the cardinal points" (Kramrisch 1946: 31f).

30 According to Kramrisch 1946: 35.

31 Interestingly enough, in Vedic times the altar consisted of thirty-two stones arranged about a central, thirty-third stone (Kramrisch 1946: 95).

32 The thirty-two regents, in Java for example, are regents of the twenty-eight provinces, standing for the heavenly regents of the twenty-eight lunar constellations, and the four ministers, standing for the four directions (Heine-Geldern 1982: 33).

33 Blondeau 1990: 97ff.

34 Lessing 1976: 31ff.

35 Lessing & Wayman 1978: 281; Kalsang Gyatso 1987: 6. According to Kalsang Gyatso, charnel grounds, places near (calm) water and so forth are favourable.

36 This is an idea also typical of Hinduism; according to *Vāstuvidyā*, VII, 2–6, the *vāstumaṇḍala* underlying a temple is covered with a great serpent which, in the course of a year, moves from the east, to the south, west and north. Each day, the head of the *nāga* moves one degree (Kramrisch 1946, Vol.1: 62, 90, n. 9; see also Becker-Ritterspach 1982: 59).

37 Likewise, before the building of a Tibetan monastery commences, the 'lord of the soil' is drawn on the ground. In the course of the consecration of the ground area, a monk then sprinkles earth taken from the consecrated spot all over the area of the future building, thus creating a kind of temple consecration mandala. A precise account of the ritual can be found in Bechert (1971: 17ff).

38 Lessing & Wayman 1978: 281.

39 The actual deities, which descend from heavenly realms and find their way into the objects; as opposed to the *samayasattvas*, or 'pledge beings', symbolic representations of the deities, which are not completely identical with the actual deities.

40 Lessing & Wayman 1978: 282–3.

41 The northeast is considered to be the direction from which (among other things) hindrances come; a mandala should not therefore be set up in the northeast of a town (from the monk Pema, Dharamsala, personal communication).

42 See also Lessing & Wayman 1978: 282, n. 16.

43 Here the Kālacakra ritual deviates once again from the usual traditions, in which the *vajra*-master turns from the east to the south, then to the west and finally to the north.

44 These assignments correspond to the Kālacakra mandala, but are atypical of most other mandalas, in which the following assignments are found:

east	– blue (white) Akṣobhya (Vairocana)
south	– yellow Ratnasambhava
west	– red Amitābha
north	– green Amoghasiddhi
centre	– white (blue) Vairocana (Akṣobhya)

45 *Sekoddeśaṭikā* (in Carelli 1941: 26). Often a *kalaśa* (*bum pa*) is indeed vase-shaped (Fig. 57), but in other cases (Beyer 1978: Fig. 44) it is a vessel with a long spout that cannot properly be called a vase, so that the translation 'flask' is more appropriate.

Gnoli and Orofino (1994: 158) give a detailed list of the different types of vases: "In the pacification rites (*śāntika*) the vases are made of crystal; in the rites of increase (*puṣṭi*) they are made of silver; a human skull is used in the rites of killing, and an iron vase in those of expulsion (*uccāṭana*) and hate (*vidveṣa*); the vases are of gold in the rites of submission (*vaśya*), of copper in the rites of attraction (*ākṛṣṭi*), of clay in the rites of paralysis (*stambhana*), and of wood in the rites of obscuration (*mohana*). There are ten vases."

These are the characteristics of the vessels to be used in the rites of reconciliation and of increase: "some sixteen fingers wide in girth, twenty fingers in height, two fingers at the final curve (lip), six fingers wide at the neck, and eight fingers wide at the opening (mouth). These vases must be pure as the moon and are to be used for no purpose except the rites of reconciliation and of increase."

46 When very large mandalas are built, as for example in previous times the ones in the Yonghe Gong, the Lama Temple in Beijing, the vases are placed directly on the table surface of the mandala (picture of a Kālacakra mandala, Beijing (Peking) 1932, in Wayman 1973: 80).

47 Lessing & Wayman 1978: 286–7; see also Beyer 1978: 408–11. It is unclear whether the *karma* vase in mKhas-grub rJe is identical with the *jaya* vase in Carelli (1941: 31).

In the consecration of the ground before building a monastery (n. 37), vases are likewise set out arranged in a mandala – they stand on the petals of a lotus flower drawn on the ground (Bechert 1971: 25).

48 Herbs, fragrant things such as saffron and incense, essences, grains and precious stones, which appear to symbolize the body, speech, mind, 'actions and merits' of the deities (see table in Wayman 1973: 81). The *Sekoddeśatikā* mentions as vase ingredients: pulses, grains, precious stones and metals; in addition, stones whose colours correspond to the direction to which they are related: black for the east and south-east, red for the south and south-west, and so forth. The two vases in the centre, according to this text, both contain black stones, not blue and green respectively as one might suspect (Carelli 1941: 31).

See also Gnoli and Orofino (1994: 175–78), who mention 25 vase-ingredients, and give a detailed description: 25 medicinal herbs, 25 cereals (and vegetables; 5 groups of 5 species), 5 precious stones, 5 semi-precious stones, 5 inferior stones, 5 metals. If stones and metals are absent, scented flowers in five different colours can be used.

49 Tucci (1961: 24): "A vase remains an indispensable adjunct in all those Hindu ceremonies designed to bring down the divine essence (*āvahana*) so that it may be projected and take up its abode in a statue or other object." *Āvahana* literally means 'bringing near'; an alternative reading could be *avahana*, 'bringing down', or *āvāhana*, 'invoking'.

50 For similar ideas in Hinduism, see Bäumer 1986.

51 The order of drawing the lines is not the same in every tradition (Lessing & Wayman 1978: 284, n.18; Lessing 1954).

52 Wayman 1971: 565. The terminology of the straight lines of the mandala grid and the cords used to draw them is readily confused. Skt *sūtra*, Tib. *thig* and indeed Eng. *line* are all ambiguous, and of course the cord and the line physically coincide at the crucial moment. mKhas-grub rJe (Lessing & Wayman 1978: 284–7) clearly implies that *las thig* ('working line') and *ye thig* ('gnosis line') refer to the mandala lines drawn and visualized, while the cords (*thig skud*) used to put them in place are the 'wet' and 'dry cords' (*rlon thig*, *skam thig*). dGe-bshes Chos-kyi grags-pa defines *ye thig* as *ye shes kyi thig drang po*, 'straight gnosis line', which seems unambiguous. Also consistent with this interpretation, *Bod rgya tshig mdzod chen mo* says a *las thig* is a symbolic line (or 'pledge line'; *dam tshig gi thig*) drawn on a mandala and the *ye thig* is the gnosis line raised in the air above the mandala. The parallel with pledge being/gnosis being (*samayasattva/jñānasattva*) means the term *ye thig* can hardly apply to a physical object.

53 Drawing the first line of a mandala is apparently performed the same way in South Indian Śaivism (Brunner 1986: 26).

54 According to mKhas-grub rJe (Lessing & Wayman 1978: 286–7) and Wayman (1971: 565), the dry cord is made of five sets of five differently coloured threads, so that altogether it comprises 25 (5 x 5) threads.

55 According to another source (Jamyang 1985: 2), the five female partners of the Tathāgata-Buddhas.

56 These colours are typical for the Kālacakra tradition but disagree with the colouring of many other mandalas (n. 44).

57 n. 16, above.

58 Lessing & Wayman 1978: 290–1; Lessing 1954: Plate 6; see p. 125, n. 13.

59 See p. 130, n. 48.

60 These are emptiness, signlessness, wishlessness and non-action.

61 In the Yamāntaka system the inner offering is offered differently:

centre – human flesh, Akṣobhya (or Vairocana)
east – cow flesh, Vairocana (or Akṣobhya)
south – dog flesh, Ratnasambhava
west – elephant flesh, Amitābha
north – horse flesh, Amoghasiddhi

On this, see for example Wayman (1973: 116).

62 white OṂ = Amitābha
red ĀḤ = Ratnasambhava
black HŪṂ = Amoghasiddhi
yellow HOḤ = Vairocana
green HAṂ = Akṣobhya
blue KṢAḤ = Vajrasattva

63 The twelve offering goddesses and offerings, which the meditator generates from his heart chakra and reabsorbs into his heart at the end, are grouped in six pairs. Each pair has to purify one of the six elements (deep awareness, space, air, fire, water, earth). It is easy to see from their colours that the six again form a mandala with the four cardinal directions plus centre above and centre below.

64 Uṣṇīṣa, Śumbha, Sarvanīvaraṇaviṣkambhin, Nīladaṇḍa, Prajñāntaka, Ṭakki, Padmāntaka, Acala, Yamāntaka and Mahābala.

65 Brahmā, Viṣṇu, Nairṛti, Vāyu, Yama, Agni, Samudra, Rudra, Indra and Yakṣa.

66 Rāhu, Kālāgni, moon, sun, Mercury, Mars, Venus, Jupiter, Ketu and Saturn.

67 Rāja, Vijaya, Karkotaka, Padma, Vāsuki, Śaṅkhapāla, Ananta,

Kulika, Mahāpadma and Taksaka.

68 Various kinds of spirits and demons, many with animal heads. All sixty deities of the protective circle after Jackson (1985b: 125).

69 These four phases are also known as 'approach', 'close approach', 'realization' and 'great realization'.

70 In this way the cosmos is apparently created 'upside down' within the body: space is related to the crown chakra, air to the brow, fire to the throat, water to the heart and earth to the navel chakra; Meru to the region from the navel to the genitals; and sun, moon and Rāhu/Kālāgni to three channels that meet at the sexual chakra (Tenzin Gyatso 1985: 417; Mullin 1985a: 159f, see also Fig. 66).

71 Channels for faeces, urine and semen.

72 Jackson 1985b: 128; Tenzin Gyatso 1985: 401.

73 It is unclear whether the syllable PHREṂ is generated in the palace.

74 In the mandala only eight Śaktis encircle the central couple, the remaining two coincide with the goddess Viśvamātṛ.

There are close correlations between the ten goddesses and the ten winds (Table 6; see also p. 100f).

75 Or wisdom/deep awareness of the individuality of things.

76 Or action-accomplishing wisdom/deep awareness.

77 *Śakti* ('mighty') is a term little used in Tibetan Buddhism. In the *Kālacakra Tantra*, however, the eight or ten goddesses are in fact described as Śakti (*nus ma*), so it seems sensible to use the word (cf. Hopkins 1985: 83; Sopa 1985a: 99).

78 e.g., Jackson 1985b: 129.

79 Details of the number of deities in the Kālacakra mandala vary. Tenzin Gyatso (1985: 253–4) speaks of 722 deities, an enumeration that we follow here; other sources give 702 or 634 deities (Hopkins 1985: 485, n. 94). The XIII Dalai Lama even speaks of 1,620 deities mentioned in the root *tantra*, whereas the abbreviated *tantra* talks about 722 deities (according to Mullin 1988: 300).

80 Correspond to the six female Buddhas.

81 Correspond to the six male Buddhas just mentioned.

82 nn. 74, 99.

83 The remaining two male and two female Buddhas are not counted here, presumably because they coincide with the central couple.

84 Another four wrathful deities are not counted here, as they are assigned not to the mind mandala but two each to the upwards direction and to the body mandala.

85 Two other Śaktis have already been included in the topmost chakra.

86 The two central deities in each group of eight are not included in this number.

87 It is hard to match the number 32 to the deities in the body mandala: possibly 24 main male and female deities in the twelve wheels (= 24) plus a protector and a partner in each of the four directions.

88 In Grünwedel (1915: 96), other correlations are mentioned:

YA – foot
RA – shin
VA – thigh
LA – hip
MA – spine
KṢA – neck to forehead
HA – crown
crescent and drop – left and right channels
nāda – central channel

89 It is unclear whether 8 or 11 represents the central energy channel. Its upper and lower parts correspond to Rāhu and Kālāgni.

90 Tenzin Gyatso 1985: 213.

91 The colouring of the crescent and the dot or 'drop' (*thig le*) is not standardized. The following assignments would seem the most sensible: white crescent – left channel – moon; red dot – right channel – sun; but when the colours are different, the correspondences with the sun and moon and channels may be changed also.

92 When visualizing Kālacakra there is a slight difference in the assignment of the syllables to the chakras (Tenzin Gyatso 1985: 245):

navel – yellow LAṂ
heart – black YAṂ
throat (neck) – red RAṂ
forehead – white BAṂ

93 It is obvious that these syllables are analogous to those from which, according to the *Kālacakra Tantra*, the individual elements of a universe arise (in that case a final Ṃ is added); on this visualization see, e.g., Mullin 1985a: 159; Tenzin Gyatso 1985: 213.

94 Two ear, nose and eye openings; mouth, opening of urethra, opening of vas deferens or vagina, anus, upper and lower openings of the central wind channel.

95 According to Tibetan tradition, from conception to birth takes nine months and ten days; the expression 'tenth month' refers to the ten days of the tenth month.

96 e.g., Wayman 1973: 180. Another account of embryonic and foetal development is given by Dhargyey (1985: 106), and Lati Rinpoche & Hopkins (1990: 95f):

first month – embryo like a fish
second month – like a turtle;
third month – like a wild pig
fourth month – foetus like a lion
fifth month – foetus like a tiny human being
(Lati Rinpoche & Hopkins 1990: 95, 'dwarf')
sixth month – development of visual ability,
earth element arises
seventh month – sense of hearing, water element

eighth month – sense of smell, fire element
ninth month – sense of taste, air element
tenth month – sense of touch, space element

97 e.g., Tenzin Gyatso (1985: 253–4), who mentions 162 main deities (the 156 enumerated in Fig. 65 plus 6 Tathāgatas), which correspond to the 162 main channels. Another tradition counts 120 main deities, corresponding to the 120 petals of four chakras (Wayman 1973: 174). In the Vajradhātu mandala of Japanese Tendai Buddhism, the regions of the mandala (or the twelve most important deities) are related to certain parts of the body (Saso 1991: 124).

98 Tenzin Gyatso 1985: 212–3.

99 The group basically includes ten goddesses; eight surround the central deity couple and two are in the centre, coinciding with Kālacakra's partner, Viśvamātṛ.

100 Kālacakra (= the meditator) is entered by way of the crown aperture, then the white *bodhicitta* flows down in the central channel and via his *vajra* (penis) finds its way into his partner, Viśvamātṛ; there the deities are generated step by step: (drop → seed-syllable → emblem → form of deity plus partner).

101 Possibly also in the sexual and crown chakras.

102 A detailed division of the initiations can be found in Tenzin Gyatso (1985: 213–4); see also Lessing & Wayman (1978: 311ff). According to them, there are four major kinds of initiation in Anuttarayoga Tantra:
'flask' (*kalaśa*) – eleven types
'secret' (*guhya*) – one type
'insight-knowledge' (*prajñājñāna*) – one type
'fourth initiation' (*caturtha*) – one type

103 The candidate for initiation is in fact described as a child (Tenzin Gyatso 1985: 178).

104 For details, Tenzin Gyatso 1985: 186–95; the idea that the six elements are of the nature of the six female Buddhas and setting the seed-syllables of the nature of the six male ones, displays parallels with the inner offering and self-protection.

105 In his commentary Nāropa has this to say: "The disciple will throw the flower (he holds) in the hollow of his hand outside the mandala, onto the vase of triumph. The flowers, etc., are not to be tossed onto the coloured powder as this would damage it; as a consequence of damaging the already marked and consecrated mandala one would succumb to the sin of destruction (*stupa*). Therefore the flower must be thrown outside the mandala, onto the vase of triumph before the gate of the East, for the purpose of observing and determining the family affiliation of the disciple." (in Gnoli and Orofino 1994: 172ff). Spiritual relationship with one of the Tathāgatas can also apparently be ascertained by the fall of a toothpick that the student throws onto the mandala surface or onto a board representing it.

106 e.g., Tenzin Gyatso 1985: 201–3, 207–8; see also Jamyang 1985: 5.

107 dGe-'dun grub (cited in Mullin 1985a: 151).

108 According to Tenzin Gyatso 1985: 264–6; Sopa 1985a: 99–100.

109 i.e., the vase assigned to the relevant direction on the side of the mandala table.

110 It was pointed out above that a flask is assigned to each direction: the four cardinal and four intermediate directions, and above and below. The conch shell on the 'vase with the water from above' ('all-victorious vase') contains water from every direction. In the initiations the initiation substances (water, crown, ribbon, etc.) are therefore broken down into their components and these mixed with the individual constituents of the initiation candidate.

111 Strangely enough, the text speaks of two seed-syllables which turn into two emblems and two deities.

112 Tenzin Gyatso 1985: 267 (adapted).

113 Hopkins (1985: 118) additionally relates the four internal initiations occurring in the first, third, fifth and seventh initiations to phases in the development of the embryo and foetus.

114 Or "fixing up the hair on the top of the child's head" (Hopkins 1985: 110, 118–9; see also Jamyang 1985: 8).

115 Jamyang 1985: 9; or according to Tenzin Gyatso 1985: 304, "a child's laughing and talking".

116 There can also be five rings, one on each finger, related to the five elements – the thumb ring, for instance, correlates with earth and is therefore yellow (Tenzin Gyatso 1985: 308).

117 Hopkins (1985: 119) rightly points out that at least four of these events in the life of a child are so-called rites of passage, and the other three events also constitute important transitions.

118 Jamyang (1985: 11) adopts a slightly different interpretation.

119 The number of spokes of the *vajra* minus one (= centre, central channel) corresponds to the number of petals in the relevant chakra lotus.

120 Also translated as: emanation body, illusory body, transformation body, radiation body, production body or incarnate physical body.

121 In Tantric Buddhism *saṃbhogakāya* refers to the speech of a Buddha and does not have the meaning of enjoyment body (Dhargyey 1985: 130; Sopa 1985 b: 157, n. 46).

122 It is not quite clear whether this drop is also related to the sexual and crown chakras.

123 'Body of own-being' (*svābhāvikāya*), also known as the 'innate body' (*sahajakāya*). See also Sopa 1985b: 157, n. 47; Carelli 1941: 10 (see p. 130, n. 39).

124 The practitioner should concentrate on the upper end of the central channel, i.e., the point between the eyebrows.

125 Or four night signs and six day signs (Dhargyey 1985: 135).

126 Dhargyey (1985: 135) speaks of a sign of bright lightning. All these visions correspond to those that appear after death. The first four arise when four aggregates (*skandha*) dissolve, the next six when the white *bodhicitta* drop descends, when the red *bodhicitta*-drop rises, when the two drops unite in the heart

chakra, etc. (Dhargyey 1985: 85–94; see also p. 130, n. 50).

127 Certainty of time, of abode, of the (empty) nature of the deity and his partner, of the body of the deities (who are one with Vajrasattva), and of aspect (the two deities in union) according to Dhargyey 1985: 135f.

128 The *vajra* recitation is described in Dhargyey (1985: 137).

129 A detailed description of the vase-type meditation is given by Dhargyey (1985: 138ff); see also Mullin (1985b: 116).

130 According to dGe-'dun grub (in Mullin 1985a: 180); see also a similar description by dGe-'dun rgya-mtsho (in Mullin 1985b: 116).

131 According to dGe-'dun grub (in Mullin 1985a: 180), the elements dissolve in this stage, which recalls the passing of a cosmos and of a person. Earth dissolves into water, and the energies involved reach the heart chakra; water dissolves into fire and flows into the throat chakra; fire becomes air and reaches the brow, air dissolves into space and is brought into the crown, and finally space becomes wisdom, which collects in the sexual chakra. According to dGe-'dun rgya-mtsho (in Mullin 1985b: 119), air dissolves into consciousness and this into clear light (see also p. 130, n. 50).

132 *Jñānamudrā* can also be called *dharmamudrā*; a slightly different interpretation of *mahā-* and *dharmamudrā* from mKhas-grub rJe is found in Wayman 1973: 127; (see also n. 3, above).

133 According to dGe-'dun grub (in Mullin 1985a: 182f).

134 Dhargyey 1985: 143; dGe-'dun grub in Mullin 1985a: 183ff; Tenzin Gyatso 1985: 420–22.

135 Tenzin Gyatso 1985: 422–3.

Chapter Six
The Mandala and the West
(Pages 121–124)

1 Cammann 1950.

2 Hummel 1958: 167.

3 Hummel 1958: 162.

4 Interesting pictorial material testifying this can be found in Argüelles 1972.

5 Jung 1981: 80ff (Eng. edn *CW* 9: I, para. 630ff); see also Jung 1938: 122 and Jung 1944: 146 (*CW* 12: para. 125).

6 Jung 1981: 81 (*CW* 9: I, para. 633. Hull's translation adapted).

7 Jung 1954: 198.

8 Jung 1954: 475; see also Jung 1981: 45 (*CW* 9: I, para. 572).

9 Jung 1954: 13 (*CW* 9: I, para. 16).

10 Jung 1981: 116 (*CW* 9: I, para. 714).

11 Jung 1948: 471.

12 Jung 1954: 387ff.

13 Jung 1972: 49.

14 Jung [1929]: 24.

15 Jung 1954: 319.

16 Jung 1954: 322.

17 Jung 1954: 327.

18 Jung 1948: 472.

19 e.g., Moacanin 1986; Kalff 1983.

20 Jung 1948: 467 (Zur Psychologie östlicher Meditation ['On the Psychology of Eastern Meditation']).

21 Oral teachings of Lama Yeshe 1979, 1980.

22 See Dhargyey 1985: 36.

23 Newman 1987: 473.

24 This worldview is astonishingly similar to that of the Russian cosmologist Andrei Linde: "Then it turned out that one cannot understand the exceedingly large without understanding the exceedingly small – from which everything came. ... The processes dependent on chance that occur before one on a small scale recur in the entire universe." Interview in *Tages Anzeiger Magazin*, 20, Zürich 1990.

25 Origen in *Leviticum homiliae*, V, 2 (in Jung 1981: 75; *CW* 9: I, para. 624).

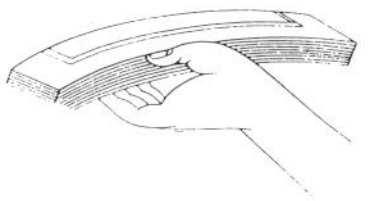

Bibliography

This bibliography lists works consulted in the preparation of the present book, and so likely to have influenced the author's thinking on the subject. Writing was completed at the end of 1991. Since then a number of important works on the Tibetan mandala have been published. These publications have been included in the bibliography but are not discussed in the text. In a few cases of especially relevant new material, however, these publications are referred to in footnotes.

Argüelles, José & Miriam. 1972. *Mandala.* Berkeley & London: Shambala Publications (Ger. edn *Das grosse Mandala-Buch. Mandala in Aktion.* Freiburg i.B. 1974).

Aung-Thwin, Michael. 1987. 'Heaven, earth and the supernatural world. Dimensions of the exemplary center in Burmese history.' In eds. Smith & Reynolds 1987.

Banerjee, Biswanath. 1985. *A Critical Edition of Śrī Kālacakratantra-rāja* (collated with the Tibetan version*).* Calcutta: Asiatic Society.

Bareau, André. 1962. 'La construction et le culte des stūpa d'après les Vinaya-pitaka.' *Bulletin de l'Ecole Française d'Extrême-Orient*, 50.ii, 229–74.

Barrett, Douglas. 1954. *Sculptures from Amarāvati in the British Museum.* London.

Bäumer, Bettina. 1986. 'Pañjara et yantra. Le diagramme de l'image sacrée.' In CNRS 1986.

Becker-Ritterspach, Raimund O.A. 1982. *Gestaltungsprinzipien in der Newarischen Architektur* ['Formal principles in Newar architecture']. Hamburg.

Bechert, Heinz, *et al.* 1971. *Buddhismus, Tibet. 'Sa-gShi Byin-rLob'. Zeremonie zur Gründung des klösterlichen Tibet-Instituts in Rikon (Schweiz)* ['Ceremony on the foundation of the Tibetan Monastic Institute in Rikon, Switzerland']. Encyclopaedia Cinematographica (E 1511/1969). Göttingen.

Béguin, Gilles. 1978. 'Un grand mandala de Kālacakra au musée Guimet.' *La Revue du Louvre et des musées de France*, No. 2: 113–21, Paris.

——. 1981. *Les mandala himâlayens du musée Guimet.* Paris.

Bénisti, Mireille. 1960. 'Etude sur le stûpa dans l'Inde ancienne.' *Bulletin de l'Ecole Française d'Extrême-Orient*, 50: 37–116.

Bernbaum, Edwin. 1980. *The Way to Shambhala.* Garden City, NY: Doubleday.

Berzin, Alexander, n.d. *The Cosmology of Kālacakra.* Unpublished manuscript.

——, n.d. *Introduction to Kālachakra* (English lecture, on cassettes).

Beyer, Stephan. 1973. *The Cult of Tārā. Magic and Ritual in Tibet.* Berkeley: University of California Press.

Bhattacharyya, Benoytosh, ed. 1949. *Nispannayogāvalī of Mahāpaṇḍita Abhayākaragupta.* GOS, Vol. 109, Baroda.

Blondeau, Anne-Marie. 1990. 'Questions préliminaires sur les rituels mdos.' In *Tibet – civilisation et société.* Paris.

Bod rgya tshig mdzod chen mo ['The Great Tibetan-Chinese Dictionary'] 3 vols. Peking, Mi-rigs dpe-skrun-khang (Nationalities Languages Press) 1985.

Boerschmann, Ernst. 1925. *Chinesische Architektur.* 2 vols, Berlin.

Brandt, Hermes (Gelong Thubten Lodroe) 1992. *An Excellent Vase of Nectar – The Practice of the Mind Mandala of the Glorious Kalacakra.* Arranged for recitation by Deti Rinpoche, trans. H. Brandt. Unpublished manuscript.

Brauen, Martin. 1994. 'Why not translate into pictures?' *Tibetan Studies: Proceedings of the Sixth Seminar of the International Association for Tibetan Studies, Fagernes 1992.* Vol. 1, 43–67. Oslo.

Brauen, Martin and Hassler, Peter. 1997. 'Computer aided 3D-animation of the Kālacakra Mandala'. *Proceedings of the Seventh Seminar of the International Association for Tibetan Studies, Schloss Seggau 1995.* Wien.

Brunner, Hélène. 1986. 'Mandala et Yantra dans le Śivaisme āgamique. Définition, description, usage rituel.' In CNRS 1986.

Bryant, Barry. 1992. *The Wheel of Time Sand Mandala. Visual Scripture of Tibetan Buddhism.* San Francisco and New York: HarperCollins.

Buffetrille, Katia. 1989. 'La restauration du monastère de Bsam yas: Un exemple de continuité dans la relation chapelain-donateur au Tibet. *Journal Asiatique*, Nos 3–4.

Burrows, E. 1935. 'Some cosmological patterns.' In *The Labyrinth* ed. S.H. Hooke. London 1935.

Cammann, Schuyler. 1950. 'Suggested origin of the Tibetan Mandala paintings.' *The Art Quarterly*, Vol. XIII, Detroit.

Carelli, Mario E. 1941. *Sekoddeśaṭīkā of Nāḍapāda (Nāropa). Being a commentary of the Sekoddeśa section of the Kālacakra Tantra.* GOS, Vol. 90, Baroda.

Chandra, Lokesh. 1972. *The esoteric iconography of Japanese Mandalas.* New Delhi.

——. 1980. 'Borobudur: a new interpretation.' In ed. Dallapiccola 1980.

Chang, Garma C.C. 1963. *Six Yogas of Nāropā and Teachings on Mahāmudrā.* 1963, repr. Ithaca, NY, Snow Lion, 1977; 'The Six Yogas of Nāropā', also in *Esoteric Teachings of the Tibetan Tantra,* ed. C.A. Musès, 1961, 2nd edn York Beach, ME, Samuel Weiser, 1982.

Chayet, Anne. 1985. *Les temples de Jehol et leurs modèles tibétains.* Paris, Edns Recherche sur les Civilisations.

——. 1988. 'Le monastère de bSam-yas: sources architecturales.' *Arts Asiatiques,* XLIII.

Chos-kyi grags-pa, dGe-bshes. 1981. *brDa 'dag ming tshig gsal ba.* (Tibetan dictionary.) Lhasa 1949; with Chinese trans. added 1957, repr. Peking: Mi-rigs dpe-skrun-khang (Nationalities Languages Press) 1981.

Clausberg, Karl. 1980. *Kosmische Visionen. Mystische Weltbilder von Hildegard von Bingen bis heute* ['Cosmic visions. Mystical world pictures from Hildegard of Bingen to the present day']. Köln.

CNRS 1986. *Mantras et diagrammes rituels dans l'Hindouisme.* Paris: Edns du CNRS.

Cochran, Tracy. 1994. '3-D dharma: the first computer mandala'. *Tricycle,* Vol. 3, No. 4, New York.

Cozort, Daniel. 1995. *The Sand Mandala of Vajrabhairava.* Ithaca: Snow Lion.

Dalai Lama I/II/III/XIII: see Mullin

Dalai Lama XIV: see Tenzin Gyatso

Dallapiccola, Anna Libera, ed. 1980. *The stūpa. Its religious, historical and architectural significance.* Wiesbaden.

Dargyay, Eva K., trans. 1977. *Das tibetischer Buch der Toten.* Bern and Munich.

Denwood, Philip. 1980. 'Stūpas of the Tibetan Bonpos.' In ed. Dallapiccola 1980.

Dhargyey, Geshe Lharampa Ngawang. 1985. *A commentary on the Kālacakra Tantra* (translated by Gelong Jhampa Kelsang). Dharamsala.

Diemberger, Hildegard, & Christian Schicklgruber, n.d. 'Beyul Khenbalung. The Hidden Valley of Artemisia – On Himalayan communities and their sacred landscape', (unpublished manuscript, expected to appear in an anthology on *Mandala and Landscape,* ed. A. Macdonald).

Doboom Tulku. 1988. 'The distinctions between the Sūtra and the Mantra Vehicles from Tibetan sources.' In *Tibetan Studies,* Vol. 2, eds. H. Uebach & J.L. Panglung, Munich.

Eck, Diana L. 1987. 'The city as a sacred center.' In eds. Smith & Reynolds 1987.

Eliade, Mircea. 1937. 'Cosmological homology and yoga.' *Journal of Indian Society of Oriental Art,* Vol. 5, Calcutta.

——. 1957. 'Centre du monde, temple, maison.' In *Le symbolisme cosmique des monuments religieux.* Serie Orientale Roma, XIV, Rome: IsMEO.

----. 1958. *Ewige Bilder und Sinnbilder. Vom unvergänglichen menschlichen Seelenraum* ['Eternal pictures and symbols. From the everlasting sphere of the human soul']. Olten.

Essen, Gerd-Wolfgang, & Tsering Tashi Thingo. 1989. *Die Götter des Himalaya.* Buddhistische Kunst. 2 vols, München: Prestel-Verlag.

Evans-Wentz, W.Y., ed. 1957. *The Tibetan Book of the Dead. Being the Bar-do thos-grol as trans. by Kazi Dawa-samdup.* 3rd edn, London: Oxford University Press.

——, ed. 1958. *Tibetan Yoga and Secret Doctrines.* London: Oxford University Press 1935, 2nd edn 1958.

Fischer, Klaus, *et al.* 1987. *Architektur des indischen Subkontinents.* Darmstadt.

Fremantle, Francesca & Chögyam Trungpa (trans. & ed.) 1975. *The Tibetan Book of the Dead. The Great Liberation through Hearing in the Bardo, by Guru Rinpoche according to Karma Lingpa.* Berkeley & London: Shambhala Publications.

Gail, Adalbert. 1980. 'Cosmical symbolism in the spire of the Ceylon dagoba.' In ed. Dallapiccola 1980.

Gar-je K'am-trül Rinpoche. 1978. 'A geography and history of Shambhala.' Trans. by Sherpa Tulku and Alexander Berzin. *The Tibet Journal,* Vol. 3, No. 3.

dGe-'dun grub (I Dalai Lama): see Mullin 1985a

dGe-'dun rgya-mtsho (II Dalai Lama): see Mullin 1985b

Gerner, Manfred. 1987. *Architekturen im Himalaya.* Stuttgart.

Gnoli, G., & L. Lanciotti, eds. 1985–88. *Orientalia Iosephi Tucci Memoriae Dicata.* Serie Orientale Roma, LVI, 3 vols, Rome: IsMEO.

Gnoli, Raniero, & Orofino, Giacomella. 1994. *Iniziazione Kālacakra (Nāropā).* Adelphi Edizione.

Govinda, Lama Anagarika. 1966. *Grundlagen tibetischer Mystik.* 1956, repr. Zürich 1966. Eng. *Foundations of Tibetan Mysticism. According to the Esoteric Teachings of the Great Mantra* OM MANI PADME HUM. London: Rider & Co., 1960, repr. NY: Samuel Weiser 1969.

——. 1971. 'Solar and lunar symbolism in the development of stūpa architecture.' *Cakra,* Vol. 3, New Delhi.

—— 1976. *Psycho-cosmic symbolism of the Buddhist stūpa.* 1935, 2nd edn Emeryville, CA: Dharma Publishing, 1976.

----. 1986. 'Die Entstehungsgeschichte des buddhistischen Mandala.' *Der Kreis,* No. 179, Apr–Jun 1986.

Grünwedel, Albert. 1915. *Der Weg nach Shambhala des dritten Gross-Lama von bKra shis lhun po, bLo bzang dPal ldan Ye shes* ['The Way to Shambhala', by the Third Panchen Lama]. München.

Guenther, Herbert V. 1972. *Buddhist Philosophy in Theory and Practice.* Berkeley: Shambhala Publications, 1971; repr. Harmondsworth and Baltimore: Penguin Books 1972.

Gupta, Sanjukta. 1988. 'The Mandala as an image of man.' In *Oxford*

University Papers on India, Vol. 2, Part 1: *Indian Ritual and its exegesis*, ed. Richard Gombrich. Delhi.
Gutschow, Niels. 1980. 'The urban context of the stūpa in Bhaktapur, Nepal.' In ed. Dallapiccola 1980.
----. 1982. *Stadtraum und Ritual der newarischen Städte im Kathmandu-Tal.* Stuttgart.
Gyalzur, Losang Paldhen, & Antony H.A. Verwey. 1983. 'Spells on the Life-Wood. An introduction to the Tibetan Buddhist ceremony of consecration.' *Studies in the History of Religion*, XLV, 1984.
Handa, O.C. 1994. *Tabo Monastery and Buddhism in the Trans-Himalaya.* New Delhi: Indus Publishing.
Heine-Geldern, Robert. 1982. 'Weltbild und Bauform in Südostasien.' *Acta Ethnologica et Linguistica*, No. 55. Wien-Föhrenau.
Henss, Michael. 1981. *Tibet. Die Kulturdenkmäler.* Zürich: Atlantis.
——. 1985. *Kalachakra. Ein tibetisches Einweihungsritual.* Zürich, 1985; 2nd edn, enlarged & revised, Ulm/Donau: Fabri Verlag, 1992.
Herdick, Reinhard. 1987. 'Death Ritual in Kirtipur in relation to urban space.' In *Heritage of the Kathmandu Valley*, eds. Niels Gutschow & Axel Michaels. Sankt Augustin.
——. 1988. *Kirtipur. Stadtgestalt, Prinzipien der Raumordnung und gesellschaftliche Funktionen einer Newar-Stadt.* Köln.
Hirakawa, Akira. 1963. 'The Rise of Mahāyāna and its relationship to the Worship of Stūpas.' *Memoirs of the Research Department of the Toyo Bunko*, No. 22, Tokyo.
Hoffmann, Helmut. 1964. 'Das Kālacakra, die letzte Phase des Buddhismus in Indien.' *Saeculum*, XV, 2.
——. 1977. 'The ancient Tibetan Cosmology.' *The Tibet Journal*, Vol. II, No. 4.
Hopkins, Jeffrey. 1983. *Meditation on Emptiness.* London: Wisdom Publications.
——. 1985. Introduction in Tenzin Gyatso 1985.
Huang Mingxin & Chen Jiujin. 1987. *Zangli de yuanli yu shixian.* Beijing 1987.
Hummel, Siegbert. 1958. 'Der Ursprung des tibetischen Mandalas.' *Ethnos*, 23.
Imaeda, Yoshiro. 1987. 'Peintures cosmiques du Bhoutan.' In eds. Gnoli & Lanciotti 1985–88, Vol. 2.
Irwin, John. 1980. 'The axial symbolism of the early stūpa. An exegesis.' In ed. Dallapiccola 1980.
Iwata Keiji & Sugiura Kohei. 1989. *Ajia-no uchukan – Bi-to Shukyo-no Kosmosu* ['Asian Cosmology and Mandalas']. Tokyo.
Jackson, Roger. 1985a. 'Kalachakra in context.' In ed. Simon 1985.
——. 1985b. 'The Kalachakra generation-stage sādhana.' In ed. Simon 1985.
Jamyang, Chö Yog Thubten. 1981. 'A Guide to the Kālacakra Initiation, Madison 1981'. In *Kalachakra Initiation Madison 1981*, Madison: Deer Park.
Jung, Carl Gustav. dates refer to first publication in the original language. *CW* denotes the complete English edition of the *Collected Works*, published in the UK by Routledge & Kegan Paul, London, and in the US by Bollingen Foundation/Princeton University Press, Princeton. English translations by R.F.C. Hull.
——, [1929]. Preface to the 2nd Edition of *Das Geheimnis der goldenen Blüte,* trans. Richard Wilhelm, Berlin, n.d. (1929). Eng. trans. 'The Secret of the Golden Flower', *CW*, Vol. 13: *Alchemical Studies*. London & Princeton 1968.
——. 1938. *Psychology and Religion. The Terry Lectures 1937.* Repr. in *CW*, Vol. 11: *Psychology and Religion: West and East*, 1958, 2nd ed. 1969. Page refs are to Ger. edn, *Psychologie und Religion*, Zürich: Rascher Verlag 1942.
——. 1944. 'Die Mandalasymbolik.' In *Psychologie und Alchemie.* Zürich: Rascher Verlag 1944. Eng. 'The Symbolism of the Mandala', *CW*, Vol. 12: *Psychology and Alchemy*, 2nd edn, London 1968.
——. 1948. *Symbolik des Geistes. Studien über psychische Phänomenologie.* Zürich: Rascher Verlag.
——. 1951. *Aion. Untersuchungen zur Symbolgeschichte.* Zürich: Rascher Verlag 1951. Eng. *Aion. Researches into the phenomenology of the Self. CW*, Vol. 9, Part II, 1959, 2nd edn 1968.
——. 1954. *Von den Wurzeln des Bewusstseins. Studien über den Archetypus.* Zürich: Rascher Verlag.
——. 1972. Preface and psychological commentary to the Bardo Thödol. In *Das Tibetanische Totenbuch*, ed. W.Y. Evans-Wentz, 1935/1953, 7th edn Olten: Walter-Verlag 1972. Eng. in ed. Evans-Wentz 1957; also in *CW*, Vol. 11.
——. 1981. *Mandala. Bilder aus dem Unbewuöten.* Olten: Walter-Verlag 1977, repr. 1981. Eng. in *The Archetypes and the Collective Unconscious. CW*, Vol. 9, Part I, 1959, 2nd edn 1968.
Kalff, Martin. 1983. 'The Negation of Ego in Tibetan Buddhism and Jungian Psychology.' *Journal of Transpersonal Psychology*, Vol. 15, No. 2, 103–24.
Kalsang Gyatso (VII Dalai Lama) 1987. *The long Kālachakra sādhana.* Trans. R.A. Thurman, hectographed, no place of publication.
Kalu Rinpoche. 1986. *The Dharma that illuminates all beings impartially like the light of the Sun and the Moon.* Ed. Kagyu Thubten Choling Translation Committee. Albany, NY: State University of New York Press.
——.1991. *Den Pfad des Buddha gehen: eine Einführung in die meditative Praxis des tibetischen Buddhismus* ['Walking the Path of the Buddha. An introduction to the meditative practice of Tibetan Buddhism']. München.
Keilhauer, A. & P. 1980. *Ladakh und Zanskar. Lamaistische Klosterkultur im Land zwischen Indien und Tibet* ['Ladakh and Zanskar. Lamaist monastic culture in the land between India and Tibet']. Köln 1980, 4th edn 1987.
Kirfel, Willibald. 1959a. *Symbolik des Buddhismus.* Stuttgart.
——. 1959b. *Symbolik des Hinduismus und des Jainismus.* Stuttgart.
Kloetzli, Randy. 1983: *Buddhist Cosmology. From single world system to Pure Land.* Delhi.

Kongtrul, Jamgön Lodrö Tayé. 1995. *Myriad Worlds, Buddhist Cosmology in Abhidharma, Kālacakra and Dzog-chen*. Ithaca: Snow Lion.

Kramrisch, Stella. 1946. *The Hindu Temple*. 2 vols. Calcutta.

Kuiper, Franciscus Bernardus. 1970. 'Cosmogony and conception: a query.' *History of Religions*, Vol. 10, No. 2. University of Chicago Press.

Lati Rinpoche & Jeffrey Hopkins 1990. *Death, Intermediate State and Rebirth in Tibetan Buddhism*. London, Rider, 1979; page refs are to Ger. trans. by Matthias Dehne, Stufen zur Unsterblichkeit, Munich: Eugen Diederichs Verlag 1983, repr. 1990.

Lauf, Detlef Ingo. 1972. *Das Erbe Tibets* ['The Legacy of Tibet']. Bern.

La Vallée Poussin, Louis de. 1923–31. *L'Abhidharmakośa de Vasubandhu*. 6 vols. Paris 1923–31; repr. as Mélanges Chinois et Bouddhiques, Vol. XVI, Brussels 1971, 1980.

Ledderose, Lothar. 1980. 'Chinese prototypes of the pagoda.' In ed. Dallapiccola 1980.

Lessing, Ferdinand D. 1935. *Mongolen. Hirten, Priester und Dämonen*. ['Mongolia: Shepherds, Priests and Demons']. Berlin.

——. 1942. *Yung-Ho-Kung. An iconography of the Lamaist cathedral in Peking. With notes on the Lamaist mythology and cult*. Reports from the Scientific Expedition to the North-western Provinces of China under the leadership of Dr Sven Hedin, VIII, Ethnography, 1, Stockholm.

——. 1954. 'The Eighteen Worthies Crossing the Sea.' In *Contributions to Ethnography, Linguistics and History of Religion*. Reports from the Scientific Expedition to the North-western Provinces of China under the leadership of Dr Sven Hedin, Publ. 38, VIII, Ethnography, 6, Stockholm.

——. 1976. 'Miscellaneous Lamaist notes, I. Notes on the thanksgiving offering.' *Central Asiatic Journal*, II.1, 58–71, 1956; repr. in *Asian Folklore and Social Life Monographs*, Vol. 91, ed. Lou Tsu-k'uang, Taipei 1976.

—— & Alex Wayman. 1978. *mKhas-grub-rje's 'Fundamentals of the Buddhist Tantras'*. The Hague/Paris 1968. 2nd edn entitled *Introduction to the Buddhist Tantric Systems*. Trans. from mKhas-grub-rje's *rGyud sde spyiḥi rnam par gźag pa rgyas par brjod*. Delhi: Motilal Banarsidass 1978.

Lo Bue, Erberto. 1987. 'The Dharmamaṇḍala-Sūtra by Buddhaguhya.' In eds. Gnoli & Lanciotti 1985–88, Vol. 2.

Lutz, Albert. 1991. *Der Goldschatz der drei Pagoden* ['The golden treasure of the three pagodas']. Zürich.

Mabbett, I.W. 1983/84. 'The Symbolism of Mount Meru.' *History of Religions*, Vol. 23.

Macdonald, Ariane. 1962. *Le Maṇḍala du Mañjuśrīmūlakalpa*. Paris: Adrien-Maisonneuve.

Macdonald, A.W. & Anne Vergati Stahl 1979. *Newar Art*. Warminster.

Majupuria, T.Ch. & S.P. Gupta 1981. *Nepal. The Land of Festivals*. New Delhi.

Markel, Stephen. 1990. 'The Imagery and Iconographic Development of the Indian Planetary Deities Rāhu and Ketu.' *South Asian Studies*, Vol. 6, 9–26, London.

Martin, Dan. 1994. *Mandala Cosmogony*. Wiesbaden: Harrassowitz.

Mémet, Sébastien. 1988. 'Le monastère de bSam-yas. Essai de restitution.' *Arts Asiatiques*, XLIII.

Meyer, Fernand. 1981. *gSo-ba rig-pa, le système médical tibétain*. Paris.

Moacanin, Radmila. 1986. *Jung's Psychology and Tibetan Buddhism. Western and Eastern Paths to the Heart*. London: Wisdom Publications.

Mode, Heinz. 1987. 'Der Chakra. Bildtradition, Symbol, Funktion.' In eds. Gnoli & Lanciotti 1985–88, Vol. 2.

Mookerjee, Ajit, & Madhu Khanna 1977. *The Tantric Way. Art, science, ritual*. London & New York 1977 (Ger. edn Munich 1987).

Mullin, Glenn H. (compiled & trans.) 1982. *Essence of Refined Gold. Selected Works of the Third Dalai Lama (bSod-nams rgya-mtsho)*. Ithaca, NY: Snow Lion.

——. 1985a. *Bridging the Sutras and Tantras. A collection of ten minor works by Gyalwa Gendun Drub (dGe-'dun grub) the First Dalai Lama*. Dharamsala, Tushita Books 1981; rev. edn, Ithaca, NY: Snow Lion, 1985.

——. 1985b. *Tantric yogas of Sister Niguma. Selected Works of the Second Dalai Lama (dGe-'dun rgya-mtsho)*. 1982; repr. Ithaca, NY: Snow Lion, 1985.

——. 1988. *Path of the Bodhisattva Warrior. The Life and Teachings of the Thirteenth Dalai Lama*. Ithaca, NY: Snow Lion.

Mus, Paul. 1932–34. 'Barabuḍur. Les origines du stūpa et la transmigration. Essai d'archéologie religieuse comparée.' *Bulletin de l'Ecole Française d'Extrême-Orient*, 32 (Fasc. 1) (1932): 269–439; 33 (1933): 577–980; 34 (1934): 175–400; also published separately, Hanoi 1935.

Newman, John R. 1985. 'A brief history of the Kalachakra.' In ed. Simon 1985.

——. 1987. *The Outer Wheel of Time: Vajrayāna Buddhist Cosmology of the Kālacakra Tantra*. PhD Thesis, University of Wisconsin, Madison.

Nispannayogāvali: see Bhattacharyya 1949.

Norbu, Thubten Jigme, & Colin M. Turnbull 1972. *Tibet. Its History, Religion and People*. London, Chatto & Windus 1969, repr. Harmondsworth: Penguin Books 1972 (Ger. edn *Mein Tibet. Geist und Seele einer sterbenden Kultur*. Wiesbaden 1971).

Olschak, Blanche Christine, & Geshé Thubten Wangyal. 1972. *Mystik und Kunst Alttibets*. Bern & Stuttgart: Hallwag Verlag 1972. Eng. *Mystic Art of Ancient Tibet*. London, Allen & Unwin and New York, McGraw-Hill 1973.

Oppitz, Michael. 1968. *Geschichte und Sozialordnung der Sherpa. Khumbu Himal*. 8 vols, Innsbruck and Munich.

Palden Yeshe (dPal-ldan Ye-shes), 3rd Panchen Rinpoche, n.d. (Ger.) *Abgekürzte Methode zur Vergegenwärtigung des (dreizehn-Gottheiten) Kalachakra Rad der Zeit, der alles überwunden hat, der alles gewonnen hat. Ein Schatzhaus voller Juwelen*. (Eng.) *Abbreviated method for Actualizing (the Nine-deity) Kālachakra, Cycles of Time, one who has overcome and gained all. A Treasure House of Gems.* (Tib. *Collected Works*, CHA, no. 919). Hectographed, no date or translators' names.

——. see also Grünwedel 1915.

Panchen Ötrul Rinpoche. 1990. 'The stages of the rite of a tantric initiation.' *Chö Yang, The Voice of Tibetan Religion and Culture*, No. 3, Dharamsala.

Perrot, Maryvonne. 1980. *Le symbolisme de la roue.* Paris.

Peterson, Kathleen W. 1980. 'Sources of variation in Tibetan canons of iconometry.' In *Tibetan Studies in honour of Hugh Richardson*, eds. Michael Aris & Aung San Suu Kyi, Warminster.

Petri, Winfried. 1988. 'Die Astronomie im Kālacakralaghutantra.' In *Tibetan Studies*, Vol. 2, eds. H. Uebach & J.L. Panglung, Munich.

Roth, Gustav. 1980. 'Symbolism of the Buddhist stūpa.' In ed. Dallapiccola 1980.

Saṃvarodaya-tantra: see Tsuda 1974

Saso, Michael. 1991. *Homa rites and mandala meditation in Tendai Buddhism.* Śata Piṭaka Series, Vol. 362, New Delhi

Schabert, Tilo. 1990. *Stadtarchitektur. Spiegel der Welt* ['Town architecture, mirror of the world']. Zürich.

Schnurr, Eugen. 1985. *Gleich dem Lotos* ['Like the lotus']. Stuttgart.

Schöne, Wolfgang. 1983. *Über das Licht in der Malerei.* 1954, repr. Berlin 1983.

Schubert, Johannes. 1953. 'Das Wunschgebet um Shambhala. Ein tibetischer Kālachakra-Text (mit einer mongolischen Übertragung).' *Mitteilungen des Instituts für Orientforschung*, I, Berlin.

——. 1954. 'Das Reis-Mandala. Ein tibetisches Ritualtext' ['The rice mandala. A Tibetan ritual text']. In *Asiatica. Festschrift F. Weller.* Leipzig.

Schuh, Dieter. 1973. *Untersuchungen zur Geschichte der tibetischen Kalenderrechnung* ['Investigations into the history of Tibetan calender computation']. Wiesbaden.

Seckel, Dietrich. 1957. *Buddhistische Kunst Ostasiens* ['Buddhist Art of Eastern Asia']. Stuttgart.

——. 1980. 'Stūpa elements surviving in East Asian pagodas.' In ed. Dallapiccola 1980.

Serkong Rinpoche. 1982. *Teaching on Kalachakra.* Trans. Alexander Berzin. Tape recordings, Deer Park, Madison, Wisconsin.

Shashibala. 1989. *Comparative iconography of the Vajradhātu Mandala and the Tattva-Saṅgraha.* Śata Piṭaka Series, Vol. 344, New Delhi.

Simon, Beth, ed. 1985. *The Wheel of Time. The Kalachakra in Context.* Madison, WI: Deer Park Books.

Slusser, Mary Shepherd. 1982. *Nepal Mandala – A cultural study of the Kathmandu valley.* Princeton.

Smith, Bardwell, & Holly Baker Reynolds, eds. 1987. *The city as a sacred centre.* Leiden.

Snellgrove, David. 1967. *The Nine Ways of Bon.* London: Oxford University Press 1967; repr. Boulder: Prajñā Press, 1980.

——. 1987. *Indo-Tibetan Buddhism. Indian Buddhists and their Tibetan successors.* London: Serindia and (in 2 vols) Boston: Shambhala.

Snelling, John. 1990. *The sacred mountain. Travellers and pilgrims at Mount Kailash in Western Tibet and the great universal symbol of the sacred mountain.* London 1983, repr. 1990.

Snodgrass, Adrian. 1988. *The Symbolism of the Stupa.* 1985, repr. Ithaca, NY, 1988.

——. 1988. *The Matrix and Diamond World Mandalas in Shingon Buddhism.* 2 vols. New Delhi: Aditya Prakashan.

bSod-nams rgya-mtsho & Musashi Tachikawa. 1989. *The Ngor Mandalas of Tibet.* Plates. Bibliotheca Codicum Asiaticorum, 2. Tokyo: Centre for East Asian Cultural Studies.

—— *et al.* 1983. *Tibetan Mandalas. The Ngor Collection.* 2 vols. Tokyo: Kodansha.

—— *et al.* 1991. *The Ngor Mandalas of Tibet. Listings of the Mandala Deities.* Bibliotheca Codicum Asiaticorum, 4. Tokyo: Centre for East Asian Cultural Studies.

Sopa, Geshe Lhundup. 1985a. 'The Kalachakra Tantra initiation.' In ed. Simon 1985.

——. 1985b. 'The subtle body in tantric Buddhism.' In ed. Simon 1985.

—— & Jeffrey Hopkins. 1976. *Practice and Theory of Tibetan Buddhism.* London: Rider, 1976 (repr. as *Cutting through Appearances*, Ithaca, NY, 1989).

Stein, M. Aurel. 1921. *Serindia – detailed report of explorations in Central Asia and westernmost China.* 5 vols, Oxford 1921, repr. Delhi 1980.

Stein, R.A. 1962. *La civilisation tibétaine.* Paris 1962; Eng. *Tibetan Civilization*, trans. J.E. Stapleton Driver, London: Faber & Faber and Stanford: Stanford University Press 1972.

Tambiah, S.J. 1976. *World Conqueror and World Renouncer* (chapter: 'The Galactic Polity'). Cambridge.

Tenzin Gyatso (XIV Dalai Lama) 1981. 'Heart of Mantra'. In Tsong-ka-pa 1981.

——. 1985: *The Kālachakra Tantra. Rite of Initiation for the Stage of Generation. A commentary on the text of Kay-drup-ge-lek-bel-sang-bo.* Ed., trans. and introd. by Jeffrey Hopkins. London: Wisdom Publications.

Tharchin, Geshe Lobsang. 1987. *A commentary on Guru Yoga and offering of the mandala.* Ithaca, NY: Snow Lion.

Thurman, Robert A.F., trans. 1987, see Kalsang Gyatso 1987.

——, trans. 1994. *The Tibetan Book of the Dead. Liberation through Understanding in the Between.* New York: Bantam Books.

Tsang Nyön Heruka (gTsang-smyon He-ru-ka). 1982. *The Life of Marpa the Translator.* Trans. Nālandā Transln Committee. Boulder: Prajñā Press.

Tsong-ka-pa. 1981. *The Yoga of Tibet. The Great Exposition of Secret Mantra: 2 and 3.* Introd. by H.H. Tenzin Gyatso, XIV Dalai Lama; trans. and ed. by Jeffrey Hopkins. London: Allen & Unwin.

Tsuda, Shinichi. 1974. *The Saṃvarodaya-tantra. Selected Chapters.* Tokyo

Tucci, Giuseppe. 1961. *The Theory and Practice of the Maṇḍala. With special reference to the modern psychology of the subconscious.* Trans. from the Italian by Alan Houghton Brodrick. London: Rider & Co. 1961, repr. 1969 (Ger. edn 1949, repr. Düsseldorf 1989).

——. 1980. *The Religions of Tibet.* Trans. from the Ger. and Italian by Geoffrey Samuel. London: Routledge & Kegan Paul, 1980 (Ger. edn 1970).

——. 1988a. *Stūpa. Art, Architectonics and Symbolism.* Śata Piṭaka Series, 347, New Delhi: Aditya Prakashan, 1988 (Eng. version of *Indo-Tibetica*, I, Rome 1932).

——. 1988b. *The temples of Western Tibet and their artistic symbolism. The monasteries of Spiti and Kunavar.* Ed. Lokesh Chandra. Śata Piṭaka Series, 349, New Delhi: Aditya Prakashan, 1988 (Eng. version of *Indo-Tibetica*, III.1, Rome 1935).

Van der Wee, Pia and Louis. 1995. *A Tale of Thangkas, Living with a Collection.* Antwerp.

Vasubandhu: see La Vallée Poussin

Vergati, Anne. 1986. 'Quelques remarques sur l'usage du mandala et du yantra dans la vallée de Kathmandu, Népal.' In CNRS 1986.

Vira, Raghu, & Lokesh Chandra. 1961–72. *A new Tibeto-Mongol Pantheon.* 20 parts. Śata Piṭaka Series, 8, New Delhi: Int. Acad. Indian Culture.

Wayman, Alex. 1959. 'Studies in Yama and Māra.' *Indo-Iranian Journal*, Vol. III. The Hague.

——. 1971. 'Contribution on the symbolism of the mandala-palace.' In *Etudes tibétaines dédiées à la mémoire de Marcelle Lalou.* Paris

——. 1973. *The Buddhist Tantras. Light on Indo-Tibetan esotericism.* New York: Samuel Weiser, and London

——. 1974. 'The ritual in Tantric Buddhism of the disciple's entrance into the mandala.' *Worship and Ritual.* Studia Missionalia, 23. Rome.

——. 1978a. Introduction to the second edition, in Lessing & Wayman, 1978.

——. 1978b. *Calming the Mind and Discerning the Real. Buddhist Meditation and the Middle View. From the Lam-rim chen-mo of Tsoṅ-kha-pa.* New York: Columbia University Press.

——. 1981. 'Reflections on the theory of Barabudur as a mandala.' In *Barabudur: history and significance of a Buddhist monument*, ed. Luis Gomez *et al.*, Berkeley.

——. 1982/83. 'The human body as microcosm in India, Greek cosmology, and sixteenth-century Europe.' *History of Religion*, Vol. 22.

Weber, Max. 1988. *Gesammelte Aufsätze zur Religionssoziologie* ['Collected Essays on the Sociology of Religion']. Tübingen.

Yamamoto, Tetsushi. 1990. 'Mandalas for world peace.' *Chö yang. The voice of Tibetan religion and culture*, No. 3. Dharamsala.

Illustration Sources

Colour Plates

1 Völkerkundemuseum der Universität Zürich. Inv. No. 19824. 65 x 55 cm. Photo: Peter Nebel.
2 Völkerkundemuseum der Universität Zürich. Inv. No. 14476. 49.5 x 49.5 cm. Photo: Peter Nebel.
3 Völkerkundemuseum der Universität Zürich. Inv. No. 13981. 64.5 x 48.5 cm. Photo: Peter Nebel.
4, 5 Photos: Martin Brauen, 1982
6 Völkerkundemuseum der Universität Zürich. Inv. No. 21299. 89 x 79 cm. Photo: Peter Nebel.
7 Völkerkundemuseum der Universität Zürich. Inv. No. 13560. 92.5 x 60 cm. Photo: Peter Nebel.
8 Private collection, Mimi Lipton, London. Detail from painting, 182 x 48 cm.
9 Private collection, Mimi Lipton, London. Detail from painting, 182 x 48 cm.
10 Völkerkundemuseum der Universität Zürich. Inv. No. 18894. 41.5 x 28.5 cm. Photo: Peter Nebel.
11 Völkerkundemuseum der Universität Zürich. Inv. No. 13196. 63.5 x 44 cm. Photo: Peter Nebel.
12, 13 Folkens Museum, Stockholm. Inv. No. 1935:50:3048 (Sven Hedin Collection). Diameter: 34 cm; height: 32.5 cm. Photo: C. Åhlin.
14 National Museums and Galleries on Merseyside, Liverpool Museum. Inv. No. 54.85.40 (Beasley Collection). Height: 53 cm.
15–21 Völkerkundemuseum der Universität Zürich. Inv. No. 21131. Size of baseboard: ca. 200 x 200 cm. Height: ca. 115 cm. Object: Pema Namdol Thaye and Ngawang Namgyal Sherpa, 1990. Photos: Peter Nebel.
22 Private collection, Pia and Louis Van der Wee, Antwerp, 68 x 43 cm.
23–45 Photos: Peter Nebel, Doro Röthlisberger and Martin Brauen. Kālacakra Ritual in Rikon, Switzerland, July–August 1985.
46 Musée Guimet, Paris. Inv. No. MA 3814. 83 x 75.5 cm.
47 Private collection. 88 x 66 cm.

Black and White Figures

1, 2 Völkerkundemuseum der Universität Zürich. Inv. No. 13808. Height: 21.5 cm. Photo: Peter Nebel.
3 Frey private collection. Diameter: 33 cm
4 Stein: 1922, CIII, vol. 2, Nr. 00186. British Museum Stein Painting 174. Ink on paper. H. 44 cm, W. 30.5 cm.
5 Model and photo: Peter Nebel (after La Vallée Poussin 1923–31: II; Berzin, n.d.; Kloetzli 1983).
6 Drawing: Peter Nebel.
7 From: Snellgrove 1967.
8 Drawing: Andreas Brodbeck.
9 Völkerkundemuseum der Universität Zürich. Model: Urs Wohlgemuth. Photo: Peter Nebel.
10 Model and photo: Peter Nebel.
11 Drawing: Peter Nebel.
12 Völkerkundemuseum der Universität Zürich. Model and photo: Peter Nebel (after a 3D computer drawing by the firm Rocad, Berne; based on Berzin, n.d.; Huang Mingxin 1987; Schuh 1973).
13, 14 Völkerkundemuseum der Universität Zürich. Inv. No. 17408. Diameter: 17 cm. Photo: Peter Nebel.
15, 16 Frey private collection. Diameter: 31 cm.
17 Photo: Martin Brauen, 1972
18 See Fig. 12. Picture adapted by: Peter Nebel.
19 British Museum, London. Inv. No. 1880 7–9 39. Eliott Collection No. 102. Height: ca. 147 cm.
20 Photo: Johannes Frischknecht.
21 Drawing: Andreas Brodbeck.
22 Author's archive.
23 Photo: Lucca Invernizzi Tettoni Photobank, Bangkok.
24 Photo: Niels Gutschow (18 April 1973).
25 Drawing: Peter Nebel (after Mémet 1988).
26 Drawing: Andreas Brodbeck (after Mémet 1988).
27 Museum für Völkerkunde, Berlin. Inv. No. I.D. 36 382. Diameter: 96 cm; height: 53.5 cm. Photo: Dietrich Graf
28 Drawing: Pema Namdol Thaye (after a design in the Jokhang, Lhasa).
29 Drawing: Pema Namdol Thaye (after a scroll painting in Shalu Monastery).
30 Author's archive.
31 Drawing: Peter Nebel and Pema Namdol Thaye.
32 Drawing: Andreas Brodbeck and Pema Namdol Thaye.
33 Drawing: Andreas Brodbeck and Peter Nebel.
34 Drawing: Peter Nebel and Pema Namdol Thaye.
35 Drawing: Andreas Brodbeck and Rita Siegfried.
36 Private collection, Mimi Lipton, London. Detail from painting, 182 x 48 cm.
37 Drawing: Robert Beer.
38 Ashmolean Museum, Oxford. Inv. No. Bod. 47.
39 Photo: Peter Nebel.
40, 41 British Museum, London. Inv. No. OA 1982. 8–4.1. Height: 21.5 cm.
42 Picture adapted by: Peter Nebel.
43 Model and photo: Peter Nebel.
44 Model and photo: Peter Nebel (after a computer drawing by the firm Rocad, Berne).
45 Drawing: Andreas Brodbeck. Model and photo: Peter Nebel.
46 Photo: Zhongguo Jianzhu Gongye Chubanshe, Beijing. (Xizang Gu Jianzhu; No. 188).
47 Photo: Peter Nebel.
48, 49 Victoria and Albert Museum, London. Inv. No. IM 91–1936. Diameter: 48 cm; height: 65 cm.
50 Photo: Annegret Nippa.
51–56 Drawings: Andreas Brodbeck.
57 Sammlung für Völkerkunde, St. Gallen. Inv. No. B 3213/43. Height: 22 cm.Photo: Peter Nebel.
58–60 Drawings: Andreas Brodbeck.
61 Drawing: Robert Beer.
62, 63 Drawing: Andreas Brodbeck.
64 Model and photo: Peter Nebel (after a computer drawing by the computer firm Rocad, Berne).
65 Drawing: Pema Namdol Thaye and Peter Nebel.
66 Author's archive.
67 Copper engraving by J.-Th. de Bry (Oppenmeimii 1617).

Index

Placenames and monuments